Contesting Ireland

For Bet

Contesting Ireland

Irish Voices against England in the Eighteenth Century

T.O. McLOUGHLIN

FOUR COURTS PRESS

Set in 10 on 12.5 point Caslon for
FOUR COURTS PRESS LTD
Fumbally Lane, Dublin 8, Ireland
e-mail: info@four-courts-press.ie
and in North America
FOUR COURTS PRESS
c/o ISBS, 5804 N.E. Hassalo Street, Portland, OR 97213.

A catalogue record for this title
is available from the British Library.

ISBN 1 85182 448 0 hbk
ISBN 1 85182 449 9 pbk

Printed in Great Britain
by MPG Books, Bodmin, Cornwall

Contents

Preface

The 1798 rebellion and the Act of Union are the closing statements in a major phase of the long argument between England, the centre of imperial power, and Ireland, the recalcitrant colony. This book is an attempt to illustrate how diverse Irish writers in English during the eighteenth century contest England's view of Ireland. They argue in political pamphlets and speeches, in histories, poems, in novels and satirical pieces that their Ireland is different from the one the English have in mind. And yet they each contest a different Ireland for themselves. They speak not with one but many voices, protesting difference from England while turning a deaf ear to one another. Although Ireland comes across as fractured by its colonial experience, there is an extraordinary energy of intellect and talent in the different strategies of the writing, thus providing a more formidable and varied body of material written during the colonial period than found in any other British colony.

This work would not have been possible without the help of many historians to whom I am indebted, but it makes no claim to challenge or contribute significantly to their research. The objective has been rather to bring history to assist in a better understanding of eighteenth-century Irish writing. The focus has been the meeting points between two kinds of discourse, that of the coloniser and that of the colonised. This has meant giving some attention to recent postcolonial criticism, an approach that is explained in the opening chapter.

I should like to express particular thanks to the following who have contributed in various ways to this book: the Research Board of the University of Zimbabwe for financing my visits to libraries and institutions; the staff of the National Library of Ireland, of Trinity College, Dublin and of the Bodleian Library, Oxford, for their professional assistance and guidance; my colleague Anthony Chennells whose critical acumen and breadth of reading in settler literature provoked much of the theoretical debate alluded to in the book. Thanks are due also to several friends north and south of the equator who have helped directly and indirectly. The book is dedicated to my wife Bet who has shared so generously in the travails of its writing and production.

CHAPTER ONE

Eighteenth-century Ireland:
a postcolonial view

CONTESTING IRELAND

Whatever the critical approach to studies of eighteenth-century Ireland, be it Lecky or Froude in the nineteenth century, or Cullen or Bartlett in recent times, the underlying issue remains the same – Ireland's relation to England. The arguments over the last two centuries about that ever-shifting connection hinge on England's power, its authority over Irish legislation, finance, religion and culture.[1] Although some critics argue that Ireland was not a colony in the eighteenth century, not least because the word did not have the same connotations then as it does now, England's treatment of Ireland had many of the characteristics of more recent examples of colonisation. Control of political power and of economic resources together with a policy of cultural and religious assimilation reflected England's determination to assert its superiority over Irish backwardness and to subject Ireland to its own imperial needs. Irish writers through the century kept returning to this colonialist perception and kept contesting it. Their protest continued in different forms until the 1916 rising and beyond. 'In every generation,' reads the proclamation in 1916, 'the Irish people have asserted their right to national freedom and sovereignty.'[2] Eighteenth-century resistance to English rule came as much from anger at what England had done and continued to do as from fear of what she might do.

1 Many of the debates are summarised in S.J. Connolly, 'Eighteenth-Century Ireland: Colony or ancien régime?' in *The Making of Modern Irish History: Revisionism and the Revisionist Controversy*, eds D. George Boyce and Alan O'Day (London, 1996), pp 15-33. 2 The Proclamation of the Republic, 24 April 1916, *Irish Historical Documents 1172-1922*, eds Edmund Curtis and R.B. McDowell (London, 1943), p. 317.

This study starts with William Molyneux, who took the English parliament to task about its presumed power to legislate for Ireland. His understanding of the relationship was different to theirs and he weighed in with considerable historical and legal evidence to justify his case. That debate was to continue through until the Act of Union (1800), with Irish voices joining in from a wide range of interests in Irish society. However much these voices disagreed with one another, they expressed a common discontent with what England claimed or presumed Ireland to be. They contested that Ireland was not a colony and should not be treated like one, or that England had colonised Ireland and her management showed all the oppressive spirit of a colonising people, or, like Theobald Wolfe Tone, that Ireland should assert its national independence from England. What exactly Ireland was they often found difficult to say. Until the time of Tone most Protestants would argue that Ireland was a kingdom, but not a nation. The concept of nation would have meant including the Catholics, and for Protestants that was not to be thought of. But the thrust of Irish writing – be it Protestant or Catholic, Anglican or Presbyterian – was to wrest Ireland away from the bonds so neatly summarised in the Declaratory Act of 1720, 'that the said kingdom of Ireland hath been, is and of right ought to be subordinate unto and dependent upon the imperial crown of Great Britain, as being inseparably united and annexed thereunto.'[3] This was not the Ireland they wanted. It was an image of subjection to the imperial centre and presumed a relationship of coloniser to colonised which they resented.

Postcolonialism

Eighteenth-century Irish writing is frequently so embedded in historical and political arguments of the day that it is important by way of introduction to outline some of the issues in that climate of debate, and one useful way of looking at those issues is provided by postcolonial criticism. The benefit of discussing Ireland from a postcolonial point of view is that it draws attention to the variety of resistance behind the colonial presence. This sense of the term 'postcolonial' needs some explanation.

Imagine the stage of an eighteenth-century comedy. The principal characters, men and women of the beau monde, occupy centre-stage. Their language and dress, like the furniture, the drapes and the art-work, signify an artistic code, a style of organising the world they inhabit. Up-stage is a panelled screen which was often decorated. In Sheridan's *School for Scandal* Sir Peter remarks to Surface, 'You make even your screen a source of knowledge – hung I perceive with maps.'[4] Its purpose is to shield from public view the more intimate or private activities,

3 Declaratory Act, *Irish Historical Documents, 1172–1922*, p. 187.   4 Sheridan, *School for Scandal* in *Sheridan's Plays*, ed. Cecil Price (London, 1971), IV. iii. 139–40.

for example a woman undressing. Its artful front is designed to distract from its actual purpose. Its beauty hides the unmentionable things that happen behind it. In many a comedy the screen serves the dramatic purpose of hiding an illicit audience. A character behind the screen can listen to the conversation of other players and with the information gained can change the direction of the drama. The screen hides and yet empowers the illicit.

Such a screen appears to the rear of one of Hogarth's prints of *Marriage à la Mode* whose subject is the beau monde attending the countess' levée. The ornamental details in the scene – the *objets d'art*, the servants, the tea, the fabrics – reflect the splendour of England's colonial achievement. However, the assembled company of English ladies and gentlemen are as unconcerned about the colonies as they are about what happens on the other side of the screen. The black serving-boy in the background may well have come from behind the screen, but what he does or thinks or wears when he goes back there is of no concern to them. The important point is only that he conform to English expectations of his manners and dress. The colonised peoples whom he represents – from Africa, Ireland, America, India – are acceptable at the levée only in so far as they acknowledge their inferiority and their difference.

The usefulness of the analogy is that it helps distinguish the Ireland which is produced by English colonial discourse from that much more complex Ireland behind the screen. This book means to listen to the voices behind the screen, to analyse how they contested Ireland, how they resisted the language of England and in doing so attempted to describe Ireland as other than what England said it was.

The term 'postcolonial' in this context has a double sense. 'Post' means both after and, as also in Latin and in medical usage, behind. The term refers therefore to events *after* the colonisation of Ireland in 1171 when King Henry II landed at Wexford, as well as to what happens in Ireland *behind* the facade of colonial discourse.[5] Postcolonial criticism tends to concentrate on resistance writing. In some cases that is oppositional, resisting the colonial presence; in others it is ambivalent, seemingly complicit yet caught between praising and berating the forces of colonial control. In all cases it is distinct from the colonial discourse emanating from the lord lieutenant and his administration, and ultimately from England. Postcolonial criticism is also interested in the tensions created by colonisation both among those who represented the metropolitan power, particularly the settlers, and among those who were colonised. One of the striking insights of postcolonial criticism is that the interaction between coloniser and colonised generates not just a shifting and unstable relationship but also recurring problems of allegiance and self-definition.

---

5 I have been unable to find a better term than 'postcolonial' to serve these two meanings at once; words like 'post-colonisation' or 'pre-independence' convey only the temporal sense of 'postcolonial'.

Discussion about postcolonial writing usually focuses on the ways in which the colonised people responded to their colonisers; how they resisted or assimilated the language, manners, values and other cultural manifestations of their foreign masters; the images they used to describe that relationship; the strategies they employed to subvert the authority of the coloniser; how they decentred that authority and eventually transformed their position from being marginal to becoming formative, from being written about to writing, from object to subject. This resistance is more than anticolonial protest, for within it lies the difficult issue of identity, and this was particularly acute among the various peoples who constituted the Irish in the eighteenth century. To insist on difference from the coloniser begs the question not just of self-identity, but of the possibility of difference among those on the side of resistance. It is true that the colonised, rejecting the supposedly normative language and images of the coloniser, aims to 'identify, valorise, and empower what colonialist discourses label the barbarous, the primitive, the provincial'.[6] But this paradigm suggests a clear delineation between coloniser and colonised, a 'them' and 'us' confrontation, which will be found too simple for eighteenth-century Ireland. What emerges from Ireland's confrontation with the English is the abandonment of essentialist cultural standpoints and a groping towards a reconciliation of divergent cultures for the achievement of a new hybrid identity.

Many commentators do not include Ireland in their analysis of postcolonial writing which has been a feature of so many literatures around the world.[7] Some critics oversimplify or dismiss Ireland's case. A recent paper arguing that the term 'postcolonialism' should apply more extensively than just to literatures of the third world mentions Northern Ireland as not yet decolonised and makes no mention of Ireland.[8] The influential critique by Ashcroft and others presumes that Ireland, meaning perhaps Northern Ireland, together with Wales and Scotland, is part of Britain, adding that their 'complicity in the British imperial enterprise makes it difficult for colonised peoples outside Britain to accept their identity as postcolonial'.[9] Homi Bhabha, Seamus Deane and others have argued that Ireland's 'complicity' with the coloniser makes it more rather than less interesting. Ireland's postcolonial history has been more harrowing than most and markedly more complex. Whether we regard Ireland as exceptional or normative of the colonial experience, its engagement with colonialism from 1171 to 1922, and especially in the eighteenth century, demonstrates a contentious resistance, constant debates within the colonised society, arguments about what colonialism means and shift-

---

6 Chris Tiffin and Alan Lawson, *De-scribing Empire* (London, 1994), p. 230.   7 Bill Ashcroft, Gareth Griffiths and Helen Tiffin, *The Empire Writes Back: Theory and Practice in Post-Colonial Literatures* (London, 1989), p. 1.   8 Daniel Mengara, 'Postcolonialism, Third-Worldism and the Issue of Exclusive Terminologies in Postcolonial Theory and Criticism', *Commonwealth* 18, no. 2 (1996), 36-45.   9 *The Empire Writes Back*, p. 33; the error is unusual in a book to which I am indebted.

ing points of appeal and targets of attack. Much of this was generated by the colonial discourse coming from Dublin Castle or from Westminster.

Fixed and fluid notions of Ireland

A feature of colonial discourse is that it sees the character of those it controls as unchanging, what Bhabha calls 'its dependence on the concept of "fixity"'. Ireland and the Irish are reduced by the English, as much in literature as in the language of the law, to an uncomplicated unit. Bhabha says this 'sign of cultural/historical/racial difference in the discourse of colonialism ... connotes rigidity and an unchanging order as well as disorder, degeneracy and daemonic repetition.'[10] What lies behind this seemingly unambiguous colonial discourse on Ireland is a considerable contest about identity, history and culture that culminated in the unsuccessful rebellion of 1798 and the Act of Union which abolished the Irish parliament. The chapters that follow illustrate that on the reverse side of colonial rigidity there was an ever-shifting conflict with the agenda and images of imperial history.

For example, the supposed starting date of colonisation, 1171, was contested through much of the eighteenth century. By hindsight we can say the year 1171 marked a foreign intrusion by Anglo-Norman forces which gradually became a colonising process. Colonisation was not a clear-cut event, not least because the English took four hundred years to claim control, and during that time the boundaries between settlers and native Irish often became blurred. As the eighteenth century progressed the English administration in Dublin gradually became other than the voice of the metropole in Westminster. With the American war in 1776 both Catholic and Protestant Irish attitudes towards Westminster changed so that by 1780 the administration which started the century as colonialist had strong anti-colonialist members and thus became divided against itself.[11]

The term 'Irish' is also contentious. As a construct of Westminster it has the undiscriminating sense of the people of Ireland, colonisers and colonised, settlers and natives. English outsiders however kept to a more simple view. In 1775 for example an English traveller in Ireland, the notorious Richard Twiss, remarked of the 'common Irish',

> Shoes and stockings are seldom worn by these beings, who seem to form a distinct race from the rest of mankind; their poverty is much greater than that of the Spanish, Portuguese, or even Scotch peasants; notwithstanding which they appear to exist contentedly.[12]

10 Homi K. Bhabha, *The Location of Culture* (London, 1994), p. 66.   11 See D. George Boyce, *Nationalism in Ireland* (Dublin, 1982), p. 94.   12 Richard Twiss, *A Tour in Ireland in 1775*, 2nd edn (Dublin, 1776), p. 33.

Twiss' bland incurious view of the Irish 'race' prompted considerable anger in Ireland. A poet dubbed him, 'This Prince of travell'd Coxcombs ... With half an Eye he saw Hibernia's Isle,/ Then wrote Remarks would make a Cynic smile.' But English prejudice was nothing new. The poet continued,

> Hibernia long has felt th' illiberal Stroke
> Of English Witlings, and the vulgar Joke;
> Like some broad Targe expos'd her hapless Lot,
> 'Gainst which the Shafts of Malice have been shot:
> But liberal Minds so base a Conduct scorn,
> And love and cherish Worth where-ever born.[13]

This was one way to contest Twiss' view of the Irish. Another was to produce chamber pots with a portrait of Twiss on the inside.[14]

Within a few decades this kind of colonial perception of the Irish as 'a distinct race' took on discernible brutish features in the drawings of James Gillray which then became strikingly negroid in nineteenth-century political drawings and cartoons.[15] Most English certainly presumed a cultural superiority to this simplified view of the Irish: the Protestant and English interest was, said Richard Cox, '(naturally and by custom) an ascendant over the Irish.'[16] The point is a frequent topic of fun in eighteenth-century English plays, novels and poetry. The Irish were characterised as backward, degenerate and unable to speak comprehensible English. Their religion and want of culture had made them that way. English culture would civilise them. The point gives further weight to Declan Kiberd's remark that 'the notion of "Ireland" was largely a fiction created by the rulers of England in response to specific needs at a precise moment in British history'.[17]

England had always been horrified at the thought that the Irish might be more complex. There had always been discernible seepage from the settler community into the native Irish culture in spite of England's attempts to stop it. For example, the Statutes of Kilkenny (1366) prohibited intermarriage, fostering of children and 'concubinage or amour' between the English and Irish, and insisted under penalty that the English speak only their own language, and 'use the English custom, fashion, mode of riding and apparel'.[18] Nevertheless intermin-

13 Mr Lewis, *A Defence of Ireland: A Poem in Answer to the Partial and Malicious Accounts given of it by Mr. Twiss and Other Writers* (Dublin, 1776), p. 22. 14 Joseph T. Leerssen, *Mere Irish and Fior-Ghael* (Amsterdam, 1986), p. 410. 15 See for example John Tenniel's cartoon, 'The Irish Frankenstein', *Punch*, 20 May 1882 in L.P. Curtis, Jnr, *Anglo-Saxons and Celts. A Study of Anglo-Irish Prejudice in Victorian England* (New York, 1968), p. 60. 16 Cited by Charles Ivar McGrath, 'Securing the Protestant Interest: the Origins and Purpose of the Penal Laws of 1695', *IHS* 30, no. 117 (1996), 29. 17 Declan Kiberd cited in Peter Childs and Patrick Williams, *An Introduction to Post-Colonial Theory*, (London, 1997), p. 70. 18 Statutes of Kilkenny (1366), *Irish Historical Documents*, p. 53.

gling went on. Spenser talks of old English families like the Butlers and Geraldines as 'much more lawless and licentious than the very wild Irish'.[19] From Anglo-Norman stock came some of Ireland's best-known nationalist voices including the historian Geoffrey Keating.[20]

Within Ireland itself the term 'Irish' has been equally difficult to pin down. When not constructed by outsiders it refers to different and changing constituencies at different times. The Irish in 1171 are non-English, but that is true only if one forgets that Britons are said to have been among Ireland's earliest inhabitants. Spenser, who refers to the Irish as an entity, acknowledges their ethnic diversity – Scythian settlers in the north, Spanish in the south and Britons on the east coast.[21] If conquest signalled the suppression of a unified Gaelic culture in Ireland, it also heralded the emergence of modified or hybridised cultures on the island.[22] By the eighteenth century the indigenous Gaelic Catholic Irish had been weakened in numbers and influence. The emergent Catholic middle-class Irish, whose cultural roots lay in the Gaelic tradition but whose business and entrepreneurial interests turned them in ever increasing numbers to international trade with France, Spain and the Americas, were a new force for change.[23] They assimilated not just the English language but English modes of living, architecture and manufacture. Their voice surfaces after decades of hardship in the mid eighteenth century, for example in pamphlets, debates about history and the Catholic Committee. Protestant families, mainly landed gentry, some dating back to settlers in the twelfth and again in the sixteeenth centuries, regarded themselves as Irish, as did the Presbyterians in Ulster. There were also the Irish exiles in France. Each of these groups experienced different histories of Ireland and were affected in different ways by the imperial legislation; each therefore held different attitudes towards the colonising power; they argued among themselves but seldom with one another. They shared a common animosity to England but not a common cause. They each objected to being colonised but as this book will show for widely divergent reasons. As critics have noted, the lines between Protestant settler stock and Catholic Gaelic Irish 'were never absolutely water-tight. Yet the distinctions between them remained as the most important forces in Irish history.'[24]

19 Although Spenser has harsh things to say about 'that savage nation', 'stubborn and untamed', 'sly', 'licentious swearers and blasphemers', he differs from later critics by admitting there had been an ancient Irish culture which mastered writing long before England (*A View of the Present State of Ireland*, ed. W.L. Renwick, Oxford, 1970), pp 1, 4, 25, 37, 40, 72. For arguments about Spenser's authorship of this work see Jean R. Brink, 'Constructing the *View of the Present State of Ireland*', *Spenser Studies* 11 (1990), 203-28. 20 Keating (*c.*1570-1649), born in Tipperary, is famous for his history of Ireland in Gaelic *Foras Feasa ar Éirinn*. 21 Spenser, *A View of the Present State Ireland*, pp 37-46. 22 E.g. The first marquis of Antrim (1609-83) is said to have adorned his castle with the latest London fashions and maintained a retinue of Irish bards and musicians in Irish dress (John Kerrigan, 'Birth of a Nation', *London Review of Books*, 5 June 1997, p. 17). 23 See Kevin Whelan, 'An Underground Gentry? Catholic Middlemen in Eighteenth-Century Ireland', *Eighteenth-Century Ireland* 10 (1995), 7-68. 24 D. Gregory Van Dussen, 'Methodism and Cultural Imperialism in Eighteenth-Century

The term 'postcolonial' is used here of those diverse eighteenth-century Irish writers in English who in some way directly contested the colonial presence, or, like Swift, Burke or Maria Edgeworth, offered an ironic view of it. They were all Irish, but different Irish. A multiplicity of meanings lies behind the phrase 'the Irish' as used either in Ireland or at Westminster.

Conquest and religion

Ireland's long history of colonialism had an unusual start and went through many more phases and modes of control than was experienced elsewhere in British history. Why the English came to Ireland was a long time in dispute. Of two theories the first was that Henry was responding to a call from an Irish faction to sort out a wrangle between Dermot MacMurrough, king of Leinster, and Rory O'Connor, high king of Ireland. He may also have wanted to establish such control over the barons in Ireland that they posed no threat to him. The second was that he hoped by subduing Ireland he would please Rome where he had fallen out of favour as a result of his treatment of Thomas à Becket. Also Rome was disturbed at the lack of discipline in the church in Ireland and was looking for ways to remedy this. Henry's invasion would be a considerable help. Behind these two interpretations lie deep ideological and religious differences which need to be considered in some detail.

Supporters of the first theory have argued over the centuries that when Henry II landed he had no intention of colonising Ireland.[25] He came at the invitation of Dermot. Various kings and other chiefs submitted voluntarily to him, and at the council of Lismore 'the laws of England were received and confirmed'.[26] Although this version was repeatedly rejected by Irish Catholic writers, and during the eighteenth century by some Irish Protestants, it had sufficient weight in the minds of Molyneux, Swift, Charles Lucas, Henry Flood and Henry Grattan to be the foundation of their argument for legislative independence. They argued that Ireland had never been a colony of England, that Henry recognised its independence. Yet even these voices complained that in practice England had forced Ireland into dependency. The point at issue in the eighteenth century was whether Henry had conquered Ireland. Molyneux following Locke argued that conquest implies force of arms resulting in 'Absolute Arbitrary Dominion over the Persons, Estates, Lives, Liberties and Fortunes of all those whom he finds in the Nation ...'[27] In Molyneux's view Henry had not done this: he established a 'com-

Ireland', *Eire-Ireland* 23, no. 3 (1988), 20. 25 E.g. Molyneux, *The Case of Ireland's Being Bound By Acts of Parliament in England, Stated*, Dublin, 1698; rpt *The Case of Ireland Stated by William Molyneux* , ed. Andrew Carpenter with an introduction by J.G. Simms and an afterword by Denis Donoghue, *Irish Writings from the Age of Swift*, 10 vols (Dublin), v (1977), pp 30f. 26 Cited by Edmund Curtis, *A History of Ireland* (1936; London, 1957), p. 53; see also Boyce, *Nationalism in Ireland*, p. 29. 27 Molyneux, *Case of Ireland*, p. 39.

pact' with the people of Ireland, 'that they should Enjoy the like Liberties and Immunities, and be Govern'd by the same Mild Laws, both Civil and Ecclesiastical, as the People of England.'[28]

Burke thought the opposite. Echoing Irish Catholic historians like Keating, he emphasised England's deliberate attempt to subject Ireland by force.[29] Henry arrived, he says, 'to secure the conquest'.[30] English families, having entrenched themselves in castles,

> partly by force, partly by policy ... took a firm root in Ireland. It was indeed long before they were able entirely to subdue the island to the laws of England; but the continual efforts of the Irish, for more than four hundred years, proved insufficient to dislodge them.[31]

What Burke perhaps remembered and Molyneux passed over was that from the early days of colonisation the English had insisted on their conquest. The Statutes of Kilkenny for example speak of 'the conquest of the land of Ireland' and distinguish the English settlers from 'the Irish enemies.'[32]

Burke also contended that Henry looked on Ireland as a pawn in his game with Rome. Henry had recently incurred the anger of all Europe for his involvement in the murder of Thomas à Becket at Canterbury in 1170. Partly to create a military diversion at home, but more importantly to be seen to be active in the pope's wishes for a restoration of order in the Irish church Henry decided to invade Ireland: he knew 'that the speedy performance of this condition would greatly facilitate his recovering the good graces of the court of Rome.'[33] Although it is not clear whether Pope Adrian IV, an Englishman, commissioned Henry many years earlier to subdue Ireland, his successor Pope Alexander III certainly instructed the Irish nobles who had sworn fealty to Henry to assist the monarch in his efforts to subdue 'the Irish race, which has fallen so far through the enormity and foulness of its vices ... to submit to the discipline of Christian faith.'[34] Horrified at the moral laxity of the Irish, Alexander was 'duly thankful' to hear from bishops in Ireland that Henry 'had assembled a stupendous force by sea and

---

28 Ibid., p. 46. 29 Keating parallels the English with the Viking invasions in his *Tri bior-ghaothe an bhais* (The Three Shafts of Death). 30 Burke, 'Abridgment of English History', *The Writings and Speeches of Edmund Burke*, 10 vols (Oxford, 1982–), i (eds T.O. McLoughlin and J.T. Boulton, 1997), p. 513. 31 Ibid., p. 514. 32 *Irish Historical Documents, 1171–1922*, p. 53. 33 Burke, 'Abridgment of English History', *The Writings and Speeches of Edmund Burke*, i, 509. 34 Letter of Pope Alexander III, *English Historical Documents, 1042–1189*, ed. David C. Douglas and George W. Greenway (London, 1953), p. 778. Pope Adrian IV is alleged to have written to Henry II that 'Ireland and all other islands which Christ ... has illumined ... belong to the jurisdiction of St. Peter and the Holy Roman Church'; he grants Henry's petition to invade 'for the extension of the boundaries of the Church, for the restraint of vice, for the correction of morals', and ends, 'you may enter that island and perform there the things that have regard to the honour of God' (The Bull 'Laudabiliter', *English Historical Documents*, pp 776–7).

land in order to subject this people to your rule, and to extirpate the foulness of their abominations'.[35] The colonisation of Ireland thus had its roots not just in the ambitions of Henry but in the wider issue of power exercised by Rome.

This religious dimension makes Ireland's colonisation different from that in more recent examples in British history. Rome's desire for Henry to civilise the wild Irish by enforcing a more disciplined Christianity was followed after the Reformation by England's attempts to restrain if not convert Catholics from a religion seen as superstitious and demeaning. Spenser says Irish Catholics were,

> so blindly and brutishly informed, for the most part as that you would rather think them atheists or infidels; but not one amongst an hundred knoweth any ground of religion and article of his faith, but can perhaps say his pater noster or his Ave Maria, without any knowledge or understanding what one word thereof meaneth.[36]

He blames their ignorance, 'lewd lives and filthy conversation' on Rome arguing that 'this general disease' can be removed 'only with very strong purgations.'[37]

Such contempt fuelled by fear led the English in the eighteenth century to legislate in such a way as to effectively outlaw the Catholic religion in Ireland. The penal laws, enacted in the main between 1695 and 1730, served two complementary purposes: they legislated against the practices, institutions and beliefs of the colonised and asserted by implication that the Catholic religion was inimical to the institutional, intellectual and social norms of English culture. The Protestant faith and English ways had to prevail. A sermon in 1661 clearly states the options and hints at an underlying anxiety: 'If the Protestants stand, Rome must fall; but if Rome stand, Rome will still be contriving our fall.'[38] Put in other terms, 'an unregenerate Catholic population would ever be both a standing reproach to Protestantism and a constant source of danger to it'.[39] The protestant bishop of Cloyne writing at the end of the eighteenth century argues that church and state have a relation in Ireland different from that in other European countries: 'In this kingdom, many peculiar circumstances render the support of the Established church more essentially interesting to the Landed Gentleman, the Protestant Government, and the British Empire.'[40] Dublin's renowned Georgian facades, the Bank of Ireland designed by the Irish architect Pearce, the Englishman Gandon's Custom House, Trinity College founded by Queen Elizabeth, the play bills of Thomas Sheridan's Smock-Alley theatre, the statue of King William

35 Pope Alexander to Henry II, c.1172, *English Historical Documents*, p. 779. 36 Spenser, *A View of the Present State of Ireland*, p. 84. 37 Ibid., p. 85. 38 W.L[ightburn], *A Thanksgiving Sermon Preached ... upon the 23 of October, 1661*, cited by T.C. Barnard, 'The Uses of 23 October 1641 and Irish Protestant Celebrations', *English Historical Review* 106, no. 421 (1991), 892. 39 Thomas Bartlett, *The Fall and Rise of the Irish Nation: The Catholic Question 1690–1830* (Dublin, 1992), p. 25. 40 Richard Woodward, Bishop of Cloyne, *The Present State of the Church of Ireland* (Dublin, 1787), p. 13.

III in College Green are all reminders of the dominating ideology of the English.⁴¹

The settlers

In most discussions about colonialism critics have little difficulty identifying the characteristics of the settler but acknowledge that the Janus-like relationship between settler and mother country and settler and indigenous people is much more complex and, as the critic Bhabha and others have emphasised, ambivalent. Just as ambivalence involves both love and hate, so both Ireland and England desired and derided one another. In desiring Ireland England sought to assure itself that it could control what threatened it. Control was attractive for its rewards of land and revenues. The derision stems from an awareness that the Irish were different, in particular they were Catholic. England's conquest of Ireland helped self-definition, not, as Bhabha puts it, as a pre-given identity or self-fulfilling prophecy, but as difference.⁴² That difference heralded the myth of England's own superior culture and more intelligent religion as well as the stereotype of the Irish as fractious, cunning, idle, barbaric. The Irish are what the English are not, though, as Kiberd remarks, the proximity of the two made it difficult 'for the English to treat the Irish consistently as their absolute Other'.⁴³ But the English perception of the Irish was a statement of Ireland's 'otherness', not as Ray Chow puts it, 'as an open-ended process but as a pre-ordained fact'.⁴⁴ With this notion comes the imperial presumption of a superior culture evident in settler discourse throughout the British empire.

Ambivalence has a further dimension in that settlers occupy an ambivalent space between the indigenes and the metropole. Drawn at times to identify with the Catholic Irish against Westminster – as Swift does in *A Modest Proposal* – and at others to assert themselves against them, the settlers moved uneasily between the wilderness to the west and their notion of civilisation across the Irish sea. As has been said of more recent times, the settler, 'is both mediator and mediated, excluded from the unmediated authority of Empire and from the unmediated authenticity of the indigene.' Caught between the authority of the metropole and the 'otherness' of the colonised, the settler tries to find an identity in this 'half-empowered limbo' where 'he fetishizes yet disparages' the metropole.⁴⁵

41 Repeated attempts to deface William's statue were made by undergraduates of Trinity College because William faced the Castle and had his back to the College (Maurice Craig, *Dublin, 1660-1860*, Dublin, 1969, p. 77). 42 See Linda Colley, 'Britishness and otherness: an argument', *Nations and nationalisms: France, Britain, and Ireland and the Eighteenth-Century Context*, eds Michael O'Dea and Kevin Whelan (Oxford, 1995), pp 61-77; also, Bhabha on Fanon in *Introduction to Post-Colonial Theory*, pp 124-5. 43 Declan Kiberd, *Inventing Ireland* (London, 1995), p. 251. 44 Ray Chow, 'Where Have All the Natives Gone?', *Contemporary Postcolonial Theory: A Reader*, ed. Padmini Mongia (London, 1996), p. 136. 45 *De-Scribing Empire*, p. 231.

For this reason perhaps Protestants held onto the idea of Ireland as a separate kingdom rather than a separate nation. Kingdom implied allegiance to the monarch as king of both England and Ireland, thus ensuring his protection, and yet allowed a sense of separateness. For Irish Protestants Ireland was thus a community of Protestants with their own historical roots in the country, a religion, culture and lifestyle drawn largely from England, and yet faced with quite different problems – due largely to the Catholic population of the kingdom – to those found in England. Such views expressed by Molyneux to the English parliament were the basic tenets of Ireland's Protestant 'patriots' who campaigned for parliamentary independence. That way, they argued, they were best able to defend their liberty and property.[46]

This is not to say that the term 'Protestant' is without its own complications. Anglicans of the Established Church in Ireland looked with some suspicion on Ulster Presbyterians who had broken with the Westminster Confession of Faith in the 1720s and established their own presbytery of Antrim.[47] Ulster was to become the seed-bed of a radical politics quite unacceptable to Ireland's Protestant administration.

The Catholic majority was an encumbrance to the Protestant vision of Ireland and put the settler stock in the uncomfortable predicament of deciding whether to pursue with vigour the colonising process or to let it lapse. As they veered between the two, colonisation took centuries to effect, and this in spite of the geographical proximity of colonised to coloniser. In the early centuries Irish chiefs in the south who resisted the English were driven westwards to the Shannon; some were left undisturbed. In Ulster a Somerset knight, John de Courcy, held sway but only over a limited area. Parts of Connaught and the north-west continued outside English control until the sixteenth century. The English took what measures they could to consolidate their thinly spread presence by building stone castles, as opposed to the wooden structures of the Irish, marrying into Gaelic families,[48] allowing only Englishmen to be appointed bishops,[49] establishing a recognised central authority in Dublin, introducing English laws. In spite of the difficulties their civilising mission is clear from the start. In 1277 Edward I wrote to his justiciar in Ireland,

> as the laws which the Irish use are detestable to God and contrary to all law so much so that they ought not to be deemed law, it seems to us and our Council expedient to grant them the laws of England ...[50]

46 See Jacqueline Hill, *From Patriots to Unionists: Dublin Civic Politics and Irish Protestant Patriotism, 1660-1840* (Oxford, 1997), pp 11-14. 47 Thomas Bartlett, 'The Origins and Progress of the Catholic Question in Ireland' in *Endurance and Emergence: Catholics in Ireland in the Eighteenth Century*, eds T.P. Power and Kevin Whelan (Dublin, 1990), pp 3-4. 48 Anglo-Norman settlers to marry Gaelic Irish nobility included de Courcy, Hugh de Lacy and William de Burgo. 49 Some sees – Armagh, Tuam and Cashel – still had Irish bishops (Curtis, *History of Ireland*, p. 69). 50 *Irish Historical Documents*, p. 32; in the same document Edward tells his justiciar that the Irish

The physical presence of the colonising power was strengthened by numerous plantations of English families, typified in the fourteenth century by the establishment of the Pale – that area of 'English land' to the east of a line drawn from Dundalk down the river Barrow to Waterford to be granted only to new settlers. Land beyond the Pale remained contested or outside the control of the colonising power for some four centuries. The king's representative in Ireland was instructed in 1530 to defend the king's lands and resist 'the king's rebellious subjects of the wild Irishry … in their attempts and their invasions'. [51] In a sense the country was reconquered in the sixteenth century – half the money spent by Elizabeth on foreign wars went to the subjection of Ireland;[52] the rising of 1641 led to Cromwell's Irish campaign which finally reduced the country to the Commonwealth government. Ireland was finally conquered, if not completely colonised.

The 'new' English who arrived in the sixteenth and seventeenth centuries, the planter families in Ulster under James I and those settled by Cromwell several decades later, regarded themselves as different from earlier settlers, the Catholic 'old' English. They made no attempt to mix with the Catholic Irish and took an aggressive stand towards them. Their colonising mission was political, religious and civilising. England had to control its back-door neighbour and believed that English values would redeem the Catholic Irish from their barbarism. Neither the style nor the religious affiliations of the new English in the wake of Cromwell endeared them to the older settler families. However, resistance continued – be it in poetry, historical writing, recruiting for the French army or harbouring banished clergy.[53] The process of colonisation was an ongoing battle for the settler. The point is implicit both in the resistance and in the military barracks built all over Ireland at the turn of the eighteenth century. The presence of 12,000 troops in Ireland through much of the century, stationed for home defence and for service abroad and financed by the Irish parliament, is another ambiguous sign of a settler presence caught between assertiveness and unease.

Many settlers came to regard themselves as Irish or what are now called Anglo-Irish. Whether born in Ireland or not, they regarded Ireland as their home. Wolfe Tone remarks of the Dissenters that though 'they were a colony of foreigners in their origin … they soon ceased to consider themselves as any other than Irishmen'.[54] As James puts it, 'the term Anglo-Irish is primarily meaningful as a state of mind, not a condition of birth or inheritance'.[55] This applied to many

---

should pay 'a higher sum of money' than the 8,000 marks they had offered for the privilege of having English laws. 51 'A Deputy's Instructions, 1530', *Irish Historical Documents*, p. 79. 52 A.L. Morton, *A People's History of England* (1938; London, 1989), p. 221. 53 After the banishment of regular clergy in 1698, 'many remained and went underground, some in the houses of wealthy Catholic patrons': Patrick Fagan, *Dublin's Turbulent Priest, Cornelius Nary (1658-1738)* (Dublin, 1991), p. 35. 54 *The Autobiography of Theobald Wolfe Tone, 1763-1798*, ed. R. Barry O'Brien, 2 vols (London, 1893), i, 40-1. 55 Francis Godwin James, *Ireland in the Empire, 1688-1770* (London, 1973), p. 247. The term

eighteenth-century settler Protestant families like the Edgeworths who had acquired land, whose children married like-minded stock and who participated in the administration as justices, members of parliament or as local landlords. Settler as a term signifying a single entity is a fiction of metropolitan critics.

Settlers and land

It was the 'new English' who brought into focus the issue which underpins and exacerbates all colonial endeavours, land. Confiscations and redistribution of land by the English were major features of postcolonial Irish history. Land gave the settlers the status and security they wanted to consolidate their power. Sir Walter Raleigh, for example, received 42,000 acres in Munster which he distributed to English settlers. Before the 1641 rebellion Catholics still owned 60 per cent of the land.[56] As a result of confiscations and counterclaims the figure varied through the years of Cromwellian and then Jacobite settlements, but by 1685 Catholics owned but 22 per cent of profitable land. After the Treaty of Limerick (1691) widespread redistribution and conversions to the Church of Ireland further reduced the figure until it reached 14 per cent in 1704 and declined to 5 per cent during the eighteenth century.[57] The bare figures indicate the move of vested interest into Protestant hands. Even so the dispossessed Catholics maintained a significant presence on the land as tenants or by taking leasehold tenure, and thus established what has been called 'a considerable hidden Catholic interest in land.'[58] A few enjoyed substantial wealth. For example, Patrick Darcy of Galway was reputed in 1760 to have an estate worth more than two thousand pounds a year.[59] However, they were well aware that the transference of ownership to settler families was the most telling sign of their own humiliation.

The majority of Protestant landlords resided on and most improved their estates; Charles O'Hara and at the end of the century Richard Lovell Edgeworth are good examples. But there were owners who preferred to live in Dublin or London or on their English estates, thus epitomising the colonial parasite. Lord Glenthorn in Maria Edgeworth's *Ennui* (1809) spends the first part of the novel living in England off the income from the family estate in the west of Ireland. The absentee landlord was disliked in Ireland not least because he took his money abroad, depriving not just his estate but the country of what was a considerable benefit. In 1729 absentees were said to be spending £621,499 per year

'Anglo-Irish' remains contentious but serves to identify those Irish who either by religion or blood have ties with Anglican England (see Boyce, *Nationalism in Ireland*, p. 94). 56 David Dickson, *New Foundations: Ireland, 1660-1800* (Dublin, 1987), p. 3. 57 S.J. Connolly, *Religion, Law and Power: the Making of Protestant Ireland, 1660-1760* (Oxford, 1992), pp 147, 309-10; Connolly questions the accuracy of the figure of 5 per cent. 58 Bartlett, *Fall and Rise of the Irish Nation*, p. 48. 59 Abbé David Flynn to James Edgar, *Ireland in the Stuart Papers*, ed. Patrick Fagan, 2 vols (Dublin, 1995), ii, 245.

abroad.⁶⁰ In addition they were often careless as to how rents and profits were acquired or at what cost to the local tenants.

The economics of colonialism

After William had driven off the Jacobite threat from Ireland, Westminster felt free to determine the Irish economy and use it if necessary to its own advantage, mainly to protect its trade and to help finance its army. Molyneux put pen to paper because England proposed legislation to protect her own woollens manu-facturers from Irish competition. Swift wrote *The Drapier's Letters* (1724) against English plans to allow a Wolverhampton ironmonger William Wood to manu-facture half-pence and farthings for Ireland. The Irish parliament objected to the scheme as self-serving and damaging to the Irish economy. The protest was eventually unsuccessful, though not until it reached the highest authorities including the privy council. Irish parliamentary protest was repeatedly sparked off by money bills, that legislative ploy whereby the English administration sourced revenue from the Irish exchequer. In 1769 Lord Lieutenant Townshend prorogued the Irish parliament after a dispute over a money bill.

England's control of Ireland's revenue was embedded in the very structures of executive power in Ireland. The lord lieutenant and his senior administrators were appointed from London. They formed an executive authority whose power-base rested in England, not in the Irish parliament. Archbishop King complained to Swift 'that every chief governor who is sent here comes with a design to serve first those who sent him, and that our good only must be so far considered as it is subservient to the main design'.⁶¹ The competence of the lord lieutenant, who until 1767 only visited Ireland for six months every two years, was measured by his ability to see to the smooth passage of money bills. It became the practice at the start of each parliamentary session for members to inspect the public accounts, draft the money bill and then, in keeping with Poynings' Law (1495), forward the bill to the privy council in London for approval. The lord lieutenant's secretary William Hamilton called Poynings' Law 'the charter and security of the British and Protestant interest in this country'.⁶² The bill would be debated on its return, but could only be accepted or rejected in its entirety. The Irish parlia-ment repeatedly contested this control over Ireland's revenue as it clearly left the Irish economy at the mercy of the English privy council.

---

60 *A List of the Absentees of Ireland* (Dublin, 1729), p. 14. The figure had risen to over one million pounds by 1783 (*Walker's Hibernian Magazine* (1783), pp 174-6). 61 King to Swift, 29 July, 1711, cited by J.L. McCracken, 'The Political Structure, 1714-60', *A New History of Ireland*, 10 vols, *Eighteenth-century Ireland, 1691-1800*, eds T.W. Moody and W. Vaughan (Oxford, 1986), iv, 59. 62 Speech to the Irish House of Commons, Nov. 1761 on the money bill, printed in *Parliamentary Logic* (London, 1808), pp 150-1.

A parliamentary confrontation in 1753 demonstrates the power-play between colonisers and colonised. The draft money bill for that session of parliament proposed to use surplus revenue to finance the national debt, but it deliberately omitted to mention the need for the prior consent of the king. On its return to Dublin the bill had been amended to include the clause concerning the king's consent. For that reason the Irish parliament rejected the bill by 122 votes to 117. People in the streets lit bonfires to celebrate, while the lord lieutenant was instructed from London to dismiss several senior officeholders for alienating people 'from that subordination and dependence upon this country which is the security of Ireland'.[63]

Confrontation: settlers and Westminster

The two principal areas of confrontation or what postcolonial criticism calls 'adversarial space' were between settler and Westminster, and between settler and the Catholic Irish. If the coloniser or settler is to survive he must control this adversarial space, and the cleanest way to do this is by legislation. In doing so, the metropole posits its imagined construct of the colonised people which because of its reductionist nature is necessarily fictional. Thus arises what Chow calls 'the politics of the image'.[64] Bhabha, citing Foucault, says the confrontation is not a battle on behalf of the truth, 'but a battle about the status of truth and the economic and political role it plays'.[65] Protestants contested so called truths about Ireland put out by Westminster and at the same time created their own about the Catholic Irish.

England's determination to maintain its hegemony over Ireland had a long history marked for example by Poynings' Law, religious persecution, trade legislation, the Declaratory Act, the appointment of the lord lieutenant and money bills. Over the centuries the colonial agenda in Ireland shifted its emphases according to the impending threat of the times to its control, whether religion, finance, parliament, rebellion or agrarian troubles. Whatever the change of tactic the principle remained the same: Ireland was to be subject to England. Swift's contemporary Philip Yorke, later Lord Hardwicke, put the matter plainly,

> the subjects of Ireland were to be considered in two respects, as English and Irish, that the Irish were a conquered people, and the English a colony transplanted hither and as a colony subject to the law of the mother country.[66]

---

63 Duke of Newcastle cited by Dickson, *New Foundations*, p. 91. 64 Ray Chow, 'Where Have All the Natives Gone?', *Contemporary Postcolonial Theory*, p. 124. 65 Homi K. Bhabha, 'Signs Taken for Wonders', *The Post-Colonial Studies Reader*, eds Bill Ashcroft, Gareth Griffiths and Helen Tiffin (London, 1995), p. 33. 66 Cited by R.B. McDowell, *Ireland in the Age of Imperialism and Revolution*

This was the image and the truth which underpinned the colonial discourse out of England. This is the discourse the settler had to negotiate or contest.

William's victory over James at the Boyne had decided the issue of whether a Protestant or Catholic should sit on the English throne, but it did little to allay fears among the new Irish about their security in what was still Catholic Ireland. They did not accept legislative dependency on Westminster, and felt better qualified to decide their own measures. Molyneux reminded the English parliament of the traditional legal argument that Ireland was equal but different to England, an argument he based on Magna Carta, first declared in Ireland in 1217. This was the original Magna Carta but with 'Ireland' substituted for 'England', 'Dublin' for London', the 'Liffey' for the 'Thames'. That Charter secured the life, liberties and lands of all freemen: 'We will sell to no man, we will deny to no man, or delay, right or justice.'[67] Magna Carta was the passport to legitimacy for the Irish of English stock, the point of origin from which they could derive their liberty and practices.[68] Thus they looked on it as their protection from England's colonising intentions. Magna Carta plainly did not provide for the colonisation of Englishmen by fellow Englishmen and so it was a powerful obstacle to England's design to treat the ever growing numbers of English in Ireland as a marginal and subservient people. For example, in the fourteenth century the earl of Desmond, Maurice Fitzgerald, himself of settler stock, led the resistance to English overlords sent by Edward III. The family was respected locally for its acceptance of the Irish language and its patronage of Irish poets. Desmond set up an alternative assembly to the Irish parliament in Kilkenny, protested that English justiciars did not understand Ireland, that they were corrupt and careless of the needs of the people. His castle at Castleisland was taken and some supporters executed for treason. Desmond's argument, like that of the patriots in the eighteenth century, kept coming back to the rights of citizens as enshrined in Magna Carta, and that was always to raise an awkward political point for the English government.

In 1690 Molyneux was pursuing points made by a Catholic, Patrick Darcy, whose *Argument* some fifty years earlier has been called 'the first fully elaborated statement of Ireland's claim to the status of a sovereign Catholic kingdom under the Crown of England.'[69] According to Darcy, 'the subjects of this his Majesty's kingdome of Ireland, are a free people' and are to be governed by the laws of England and statutes made by the Irish parliament.[70] Later in the eighteenth century Burke continued the point, adding that 'subjects' meant Catholics as well as Protestants.

(Oxford, 1979), p. 131. 67 *Irish Historical Documents*, pp 28-31. 68 See Seamus Deane, Introduction to Terry Eagleton, Frederic Jameson, Edward Said, *Nationalism, Colonialism and Literature* (Minneapolis, 1990), p. 17. 69 Brendan Bradshaw, 'Geoffrey Keating: Apologist for Irish Ireland', *Representing Ireland: Literature and the Origins of Conflict, 1534-1660*, eds Brendan Bradshaw, Andrew Hadfield and Willy Maley (Cambridge, 1993), p. 186. 70 Patrick Darcy (1598-1668), *An Argument*

> I cannot conceive how any thing worse can be said of the Protestant religion of the church of England than this, that wherever it is judged proper to give it a legal establishment, it becomes necessary to deprive the body of the people, if they adhere to their old opinions, of 'their liberties and of all their free customs,' and to reduce them to a state of *civil* servitude.[71]

Burke enunciates an argument which would surface frequently in later eighteenth-century Irish writing for the extension of civil liberties to the Catholic majority.[72] The point in much of his protest on behalf of Ireland's Catholics was that the English constitution which he so admired in theory had shown itself no more than a system of oppression in Ireland. His argument implicitly challenged the colonising purpose and was only begrudgingly accepted late in the century.

The appeal to Magna Carta was a strategy of resistance, but not a plea for independence, and this anomaly is a reminder that until Wolfe Tone no Irish protester argued for complete independence from England.[73] Catholics in 1644 for instance sent a number of demands to the king in Oxford, one of which read,

> That an act shall be passed in the next parliament, declaratory that the parliament of Ireland is a free parliament of itself, independent of, and not subordinate to, the parliament of England, and that the subjects of Ireland are immediately subject to your majesty as in right of your crown, and that the members of the said parliament of Ireland, and all other the subjects of Ireland are independent, and in no way to be ordered or concluded by the parliament of England, and are only to be ordered and governed within that kingdom by your majesty and such governors as are or shall be there appointed, and by the parliament of that kingdom according to the laws of the land.[74]

Protestant members of the Irish parliament in the eighteenth century argued passionately along exactly the same lines. Like the American colonists later they wanted jurisdiction over their own affairs, not severance from the metropole.

---

delivered by Patricke Darcy Esquire, By the express order of the House of Commons in the Parliament of Ireland (Waterford, 1643), p. 130.   71 Edmund Burke, 'Letter to Sir Hercules Langrishe', 1792, *The Writings and Speeches of Edmund Burke*, ix, ed. R.B. McDowell (1991), 611.   72 E.g. The Loughgall Volunteers resolved on 5 June 1784, 'That Rejoicing in the late relaxation of the penal laws against our Roman Catholic Brethren, and firmly persuaded that the descendants of those brave Irishmen who obtained the Magna Charta of this too long oppressed kingdom, can never prove inimical to her Liberties, we most cordially invite the Roman Catholicks ... to flock to the standard and strengthen the ranks of the Loughgall Volunteers' (*Peep o' Day Boys and Defenders: Selected Documents on Disturbances in County Armagh, 1784-1796*, ed. David W. Miller, Belfast, 1990, p. 16).   73 In a controversial letter of 1791 Wolfe Tone speaks of 'separation', adding 'such an event would be a regeneration for this country' (cited by Frank MacDermot, *Theobald Wolfe Tone and His Times*, 1939; Tralee, 1969, p. 62).   74 *Irish Historical Documents*, p. 154.

According to Molyneux, Ireland was 'a Separate and Distinct Kingdom by it self from the Kingdom of England', and therefore not a colony.[75] He had no thought of complete separation. The debate he started was confined to Protestant Irish writers who wanted an independent legislature so that they could, inter alia, safeguard their 'Rights and Liberties', not least against the Catholics, 'in our own Methods regularly in our own Parliament'.[76] This is Molyneux's response to English claims to 'the Lands and Inheritances of the Rebels, and to the absolute Disposal thereof in their Parliament'.[77] Protestants were anxious to control legislation, particularly regarding their land and revenues.[78] But they also needed England. There was no question of foregoing either the authority of 'your majesty' or the legitimising power of England's church and army. These were the lynch pins of settler security and the source of an ongoing ambivalence in settler protest. England was both oppressor and defender. The heart of the problem, as William Drennan was to tell Burke later in the century, was that England's notion of liberty was contradictory,

> A liberty which includes not only a desire of a free government at home, but the power of arbitrary rule over every country that may have the misfortune of being connected with Britain.[79]

Nowhere is settler ambivalence more strikingly evident than in Swift, the Protestant clergyman of settler ancestry, one of the most bitter and ironic Irish voices against English oppression. *Gulliver's Travels* includes one of the most formidable attacks on the colonising process in the English language. Gulliver reflects on why he does not want the lands he has visited to be colonised by England. He deliberately pauses in his narrative to describe what in fact happens behind the national rhetoric on the glories of an expanding empire. His closing remarks echo with sarcasm what Pope Alexander so applauded in Henry II's expedition to Ireland. After 'a crew of pyrates' has claimed a new territory,

> Ships are sent with the first opportunity; the natives driven out or destroyed, their princes tortured to discover their gold; a free licence given to all acts of inhumanity and lust; the earth reeking with the blood of its inhabitants; and this execrable crew of butchers employed in so pious an

---

75 Molyneux, *The Case of Ireland*, pp 47-8, 115-16.   76 Ibid., p. 113. Charles Lucas said an independent parliament was 'the great Bulwark of our Liberty' (Lucas, *The Censor*, v (1 July 1749) in *The Political Constitutions of Great Britain and Ireland*, 2 vols (London, 1751), ii, 473.   77 Molyneux, *Case of Ireland*, p. 112.   78 Molyneux argues that laws imposed by England without Ireland's consent 'will naturally introduce Taxing us Without our Consent; and this as necessarily destroys our Property. I have no other Notion of Property, but a Power of Disposing my Goods as I please, and not as another shall Command' (*Case of Ireland*, p. 129).   79 William Drennan, *A Letter to Edmund Burke, Esq; by Birth an Irishman, by Adoption an Englishman* (Dublin, 1780), p. 6.

expedition, is a *modern colony* sent to convert and civilize an idolatrous and barbarous people.[80]

The passage sums up the processes and the goal of all colonising endeavours. But if we think of Swift as an Irishman the example is fraught with complications. Having condemned colonialism Gulliver goes on to say that English colonies are the exception. His *Drapier's Letters* and much of his poetry demonstrate that Swift did not believe that. Swift like Molyneux protested that England treated Ireland like a colony but had no grounds in law or reason to do so. He typifies the predicament of what Simms calls 'colonial nationalism', wanting the benefits of colonialism without the subservience.[81] He is caught between coloniser and colonised, loving English liberty but hating the 'blood-suckers' of Westminster.[82] Swift speaks up for 'the whole people of Ireland' yet is disgusted by the Catholics for their poverty and their breeding. Ambivalence is a key characteristic of Swift's resistance.

Confrontation: settlers and Catholics

The confrontation between settlers and the Irish Catholics was less ambivalent. The body of laws against Catholics known as the penal laws described the Catholics not just as subservient but as outcasts. One of the ways in which such legislation gives status to truth is that it assumes power to describe and then to curtail what opposes it. A feature of colonial legislation, be it in Ireland, India or Africa, is its ability to confine the opposition to an essentialist meaning. The derogatory nature of this discourse, imagining a unitary set (Irish Catholics) where there is variety, empowers the coloniser to dismiss the opposition en masse from the adversarial space. This the penal laws did with clinical thoroughness.[83]

For instance, the first two laws of 1695 removed any military threat by disarming Catholics who were forbidden to carry weapons or to own a horse worth more than five pounds. Education abroad was forbidden, and later at home unless in a Protestant school. Bishops and regular clergy were banished in 1697; parish clergy had to register on penalty of arrest and transportation in 1704, and in 1709 were required to swear an oath accepting Queen Anne and denying the claims of the Stuarts. Pilgrimages and religious assemblies were banned on the grounds that the 'many thousands of papists' who participated posed a threat to public order and 'the safety of the government'.[84] Later acts forbade Catholics to

80 Swift, *Gulliver's Travels* (London, 1956), p. 315. 81 J.G. Simms, *Colonial Nationalism, 1698-1776*, Cork, 1976. 82 *The Drapier's Letters*, Letter I, *The Prose Works of Jonathan Swift*, ed. Herbert Davis, 14 vols (Oxford, 1939-68), x, 7. 83 The laws were modelled on penal laws against Catholics already operative in England through the seventeenth century; see Charles Ivar McGrath, 'Securing the Protestant Interest: the Origins and Purposes of the Penal Laws of 1695', *Irish Historical Studies* 30, no. 117 (1996), 26-7. 84 Act to prevent the growth of Popery (1704), *Irish Historical Documents, 1172-*

inherit or purchase property or to lease land for longer than 31 years. Unregistered deeds and conveyances were declared void. Catholics were forbidden to practise in the professions, be apprentices in the guilds, or be guardians to or educate orphans. Catholics were barred from election to parliament. They could vote if they took an oath of abjuration in 1709, but this franchise was removed from them and from those married to Catholics in 1728 and remained in force until 1793.[85]

The stereotype Irish Catholic imaged here, echoing passages in Spenser, is fixed and predictable. He likes fighting, he blindly follows an irrational, supersti-tious religion, he is therefore not fit for any responsibile position in society. Although many of these laws fell into disuse as the century progressed they effectively barred Catholics from participating in Ireland's governance.[86] Furthermore they implied that the Catholic religion was inimical to the institu-tional, intellectual and social norms of English culture. The Irish stereotype was an offence to the English myth and was treated with severity in the laws and with ridicule in the arts.

Ironically the laws also helped generate that sense of a recognisable undiffer-entiated entity among Catholics which became a starting point for the very resis-tance the English feared. The laws helped fashion an identity for Catholics who in fact had developed differences among themselves over the centuries of colo-nialism. The Catholic nobility, the dispossessed landowners, graziers, tradesmen, beggars, tenant farmers, agents for absentee landlords, Gaelic speakers, English speakers constituted a complex amalgam of people. What they shared was a common stigma – their religion, together with the penalties, especially the loss of their land. In terms of Bhabha's notion of ambivalence the penal laws were a frightening expression of derision. The Ulster radical John Toland remarked that Ireland presented 'the most deplorable scene of wrongs in the Universe ... where the stronger under colour of Law might oppress the weaker'.[87] This legislation was a forerunner of much reductionist and excluding legislation formulated else-where in the British empire during the nineteenth and twentieth centuries.

1922, p. 194. 85 J.L. McCracken, 'The Political Structure, 1714-60', *New History of Ireland*, iv, 74-5. Many commentators have shown the penal laws were not consistently or vigorously implemented, e.g. Maureen Wall, *The Penal Laws, 1691-1760: Church and State from the Treaty of Limerick to the Accession of George III* (Dundalk, 1976), p. 24 et passim. Also Catholics found ways to circumvent some of the restrictions; for example a report on the Cloyne Diocese in 1732 indicates that 530 Catholic children were at Protestant schools (L.M. Cullen, 'The Blackwater Catholics and County Cork Society and Politics in the Eighteenth Century', *Cork History and Society*, eds Patrick O'Flanagan and Cornelius Buttimer, Dublin, 1993, p. 563). 86 For an important revised view of Catholic prosecutions under the penal laws see Neal Garnham, *The Courts, Crime and the Criminal Law in Ireland, 1692-1760* (Dublin, 1996); Garnham's argument that poverty rather than religion or political principles was the main reason for Catholics coming into conflict with the law seems not to allow that the poverty could be read, at least in part, as the product of the penal laws (ibid., p. 224). 87 John Toland, *Reasons ... why ... An Act for the better Securing the Dependency of the Kingdom of Ireland upon the Crown of*

A peculiar feature of the penal laws was that they allowed redemption from their own essentialist image. If Catholics would renounce their Catholic religion and conform to the established church they would be admitted to all the privileges of the coloniser. Caste and colour made such transference impossible in, say, India or Africa. Many Irish Catholics took the option which meant they could go to university, follow a profession, stand for public office, inherit or lease land. They could cross the dividing line and enjoy the privileges of the coloniser. Burke's parents had renounced their Catholic faith and conformed to the established church with the result that Burke's father could practise as a lawyer in Dublin and the young Edmund could attend Trinity College in Dublin – a career path not open to his Catholic relations in Munster nor to his close friend, Richard Shackleton, who was a Quaker. Bishop Berkeley sums up the colonial policy in the form of a question,

> Whether ... it doth not greatly concern the State, that our Irish natives should be converted, and the whole nation united in the same religion, the same allegiance, and the same interest? and how this may most probably be effected?[88]

The repetition of the word 'same' signifies the ultimate goal of the penal laws.

However, control did not mean the absence of resistance. Nor did the divisions among the Catholics prevent them contesting colonisation in a variety of ways. For example, those with Jacobite sympathies who remained after the Treaty of Limerick put what spirit of resistance they had left into the writing of poetry or history, hoping for the restoration of their lands and king. Even though the penal laws shut them out from overt political resistance, their poetry spoke nostalgically about the past and was watchful of Jacobite fortunes abroad; their histories were full of genealogies tracing their families back to pre-invasion kings. The defeat of James had been the defeat of a legitimate royal authority which Irish genealogists traced back to the pre-colonial times of King Fergus.

Other Catholics, in spite of the penal laws, consolidated agricultural, trade and business interests within the Irish economy which showed considerable expansion in the latter half of the century. Not least of their advantages was their contact with emigrant Irish in the Americas and on the continent. Some acquired power as middlemen on or near ancestral lands which had been taken from their families. Some of these, as Maria Edgeworth shows in *Castle Rackrent*, had no scruples in exploiting fellow Catholics. The informal influence of the middlemen among tenants and local Catholics was considerable.[89] Nor were all

Great-Britain, should not Pass into Law (London, 1720), p. 14.   88 George Berkeley, 'The Querist' (1735), *The Works of George Berkeley*, ed. Alexander Campbell Fraser, 4 vols (Oxford, 1901), iv, 573 (item 289).   89 See Whelan, 'An Underground Gentry?', *Eighteenth-Century Ireland* 10 (1995), 25.

tenant farmers living on the bread-line. Moll Flanders' Lancashire husband, who is Catholic, thinks of taking her to farm in Ireland, a prospect almost as attractive as going to Virginia. He has heard that in Ireland,

> a man that could confine himself to a country life, and that could but find stock to enter upon any land, should have farms there for £50 a year, as were here let for £200 a year; that the produce was such, and so rich the land, that if much was not laid up, we were sure to live as handsomely upon it as a gentleman of £3000 a year could do in England.[90]

By contrast Catholics were also involved in outbreaks of specific local resistance, often to do with taxes, tithes and rents – the 'Houghers' in Connaught in 1710-13, the 'Whiteboys' in Munster and the 'Oakboy' movement in Ulster in the 1760s, and the 'Rightboy' disturbances of the 1780s. This rural protest has been read as an undercurrent of populist action which asserted 'popular notions of legitimacy' over against official legislation.[91]

An alternative response was to conform to the established church. The powerful McDonnells in Ulster were among notable Catholic families who took this option. A major benefit of conformity was the title to land and acceptance into the professions. An argument in favour of conformity was that it would be easier to reconvert to Catholicism than to repossess ancestral land.

A relatively small but influential number of Catholics continued the trend of emigration to France.[92] Not until the Catholic Convention of 1792 did lay Catholics come together for a common purpose.[93]

Resistance came not just from Catholics. Presbyterians in Ulster, hostile to Catholics and rejected by the Church of Ireland, had few allies until later in the century.[94] Many of them had come from Scotland during the seventeenth century and were regarded by Protestants as hostile to episcopacy and monarchy. Lady Orrery writing to her husband in 1751 blamed Swift's 'bitterness' against them 'for keeping up that spirit of division amongst us, so unworthy in X-tians', and she admits to having once 'held both Presbiterian and Roman Catholick in the utmost abhorrence'.[95] Ulster witnessed the most radical theological and political ideas during the century, starting with the Dissenter John Toland's *Christianity not Mysterious* (1696) through to the writings of

90 Defoe, *The Fortunes and Misfortunes of the Famous Moll Flanders* (1722; London, 1978), p. 161. 91 Roy Foster, *Modern Ireland, 1600-1972* (London, 1988), p. 224. 92 E.g. Philip O'Sullivan Beare names 29 Irishmen who were professors on the continent in the early seventeenth century (Benignus Millett, 'Irish Literature in Latin, 1550-1700', *New History of Ireland*, iii (1976), 562. 93 L.M. Cullen, 'Catholics under the Penal Laws', *Eighteenth-Century Ireland* 1 (1986), 35. 94 See James Kelly, 'Relations between the Protestant Church of Ireland and the Presbyterian Church in Late Eighteenth Century Ireland', *Eire-Ireland* 23, no. 3 (1988) 38-56. 95 Lady Orrery to Lord Orrery (8 January 1751), *The Orrery Papers*, ed. the countess of Cork and Orrery, 2 vols (London, 1903), ii, 254.

Drennan in the 1780s. It has been argued that the influence of Freemasonry from northern Ireland on the Irish Volunteers in the closing decades of the century generated a new sense of non-sectarian nationalism which led to the 1798 rebellion. As A.T.Q. Stewart writes, Freemasonery was 'almost the only sphere in which Catholics and Protestants could meet on equal terms'. That explains why,

> the old asperities between Protestants and Catholics seemed suddenly to melt, and both persuasions, especially in the North of Ireland, seemed eager to create a new Irish nationality, one more liberal than the 'Protestant nation' or a hypothetical theocracy dominated by the Catholic Church.[96]

In the closing decades of the century radicalism from the North become a major force in Irish politics. Protestant, Dissenter and Catholic strands of engagement can be read metonymically as a process of subversion, but the subversion sprang from very different histories as well as divergent economic and political contexts.

Irish postcolonial writing

For a host of reasons the corpus of postcolonial writing before independence in many colonial countries is slight. The limitations are well-known – educational opportunities, availability of books, access to publication. Achebe published his first novel two years before Nigeria's independence, Ngugi one year after Kenya's independence. There is a tendency to equate postcolonial writing with work written after independence. South Africa is an interesting exception. Literature had a difficult but striking history there before and during the apartheid era with work by black writers like Plaatje, Mphahlele and La Guma and whites like Schreiner, Gordimer and Coetzee. Their work has been described as 'part of a continuing struggle for survival' because it persistently and imaginatively resisted oppression.[97]

Ireland presents a more complex example not least because there is so much material written during the colonial period. The many voices refusing to acquiesce disagreed with one another and targeted quite different aspects of the colonial presence. Apart from Irish Protestant voices contesting the legitimacy of government – like Molyneux, Swift, Grattan and Tone – there were several Catholic voices – Keating, Lynch, Mac Cruitín, O'Conor, Curry, MacGeoghegan – engaged in rewriting Irish history. They were retaliating against views of Ireland by Englishmen like Davies, Temple and Clarendon. These camps pro-

96 A.T.Q. Stewart, *A Deeper Silence: The Hidden Roots of the United Irish Movement* (London, 1993), p. 177.   97 *The Empire Writes Back*, p. 83.

duced radically different versions of Ireland in a contest that was frequently passionate and prejudiced. For example, in the brief time that James II's Dublin parliament held sway it denounced Temple's *Irish Rebellion* (1646) as seditious, which made it all the more celebrated among Protestants.[98] Catholic historians wrote from the point of view of the victim, and some of them would have regarded Molyneux and his followers with scorn.

That the texts discussed in this book were written in English is not to deny the pertinence of writing in Irish. Indeed, Geoffrey Keating, who wrote in Irish in the seventeenth century, is a seminal figure in the development of Ireland's historical consciousness throughout the eighteenth century.[99] Keating, Lynch and their followers like O'Conor and O'Halloran argued against writers from across the Channel, such as Giraldus Cambrensis, Spenser, Camden, Davies who presented Ireland as uncivilised, with no historical records, no significant culture.[100] O'Conor pointed out that Ireland's political institutions, its records of civil law and jurisprudence dated back to the fourth century BC; hence Ireland was far from being barbaric at the time of England's invasion. The case is closer to that of, say, India with its ancient written culture at the time of colonialism than, say, Africa, North America or Australia.[101] Ireland's was not a purely oral culture about to be subjected to the written word with its peculiar claims to authority and knowledge, as was to happen in much of the British empire. Irish monasteries and schools had produced the renowned artistry of the Book of Kells and the Book of Durrow; the Irish boasted the Brehon Laws, much poetry and a delicate material culture often in gold. The Anglo-Normans faced a people with a literary and cultural heritage every way as old and as sophisticated as their own.

The point is worth recalling because this established culture was a considerable obstacle to colonisation, as is evidenced by England's shifting attitude to it over the centuries. Since Irish, the language of the Catholic majority, had the support of the Catholic clergy until well into the eighteenth century, a recurring issue for the English administration was whether to ignore it, discourage it, or use it to proselytise the majority. Successive governments differed as to how to react. Elizabeth had agreed to its use to try to consolidate the Protestant faith. In 1665 an act of Charles II legislated in typically colonial terms that all place names be anglicised: 'His Majestie taking notice of the barbarous and uncouth names, by which most of the towns and places in this kingdom of Ireland are called' ordered that new names be given, 'more suitable to the English tongue'.[102] A bill

---

98 T.C. Barnard, 'The Uses of 23 October 1641 and Irish Protestant Celebrations', *English Historical Review* 106, no. 421 (1991), 894. 99 Keating wrote an account of Ireland down to the twelfth century, *Foras feasa ar Éirinn*, which circulated widely in manuscript. 100 John Lynch (*c*.1599-*c*.1673), a Catholic from Galway, wrote a riposte in Latin to Giraldus, *Cambrensis Eversus* (1662). 101 Burke called the people of India, 'a people for ages civilized and cultivated; cultivated by all the arts of polished life, whilst we were yet in the woods': Speech on Mr Fox's East-India Bill, 1783, *The Writings and Speeches of Edmund Burke*, ed. Paul Langford, ii (1982), 182. 102 17 & 18 Charles II, c. 2, 234 (1665),

of 1697 proposed to ban Irish, and in 1710 an act was passed to encourage its use.[103] There were moves in the early eighteenth century to train Protestant clergy to conduct services and preach in Irish.[104] Preaching in Irish was not regarded as an encouragement of the Irish interest.[105] However, these developments were soon rejected. Although the Methodists encouraged evangelisation in Irish, most Protestant clergy came to ignore the language.[106] Meanwhile poets like O'Rahilly and Merriman continued writing in Irish for a Gaelic audience. About two thirds of the population of approximately two million were Irish-speaking in 1731 and about a half in 1799. As might be expected, the figures are higher the further westwards one goes from Dublin, though even in Dublin there was a small and active circle of Irish scholars and poets well into the eighteenth century.[107]

The fact that Irish as the language of resistance began to wane in the mid-eighteenth century may be an indication that finally the language of the coloniser had broken down that resistance. The growing acceptance of English could imply that the Irish realised their own culture had been defeated.[108] But other forces have to be considered. Ireland's growing trade and prosperity were dependent on English. The emergent Catholic middle class who acted as entrepreneurs between rural Ireland and the English speaking world had to have the language. It paid to be able to speak English. In addition English was the language of political debate and of controversy among antiquarians and historians. For writers in Ireland to argue against English prejudices, to contest a dignity and identity for themselves, they had to do so in English. That was the medium for economic security as well as of effective resistance.

It might be thought strange that by the eighteenth century the settler community had made no attempt to write a distinctive imaginative literature of their own to capture their experience in this new place. There is no equivalent of Fenimore Cooper, Hawthorne or Whitman attempting to forge a new literature, no figure exhorting writers and thinkers to focus on their new home and not England as Emerson did in nineteenth-century America – 'We will walk on our own feet; we will work with our own hands; we will speak our own minds.'[109] Spenser's poetry which reflects much about the places and experiences of his stay

Irish Statutes, revised edn, intro. W.N. Osborough (Dublin, 1995), p. 289. 103 See T.C. Barnard, 'The Uses of 23 October 1641 and Irish Protestant Celebrations', *English Historical Review* 106, no. 421 (1991), 904-6. 104 Brian Ó Cuiv, 'Irish Language and Literature, 1691-1845', *New History of Ireland*, iv, 374-5. The first Irish lectureship was introduced at Trinity College, Dublin in 1710 (Leerssen, *Mere Irish and Fior-Ghael*, p. 330). 105 Leerssen, *Mere Irish and Fior-Ghael*, p. 331. 106 Van Dussen, ' Methodism and Cultural Imperialism in Eighteenth-Century Ireland', *Eire-Ireland* 23, 23-4, 36. 107 Ó Cuiv, *New History of Ireland*, iv, 383, 393. 108 See David Cairns and Shaun Richards, *Writing Ireland: Colonialism, Nationalism and Culture* (Manchester, 1988), p. 21. 109 Emerson, 'The American Scholar', 31 August 1837, *Anthology of American Literature*, 2 vols, 2nd edn, ed. George McMichael (London, 1980), i, 1036.

in Munster shows no sign of attempting radically new forms. For many there was no need to assert difference from England. Their reasons have already been implied. Ireland's physical proximity to England, the colonising agenda, the limited success of the conquest, at least until the seventeenth century, all contributed to a sense that the settler community were not so far removed from the metropolis as to constitute exile status and near enough to make Dublin the second city of the realm. Writers of talent like Farquhar, Congreve and Goldsmith moved to London largely because that was where fame and money were to be made. Their work gave English conventions a new comic impetus, the amusing spice of an ironic tension between highly refined manners and natural good sense, between an appearance of English craft and Irish naïveté. These were attractive innovations so long as they did not threaten English taste. As Seamus Deane writes,

> Culturally speaking, the virtues of Irish warmth, enthusiasm and spontaneity could be sponsored up to a certain point; when that was passed, those virtues became political vices, characteristic of an ungovernable and unruly race.[110]

The English often reinforced the point by making Irish characters a laughing stock. Their badge of difference and inferiority was that they were no more able to master the English language than to acquire English manners. In Farquhar's *The Beaux' Stratagem* the Irishman Mackshane poses as a French priest and is discovered by the gentleman Aimwell: 'The son of a bogtrotter in Ireland,' exclaims Aimwell, 'Sir, your tongue will condemn you before any bench in the kingdom.'[111] But there is a danger in presuming that because, say, Farquhar or Macklin or O'Keefe moved to London and wrote for English audiences at the centre of the empire they therefore colluded with and were assimilated into the colonising ethos.[112] Irish writers and artists who went to London did so for economic not political motives. It is therefore interesting to question whether their work reads any differently if we stress the Irish background of the writer instead of the English context in which the work appeared.

For all the social, religious and cultural differences among writers who remained in Ireland and who wrote against the English, they produced a markedly similar kind of abuse. The Gaelic poet Egan O'Rahilly, for instance, laments the arrival of the upstart English gentry in a poem addressed to one of the new Anglo-Irish landlords, Lord Kenmare, whom he belittles by using his former common name, Browne,

---

110 Seamus Deane, *A Short History of Irish Literature* (London, 1986), p.119.   111 Farquhar, *The Beaux' Stratagem* (1707), ed. Charles N. Fifer (London, 1977), IV. ii, 61-2.   112 Leerssen's discussion of Irish dramatists in London points up some of the complexities of presenting Irish characters to an English audience (*Mere Irish and Fior-Ghael*, pp 113-20).

> That my old bitter heart was pierced in this black doom,
> That foreign devils have made our land a tomb,
> That the sun that was Munster's glory has gone down
> Has made me a beggar before you, Valentine Brown.[113]

The 'foreign devils' were described variously in all quarters of Irish writing as treacherous, heartless, insolent, plunderers. Voices of protest established a counter-text to England's derogatory images. From Molyneux through to Tone and Edgeworth Irish writers retaliate with their various images of the English, a counter-text which rejects England's image of itself and implicitly asserts a rhetorical power-base from which to define and judge the coloniser. Whereas Philip Yorke had referred to England as the 'mother country', Swift and his followers imaged England as a deceitful suitor. This critical thread of discourse will be a major topic of analysis in each of the chapters that follow.

Cultural identity

Many of the texts discussed below contest the issue of identity, particularly the images given by English writers.[114] They either construct alternate identities by rewriting their history or by subverting the identity imposed from England. Often Irish writers disagree as to what it means to be Irish, or what political, religious, cultural factors should contribute to such an identity. For most eighteenth-century Irish writers identity is a matter of negotiation between competing identities – past and present, idea and practice, and between coloniser and colonised. Gulliver's experiences in his fourth journey to the Houyhnhnms encapsulates many of the issues: he is horrified to be likened to the Yahoos, a race whose filthy habits, rebelliousness, laziness remind us of the Irish as perceived by the English. He adulates his masters, the Houyhnhnms, who reflect certain English characteristics – lack of emotion, clarity of thought, cleanliness. Yet when he returns home he is so deranged as to be incapable of identifying with his wife or his culture. Mentally colonised by the Houyhnhnms he ends up deracinated, with no meaningful identity. In the writings of O'Conor and Burke there are tensions between their family cultural roots and their roles as public figures. After five centuries of colonialism there was less reason than ever for the invocation of an essentialist Irishness, or for a homogenous alternative to the English system. What Irish dissenting voices shared was the desire that England should recognise difference. Irish experiences of English rule together with their

113 Egan O'Rahilly, 'A Grey Eye Weeping', trans. Frank O'Connor, *The Penguin Book of Irish Verse*, ed. Brendan Kennelly (London, 1970), p. 71. 114 For a study of this in the seventeenth century see *Representing Ireland: Literature and the Origins of Conflict, 1534–1660*, eds Brendan Bradshaw, Andrew Hadfield, and Willy Malley, Cambridge, 1993.

cultural heritages had produced identities in Ireland that were different from the reductionist images insisted upon by English historians and dramatists. History is repeatedly invoked both by Catholics and Protestants to validate these separate and discrete identities.

Colonialism affected the various communities in Ireland in different ways and thus authored different identities – Catholic or old English, new English, 'mere' Irish as the English termed the majority of the Catholics, patriot Anglo-Irish. The problem is to know which if any of those identities had or should have precedence in the several histories of Ireland, whether they could co-exist or might in some respects merge. Ireland's case throws up the complex issue of competing identities within a colonised country. Awareness of difference from the metropolitan did not produce among the people of Ireland a recognisable or unified counter-identity. All postcolonial societies, it has been said,

> are constituted by their difference from the metropolitan and it is in this relationship that identity both as a distancing from the centre and as a means of self-assertion comes into being.[115]

This did not happen in eighteenth-century Ireland. Differences within Ireland, encouraged by the English over the centuries, prevented a unified sense of difference against the metropolitan centre.

The resulting diversity could be said to have enervated attempts by writers like Walter Harris, John Curry, Thomas Leland, or O'Conor to take the initiative in establishing a version of Irish history acceptable to Protestants and Catholics alike and based on the scholarly evidence of written and archaeological sources.[116] In the 1760s both the Catholic O'Conor and the Protestant Burke believed that Thomas Leland, respected scholar, librarian, Professor of History and Fellow of Trinity College, was the person best equipped to write such a history. The bias towards English historiography in his *History of Ireland* published in 1773 disappointed both of them. Burke's disgust is summed up in a remark to his son twenty years later: Leland, he wrote, 'thought only of himself and his bookseller'.[117] O'Conor continued to work in the field, producing in 1775 *The Ogygia Vindicated*, an edition of Roderic O'Flaherty's work, and in 1786 a second edition of his long-standing friend John Curry's work *An Historical and Critical Review of the Civil Wars in Ireland*. His enthusiasm for these fellow historians is consistent with the nationalist undercur-

115 *The Empire Writes Back*, p. 167. 116 For a discussion of the study of Irish antiquities as a ground for reconciliation between Protestant and Catholic scholars see Clare O'Halloran, '"The Island of Saints and Scholars": Views of the Early Church and Sectarian Politics in Late Eighteenth-Century Ireland', *Eighteenth-Century Ireland* 5 (1990), 7-20, and Colin Kidd, 'Gaelic Antiquity and National Identity in Enlightenment Ireland and Scotland', *English Historical Review* 109 (1994), 1197-1205. 117 Burke, *Correspondence of Edmund Burke*, ed. T.W. Copeland, 10 vols (Cambridge, 1958-78), ii, 285, n. 5 (20 March 1792).

rents of his *Dissertations*. But his disappointment with Leland was evidence that one of the hopes implicit in the *Dissertations*, a convergence of Catholic and Protestant voices in Irish historiography, was not to be realised in his lifetime.

Such a convergence might have given coherence and a different direction to Ireland's nationalist endeavours at the end of the eighteenth century. Instead, arguments continued as to the acceptable version of Ireland's history, Clarendon or Keating, Hume or O'Conor. The English version of Irish history, evidenced and enforced the enabling legislation and determined identities until well into the eighteenth century. Yet there were always Irish voices contesting the authority of that version – some close to, some far from the metropolitan centre – Keating, Molyneux, Farquhar, Swift, Mac Cuirtín. These voices contend for an identity distinct if diverse from that given by England. It was a contest that took a new course after the 1798 rising.

Predominant discourses in eighteenth-century Ireland

In comparison with twentieth-century postcolonial writing around the world there is a curious paucity of novels in eighteenth-century Irish writing. In many former colonies fiction and poetry were seen as the way of escape 'from the politics of dominance and subservience.'[118] Major Irish writers – Congreve, Farquhar, Swift, Berkeley, Burke, Goldsmith, Sheridan – give the impression that this was one of Ireland's great periods for drama and non-fictional prose; indeed, in terms of conventional imaginative literature Ireland only offers Swift's *Gulliver's Travels*, Goldsmith's *Vicar of Wakefield*, Edgeworth's *Castle Rackrent* and a few other novels against the copious output of English writers like Defoe, Fielding, Richardson and Smollett. The novels of lesser known Irish writers, Chaigneau, Brooke, Amory, soon disappeared from public attention.[119] Apart from the drama the overwhelming corpus is writing on historical, political, religious and economic affairs – suggesting a preoccupation, not with imaginative escape from the colonial presence, but with engagement, with the language of argument, debate, persuasion. The century is famous for the rhetoric of Burke, Flood, Grattan, Curran, whose speeches create a more overtly political discursive contest than any other in postcolonial literature. Here the empire comes close to literally talking back, and in doing so proffers political rhetoric as an important area of postcolonial discourse for analysis.

The century ends with a rebellion, a progress suggesting the abandonment of political debate for arms. It is ironic that at the same time as the Union is being debated in the Irish parliament Edgeworth's *Castle Rackrent* is published. That

118 *The Empire Writes Back*, p. 35. 119 E.g. William Chaigneau, *The History of Jack Connor* (1752), Thomas Amory, *The Life of John Buncle, Esq.* (1756-66), Henry Brooke, *The Fool of Quality, or the History of Henry, Earl of Moreland* (1766-70).

novel signals the end of a century of political debate and a new direction for writing in Ireland. It was followed by much patriotic if romantic poetry and is accepted as the seminal work in regional and by implication national literatures. Edgeworth completely changes the axis of the postcolonial debate by handing over her narrative to the Irish serving-man narrator, Thady Quirk. He is a product of and experienced only in the ways of service on an estate in rural Ireland, 'an observer fully within a society he exemplifies as well as describes'.[120] Parliament in Dublin, not to mention Westminster, is but a name to him. And yet the issues which so plague the Rackrent family and which his son Jason so deviously manipulates to his advantage are inextricably entwined in the debates in those parliaments. To appreciate the terms of those debates it is necessary to go back to William Molyneux's *Case of Ireland Stated* published just over a hundred years earlier.

Molyneux, a member of the Irish parliament addressing members of the English House of Commons, writes to the heart of the empire. The importance of Molyneux to this study is that he establishes Ireland's stance towards Westminster which was to be rewarded only in 1782 when Grattan exclaimed, 'Your genius has prevailed. Ireland is now a nation.'[121] Well-informed on constitutional law and historical precedents, his argument never wavers from the premise that the Irish legislature had always been independent of Westminster. He also typifies that line of Irish protest by well-educated Protestants who stressed equality with rather than difference from England, a point that would be taken up by Benjamin Franklin and the American colonists later in the century.

Molyneux was one of many who had fled to England in 1689 frightened by the prospect of a Jacobite parliament in Dublin. As Simms has shown, Molyneux advocated a 'colonial nationalism' which meant an Irish parliament independent of England's privy council, yet loyal to the British crown.[122] The formula remained tempting until the fateful Treaty of 1922. This bonding with the metropole, denying subservience or constraint, yet stressing loyalty, meant Molyneux located himself as independent yet within the colonial space. Swift, for all his acerbic indignation, as well as Maria Edgeworth, occupies much the same position. Other writers covered by this study do not. Although Burke in the House of Commons stands at the centre of the empire his writings on Ireland indicate that his sympathies were across the Irish sea. The historian Charles O'Conor moves from Gaelic Ireland to Dublin, crossing the boundary between cultures

---

120 George Watson, Introduction, *Castle Rackrent* (Oxford, 1969), p. xix.   121 Cited by J.G. Simms, Introduction, *The Case of Ireland Stated by William Molyneux*, in Irish Writings from the Age of Swift series, vol. 5 (Dublin, 1977), p. 14. The fact that Grattan may have fashioned this remark for the published version of the speech and did not use it on the day does not affect the argument.   122 J.G. Simms, *Colonial Nationalism, 1698-1776*. For the view that 'colonial nationalism' should be seen as 'an important strand in the complicated skein of Irish nationalism' see Boyce, *Nationalism in Ireland*, p. 107.

and political histories with a view to obliterating it. Irish exiles in Bordeaux and elsewhere write from outside the colonial space and look upon it with markedly different eyes. Attention to Molyneux and the Protestant writers who followed him is essential to an understanding of eighteenth-century Irish writing, but it has tended to marginalise these and other writers and to neglect the many differences they reveal.

These writers have in common a spirit of resistance which they share with several others not dealt with in this study like William Drennan. The largely Presbyterian radical tradition stemming from Locke prompted the radical resistance voiced by Drennan and the United Irishmen at the close of the century.[123] The rebellion brought to a dramatic conclusion a spirit of resistance that had hitherto been too diverse and unfocused to make so dramatic an impact. Nevertheless the urge to contest had long been there. Ireland was other than England claimed. By reading texts from a wide variety of protesters in relation to one another we recuperate the scene behind the screen of colonialism. If the impression is of *quot homines, tot sententiae* that is a further manifestation of the divisions colonialism had wrought in Ireland, but it does not deny that the Irish, whoever they were, considered themselves oppressed. As Burke's friend Beaumont Brenan put it,

> Here had Oppression fix'd her harpy Claws,
> And reign'd secure, beneath the Show of Laws.[124]

How to deal with that oppression and what was envisaged beyond it prompted the large body of writing hinted at in this study. Postcolonial writing in Ireland during the eighteenth century is a much more complex phenomenon than has hitherto been recognised.

123 Norman Vance, 'Celts, Carthaginians and Constitutions: Anglo-Irish Literary Relations, 1780-1820', *IHS* 22 (87) 1980, 230.   124 Beaumont Brenan, *The Patriots: A Poem* (Dublin, 1754), ll, 28-9.

CHAPTER TWO

William Molyneux's *Case*: the rhetorical myth

WILLIAM MOLYNEUX: THE VOICE OF SETTLER PROTEST

The seminal work of Protestant protest in eighteenth-century Ireland is William Molyneux's *Case of Ireland's Being Bound by Acts of Parliament in England, Stated* published in Dublin in 1698.[1] Regarded for nearly a century 'as the classic assertion of the legislative independence of Ireland',[2] it argued that Ireland was not subject to the English parliament, that Ireland was a separate kingdom with equal rights to self-determination, and that while it enjoyed the benefits of Magna Carta and English Common Law it did so 'by the free Consent, Allowance and Acceptance of the People of Ireland'.[3] The *Case* was 'an immediate sensation' and its arguments were quickly contested both in parliament and the press.[4] It is essentially a letter of grievance to the English parliament about its colonial attitudes: it was quite wrong in law and policy to treat Ireland as subservient to England, even more so as a colony. Molyneux's argument illustrates much of the complexity and ambivalence inherent in Protestant attempts to reconstruct their relationship with the metropole.

The voice of Protestant protest was much more audible for most of the century than that of Catholics, Dissenters or exiles for the good reason that the Protestants as the ruling class in Ireland occupied all the positions of influence – parliament, the law, the church, the army, the press, banking and education. Consequently the ideas of a writer as serious and well-informed as Molyneux

---

1 *The Case of Ireland's Being Bound by Acts of Parliament in England, Stated*, Dublin, 1698; rpt *The Case of Ireland Stated by William Molyneux* , ed. Andrew Carpenter, with an introduction by J.G. Simms and an afterword by Denis Donoghue, Irish Writings from the Age of Swift series, 10 vols Dublin, vol. 5, 1977. 2 J.G. Simms, Introduction, *Case of Ireland*, p. 7. 3 *Case of Ireland*, p. 56. 4 *DNB*, xiii, 587 and *Parl. Hist.* v, 1181. Details of four replies in 1698 are given by Carpenter in Appendix A, *Case*

would be quickly current and remain so among fellow Irish Protestants. It might also be mistaken for the voice of 'the people of Ireland', a favourite phrase of Molyneux and Swift. Protestant writers could readily converse with members of the Irish parliament or the university or the city corporation, could read Faulkner's *Dublin Journal* as reflecting their interests and contribute to the day-to-day debates about national policies and affairs. They were what Anderson calls an 'imagined' community,[5] imagining themselves as bonded by the same political, religious and economic concerns and distinct as a group from the Catholic Irish. Their ready access to people and positions of influence not only contrasts with the very subdued voice of other groups, notably the Catholics, but tends to draw inordinate attention to their point of view. For at least the first half of the eighteenth century this was the voice that mattered in debates between Ireland and England, and Molyneux was their learned and eloquent spokesman.

Molyneux's pertinence to this study is that he exemplifies the underlying ambivalence of Protestants towards Westminster, the contradictory feelings of respect and scorn, of loyalty and resistance. He occupies that problematic space between Westminster and the majority of the Irish people. It is a position in settler writing described as lying between oppressor and oppressed, which nevertheless entails 'a complicity with colonialism's territorial appropriations' while at the same time 'forging a resistance to its foreign rule'.[6] Resistance so operates in Molyneux and his disciples as to rewrite the terms of complicity.

Molyneux both in his personal background and in the character of his writing displays all the characteristics of the eighteenth-century Irish Protestant protester. He was of settler stock dating back to the sixteenth century. His ancestor Sir Thomas Molyneux (1531-97) was born in Calais, moved to Ireland where he became chancellor of the exchequer (1590) and contributed to the building of Trinity College in Dublin under the patronage of Queen Elizabeth. Service in government was a family trait. Both Sir Thomas' sons became members of the Irish parliament, as William himself was to do for Dublin University in 1692 and 1695. William's wife, Lucy, was the daughter of the attorney-general in Ireland, Sir William Donville. Family ties with the establishment are more pronounced than for any other major protester in the century.

His intellectual career was more academically striking than that of say Swift, Burke, Grattan or Curran. Like them he was educated at Trinity College, Dublin and soon developed an interest in philosophy and astronomy. He translated Descartes' *Méditations* (1680), helped found the Dublin Philosophical Society in 1683, was elected to the Royal Society in 1685 and became a friend and corre-

of Ireland, pp 143-44. The *Case* prompted an Address from the Commons 'Against any Claim of Independence for Ireland 1698': *English Historical Documents*, viii, ed. Andrew Browning (London, 1953), 777-8. 5 Benedict Anderson, *Imagined Communities: Reflections on the Origin and Spread of Nationalism* (1983; rev. London, 1991), pp 6-7. 6 Childs and Williams, *Introduction to Post-Colonial Theory*, p. 84.

spondent of John Locke. He wrote the first treatise in English on optics (1692) and received an honorary doctorate from Trinity College in 1693. There can be little question that he was a leading intellectual in Ireland, brought up in an essentially English academic tradition, who had no hesitation in calling himself Irish. Yet, like Swift and Lucas he is silent about the political aspirations of the Catholic majority in Ireland.[7] His audience lies not westwards in Gaelic-speaking Ireland but across the Irish sea in England. Dublin-London was the axis of his political interests. Swift and Grattan had a similar perspective and spoke accordingly. Burke with his roots in rural Munster was much more hesitant, always conscious that the political power struggle between Westminster and Dublin and the warped legislation which resulted from it reverberated down through the country to his Catholic relations and friends who suffered accordingly. Molyneux by contrast had no such family links. He passes over the grievances of rural Catholic Ireland in silence. His concern is Protestant Ireland and its claims to legislative equality with England. Calling on Magna Carta and the philosophy of Locke he raises the debate to a level of moral and universal principle, which is ironic since there is no place in the argument for the Catholic majority. After citing Prynne on Magna Carta he says,

> Here we have a free Grant of all the *Liberties of England* to the *People of Ireland*. But we know the *Liberties* of Englishmen are Founded on that Universal *Law of Nature*, that ought to prevail throughout the whole World, *of being Govern'd only by such Laws to which they give their own Consent by their Representatives in Parliament.*[8]

This was the Protestant anti-colonial argument which Grattan's parliament brought to fruition in 1782 and was used to such effect by the American colonists. The crux is that England's liberties are Ireland's liberties. For Westminster to think otherwise is a betrayal of history and has to be resisted as much on moral as political grounds. To think of Ireland as a colony is to deny the relationship embedded in Magna Carta.

Why then, one might ask, was Molyneux so anxious to make the point? Recent debates on Ireland at Westminster and the ongoing dispute between parliament and King William over the redistribution of hundreds of thousands of acres of Irish land confiscated from Jacobite supporters indicated that England presumed to settle Irish affairs as it thought fit: Ireland was a dependency and England proposed treating her as such.[9] This attitude challenged the very iden-

---

7 An example of what Ashcroft, Griffiths and Tiffin call, 'the silencing and marginalisation of the post-colonial voice by the imperial centre' (*The Empire Writes Back*, p. 83); also Bhabha, *The Location of Culture*, pp 123-7. 8 *Case of Ireland*, pp 52-3. 9 William wanted to grant the land to his Dutch and English supporters whereas the Commons and many Protestants in Ireland thought they should have preference (see Dickson, *New Foundations*, pp 50-1).

tity of Irish Protestants. The presence in Ireland of James II had threatened their lands, their political power and their very raison d'être for being in Ireland. Accordingly William's victory at the battle of the Boyne in 1690 not only restored Protestant settler fortunes but confirmed old ties with their spiritual and physical kith and kin in England. That relationship stretching back over centuries was one of common cause, not subservience. The spirit of liberty in Magna Carta was a crucial reference point 'not because Ireland was a colony, but – on the contrary – because Ireland was *not* a colony'.[10] The markers of Protestant Irish identity would change dramatically if Westminster insisted on treating Ireland as subservient and this is Molyneux's underlying anxiety. Ireland would have a new character in which the distinction between settlers and native Irish would be less clear in English eyes. The move would imply a geographical if not cultural entity within which such oppositions as did exist would be less significant than the comprehensive entity known to the English as 'Ireland'. That would be the beginning of the end for the Protestant Irish.

The particular issues which prompted Molyneux to write his *Case* were first, a bill before the English parliament to prevent the export of Irish woollens, and second a lawsuit over land rights between Bishop William King of Derry and the London Irish Society. In this latter debate the question was whether the Irish or the English House of Lords was the higher court of appeal in an Irish dispute. Both issues raised the key problem: had England the right to legislate for Ireland? The question was to surface several times during the eighteenth century, and on every occasion Molyneux was cited and republished.[11]

Irony and myth-making

Molyneux's implied audience is English. Writing to Locke about the *Case* he says, 'I think I have treated it with that caution and submission that it cannot justly give any offence,' a sentiment which sums up much of the gentle manner with which he advances his arguments.[12] However, the gentleness contains a lurking ambiguity, leaving the reader uncertain whether it stems from respect for, even wariness of his English readers, or whether this is an ironic pose, a mark of hidden ridicule. The opening address to the king confirms this desire not to offend but rather to reaffirm age old principles. Only in one passing subordinate clause does Molyneux avert to the fact that anyone disputes Ireland's rights and liberties under the English crown, 'which some of late do Endeavour to Violate'.[13] Far from showing any desire to confront or accuse English readers, Molyneux cultivates a tone of cooperation. He tells the reader he presents his reasons 'with

10 Boyce, *Nationalism in Ireland*, p. 103. 11 *The Case of Ireland* was printed nine times during the eighteenth century; details are given in Appendix A, *Case of Ireland*, pp 141-2. 12 Cited by Simms, *Case of Ireland*, p. 10. 13 Ibid., p. 17.

all Modesty and Submissiveness'.[14] Referring to the English parliament, he declares 'a Submissive Acquiescence in whatever they Resolve for or against what I offer'.[15] The point belies the underlying purpose of the *Case* which is to contest and refute English claims to a right to legislate for Ireland. Even if the choice of words like 'Submissiveness' and 'Acquiescence' is a rhetorical pose, there is nevertheless an underlying sense that he had no desire to offend or stir up trouble for either himself or Ireland. The ambiguity however remains elusive. The writing moves between the well-intentioned and the ironic, and sometimes both levels operate at once.

For Molyneux and his successors England is admirable, at least in theory, because it avows justice, which in turn rests on the universal principle that 'Liberty seems the Inherent Right of all Mankind'.[16] Therefore Ireland's claim to the freedom to make its own choices is at one with England's sense of justice and liberty. That is the direction of the argument. His fulsome praise of the English parliament is so crucial to this argument that his images of the English border on the mythical. This is apparent from the start. The opening sentence reads,

> I have ever been so fully perswaded of the strict Justice of the Parliament of England, that I could never think that any of Their Proceedings, which might seem to have the least Tendency to Hardship on their Neighbours, could arise from any thing but want of Due Information, and a right State of Business under their Consideration.[17]

Yet the praise is undercut by the innocent sounding suggestion that 'strict Justice' towards Ireland could be thwarted by so correctable a fault as 'want of Due Information'. This critical undertow could be missed by English readers not ready to be treated ironically. Molyneux argues that in normal circumstances the deliberations of Westminster do not err, and, if they do, the blame is not to be placed on parliament, 'that August Senate',[18] but on those 'whose Affair is Transacting, and who permit that Illustrious Body of Senators to be Mis-inform'd.'[19] Molyneux has nothing but praise for 'those Great Assertors of their Own Liberties and Rights.'[20] Far from being conquerors or even hostile to Ireland, their actions are typified by Henry II's conduct in Ireland when, 'all was transacted with the greatest Quiet, Tranquility, and Freedom'.[21] Henry 'rectified many Abuses in the Church', and introduced 'Mild Laws'.[22] At the 1641 rebellion the English acted 'for our Relief and Safety',[23] and in 1689 when the likes of Molyneux felt threatened by James II England provided a refuge and a charity that he terms 'munificent'.[24] This reading of the English culminates in the image of them as 'Men of Great Wisdom, Honour and Justice'.[25]

---

14 Ibid., p. 22. 15 Ibid., p. 24. 16 Ibid. 17 Ibid., p. 23. 18 Ibid., p. 30. 19 Ibid., p. 23. 20 Ibid. 21 Ibid., p. 30. 22 Ibid., pp 45-6. 23 Ibid., p. 86. 24 Ibid., p. 89. 25 Ibid., p. 131.

Such images have an idyllic generosity. Not unlike Burke's panegyric on the English constitution – 'the well compacted structure of our church and state, the sanctuary, the holy of holies of that ancient law, defended by reverence, defended by power, a fortress at once and a temple'[26] – they establish an ideal against which the reader is free to measure the vagaries of history. As Molyneux hints from time to time, such idealism sometimes jars with political realities. William III had come to the throne 'to Assert the Rights and Liberties of these Nations',[27] and yet during his reign the rights of Ireland 'have received the greatest Weakening'.[28] Molyneux's praise of the English Commons stands awkwardly too against the proceedings in the debate on 21 May 1698 when members attacked the *Case* because it 'denied the Dependence of Ireland upon the authority of the parliament of England'; members insisted on 'the subordination and dependence that Ireland has'.[29] When Molyneux praises the English as 'Great Patriots of Liberty and Property'[30] he omits the likes of the testy Mr Garroway who in a debate on the state of the nation had told the House, 'If you will do no more, let us consider in the house how to raise money to conquer Ireland.'[31] Molyneux's rhetorical praise bears little relation to the mind of the English parliament at the time he was writing.

But the myth of a wise and just assembly has a purpose for Molyneux beyond validating the past or flattering present politicians. It provides a moral framework on which to build the future. Ireland's liberty within the English vision of empire will be secure only if the English see themselves as Molyneux here presents them. Ireland has no future if he stresses how often England has deviated from the norms of Magna Carta or if he images the English as oppressive and domineering. Those images became a part of later protest literature. Swift, for example, ridicules and berates the English in *The Drapier's Letters*. The arrogance and perfidy of the English are regular butts in the protest of Grattan and Curran. Molyneux avoids any such direct abuse or remonstration, preferring an elusive ironic rhetoric that posits an image of the English that will stand as a counsel to perfection.

In the closing pages of the *Case* the idyll is surrounded by issues which throw it into critical relief. There is even a note of threat in Molyneux's voice,

> I believe there will need no great Arguments to convince the Wise Assembly of English Senators, how inconvenient it may be to England, to do that which may make the Lords and people of Ireland think that they are not Well Used, and may drive them into Discontent.[32]

Praise of parliament is here again equivocal. What sounds like a compliment bears the message that parliament had better be wise if it is to avoid trouble from

---

26 'Letter to a Noble Lord' (1796), *Writings and Speeches of Edmund Burke*, ix, 172.   27 *Case of Ireland*, p. 95.   28 Ibid. p. 94.   29 *Parl. Hist.*, v, 1181.   30 *Case of Ireland*, p. 130.   31 *Parl. Hist.*, v, 478 (14 Dec. 1689).   32 *Case of Ireland*, p. 130.

Ireland. The sentence is anchored, not on the phrase 'the Wise Assembly of English Senators', but on the final word 'Discontent.' That modifies the confidence of the opening and leaves the praise as an open issue.

Molyneux's *Case* is designed to provide such information as the English need, particularly on the historical status of the Irish parliament and its right to an independent and representative legislature, so as to bring Westminster back to its proper sense of justice. Reconciliation with the myth is the aim, not confrontation. The myth is the principal strategy for persuading the English to accept Ireland as an equal in terms of natural and institutional law.

Debates about conquest

Molyneux traces the myth back to that highly contentious point in Ireland's history, the first landing of the English in Ireland under Henry II. If it can be established that Henry was no conqueror but a peacemaker then the original bond between the two countries is one of mutual respect and Ireland has a clear case that England has no business 'to intermeddle with the Affairs of Ireland'.[33] However, there was a strong body of opinion that had no doubt but that in 1171 the English had conquered Ireland. From the outset Molyneux dismisses the claim as deceptive. The right England pretends to 'for Binding us by their Acts of Parliament' rests on 'the Imaginary Title of Conquest or Purchases, or on Precedents and Matters of Record'.[34] Conquest comes first in this list, partly because it had substantial support in seventeenth-century English thought about Ireland; furthermore conquest was an uncomfortable notion because it left the conquered with no room for negotiation. Conquest as enunciated by, say, Hobbes would leave Ireland with no case. Hobbes wrote,

> *Conquest* ... is the acquiring the right of soveraignity by victory. Which right, is acquired in the people's submission, by which they contract with the victor, promising obedience, for life and liberty.[35]

The spirit of this definition is evident in comments about Ireland in the debate in Westminster on Molyneux's *Case* when it was first published. The book was regarded as subversive because it 'denied the Dependence of Ireland upon the authority of the parliament of England'.[36] This was particularly alarming to those members of parliament who wished to curb the king's power and saw in Molyneux's book an argument to recognise the monarch but not Westminster.[37] Some months earlier when petitions were coming to parliament from English

---

33 Ibid., p. 25.   34 Ibid.   35 Hobbes, *Leviathan* (1651; Oxford, 1960), p. 721.   36 *Parl. Hist.*, v, 1181.   37 See Dickson, *New Foundations*, p. 48.

tradesmen asking for protection against Ireland's increasingly prosperous woollen trade the language of protest had at its core the presumption that Ireland was a subject nation and therefore had no business competing with or challenging English trade. The petitions refer for recent proof of this to King William's victories in Ireland in 1690 as the 'Reduction of Ireland'; the phrase is used frequently.[38] Although there was considerable disagreement in England on these issues, parliament took a strong line that Ireland was a subject nation, a presumption based on notions of superiority, a confidence in military prowess and a sense of benificently introducing order where there had been and at times continued to be chaos.[39] This patronising and uncompromising attitude found support through to the end of the century, as is reflected in an Irish satire on 'The Lion of Old England': 'The laws of conquest are the mightiest laws;/ This said, the generous lion roared applause.'[40] Regardless of Molyneux the Commons passed the Irish Woollens Act (1699) which prohibited Ireland from exporting woollen cloths except to England.

This was the English parliamentary discourse Molyneux was writing against. From the opening pages of the *Case* he is aware that the tradition informing his opponents goes back to the issue of Henry II's landing in Ireland. The view that Henry conquered Ireland was stated by the twelfth-century Welsh historian Giraldus and continued by writers like Spenser, Sir John Davies, and Sir James Ware. Davies writes, 'The State of England did earnestly desire ... to perfect the Conquest of this Kingdom.'[41] Molyneux rejects this reading and with it the traditional English attitude that England therefore had a right to govern Ireland, with or without the consent of the people.

The confidence with which English parliamentarians talked about Ireland's subservience in the 1690s belies the fact that in England itself conquest had long been a contentious issue.[42] The principles as applied to Ireland were by no means so clear when applied to recent events in England such as the 1688 Revolution and the circumstances leading up to it. Debates between Tories and Whigs about the Stuarts centred on the legitimacy and source of the king's right to rule. An important contingent concern, raised, for example by the arrival of William, was usurpation. In brief, England had a number of awkward questions to answer: was William a usurper of the throne? Was William or James II the rightful king of England? If James returned to conquer William, would that conquest legitimise his authority?

---

38 See *Journal of the House of Commons*, Petition from Barnstable, 11 January 1698, xii, 40 and Petition from Tiverton, 26 January 1698, xii, 64.   39 See C.D.A. Leighton, *Catholicism in a Protestant Kingdom: A Study of the Irish 'Ancien Régime'* (Dublin, 1994), pp 31-2, 36-7.   40 James Porter and T. Russell, *Review of the Lion of Old England*, 2nd edn (Belfast, 1794), p. 7.   41 *A Discoverie of the True Causes why Ireland was never entirely Subdued, nor brought under Obedience of the Crowne of England, untill the Beginning of His Majestie's happie Raigne, James 1st* (1612; Dublin, 1761), p. 7.   42 Jacqueline Hill gives an analysis of this in 'Ireland without Union: Molyneux and his Legacy' in *A Union for Empire:*

Hugo Grotius (1583-1645), the Dutch jurist, had argued that conquest was a legitimate basis for a government's power. Sir Robert Filmer (*c*.1590-1653) disagreed, but also rejected the idea that if the conqueror obtained the consent of the conquered his government thereby became lawful. John Locke in *The Second Treatise of Civil Government*, published anonymously in 1690, contended that conquest gave no rights to the conqueror save over the persons who had actively opposed the conquest. A more moderate line was taken by the royalist Robert Jenkin in *The Title of a Thorough Settlement Examined* (1691) where he argued that conquest itself gave no rights, but that position could change after a period of time, say a hundred years. Even so, 'where-ever there is Actual Dominion and Government, there is Kingship and the Obligations to Subjection and Allegiance with it'.[43] Like other royalists Jenkin was looking for an argument that would allow conquest to gradually acquire legitimacy.

A key question in English minds in Molyneux's day was how to preserve liberty against despotism. Both Charles II and James II were suspected of wanting to replace English liberties with a style of government associated with the supposed tyranny of the Catholic Church. The nation had been divided in the 1680s between Tories who stressed the rights of James and monarchical power and a variety of opponents who wanted controls on the king, parliament and the army in order to preserve liberty. The Revolution of 1688 was 'glorious' for the Whigs because it reasserted the principles of English liberty enshrined in Magna Carta against the threat of a tyranny posed by the Catholic Stuarts. However, a rationale had then to be found for the legitimacy of William's presence on the throne as against James II's. In addition there was the problem that if the Stuarts were to return, on what grounds would their power be valid? Would they need the consent of the people? Would conquest or usurpation legitimise their presence on the throne? Such problems were still a part of the English climate of political debate when Molyneux presented his *Case*. Not surprisingly he made much of two points which were particularly attractive to Williamite supporters – Locke's argument that conquest gave no rights, and second, that any government required the free consent of the people.

One of the anomalies of the way the English approached the problems of Ireland is that while they argued among themselves about the rights of conquest they accepted without question the unequivocal stance of Giraldus and Spenser, of Grotius and Hobbes, as those rights applied to Ireland. They wanted Molyneux punished for subverting the relationship between the two countries as enunciated, for example, by Sir Isaac Newton: 'Ireland is one of the English plantations ... and is, and ought to be, inferior to this kingdom and subservient to its interests.'[44]

Political Thought and the British Union of 1707, ed. John Robertson (Cambridge, 1995), pp 278-84. 43 [Robert Jenkin], *The Title of a Thorough Settlement Examined* (London, 1691), p. 20 and Appendix, p. 11. 44 Cited by J.G. Simms, *Colonial Nationalism*, p. 39.

England's uncompromising stance was evident in the two topical issues of the day – the move to restrict Ireland's woollen trade and the assertion that the Irish House of Lords was subject to the English legislature as a final court of appeal. Molyneux meets this aggression with gentlemanly good reason. He marshals the arguments of Locke that conquest gives no such powers over Ireland. His deferential and appeasing language quickly assures his readers that, though he holds opposite views, his intention is quite other than to mount an attack. Molyneux's ploy is to reconcile the English to an image of themselves far more attractive than that of ruthless conquerors. He invokes Locke in order to get rid of the issue of conquest, and thereby to allow concentration on his case that Henry, far from being a conqueror, acknowledged Ireland's right to legislate for itself. Henry worked with the consent of the people and thus established a base for mutual respect. Henry's example remains an implicit if ironic guide to present English conduct. Molyneux's argument that England has no right to meddle in Irish affairs goes hand in hand with a reminder that the English have a tradition of liberty and probity to live up to.

Establishing the myth

The foundation of Molyneux's approach is his presentation of Henry's landing in the opening section of the *Case*, and what is immediately evident is his desire to convey an ambience of peaceableness. Given that climate, he poses the question whether in fact England conquered Ireland in 1171, and then examines what rights or moral obligations flow from the answer to that question.

The events surrounding Henry II's arrival are described in 'a faithful Narrative' of two separate events – an expedition to Ireland by Welsh supporters of Dermot, and the arrival of Henry II in October 1171. The first he passes over briefly as a successful 'Descent of these Adventurers' to settle Dermot's problems in Leinster.[45] Although he gives bare hints of a violent campaign against the local people – they 'were successful in Treating with the Irish, and Taking Wexford, Waterford, Dublin and other Places'[46] – he passes over it as a minor and separate incident to the main event which followed. As if to enforce the point, he says that at the time of the expedition Henry 'does not appear to have any Design of Coming into Ireland, or of Obtaining the Dominion thereof'.[47] This first expedition therefore cannot be tied in with arguments about conquest.

By highlighting Henry's landing and playing down the preliminary expedition, which all commentators agree was a violent and unscrupulous affair, Molyneux tries to preempt the objection put by many that the one was the forerunner of the other: if the Irish submitted willingly to Henry, it was because they

---

45 *Case of Ireland*, p. 27. For the Welsh barons in support of Dermot see *The Oxford History of Ireland*, ed. R.F. Foster (Oxford, 1992), p. 48.　46 Ibid.　47 Ibid., p. 32.

had already suffered at the hands of the preliminary task force. Henry had come, it could be argued, in the wake of a conquering expedition to receive oaths of loyalty. Molyneux's counter-argument is that Henry did not order such a conquest and his ready acceptance by the Irish confirms his good intentions. Force was not used and the Irish freely submitted. Molyneux then details the homage paid by local kings, 'et fere omnes Hiberniae Potentes'.[48]

Molyneux accepts that the title 'Conqueror' can mean either peaceable acquisition or hostile subjugation, but he quickly adds that where Henry was concerned, 'His Conquest was no violent Subjugation',

> For here we have an Intire and Voluntary Submission of all the Ecclesiastical and Civil States of Ireland, to King Henry II, without the least Hostile Stroke on any side; we hear not in any of the Chronicles of any Violence on either Part, all was Transacted with the greatest Quiet, Tranquility, and Freedom, imaginable.[49]

Molyneux closes the first phase of his argument with a claim that the English and Irish interacted in a willing and dignified way. The Irish 'came in Peaceably, and had large Concessions made them of the like Laws and Liberties with the People of England, which they gladly Accepted'.[50] The stress on the absence of violence fortified by words like 'peaceably,' 'large,' 'gladly' is a clue to a carefully organised rhetorical performance, both assertive in itself, evasive of other versions of the events and sometimes selective. This partiality is evident in less obvious ways.

For example, Molyneux bases his account on 'our best Historians'.[51] Among these is the surprise inclusion of the Welsh writer Giraldus who gave the lead for several centuries in regarding the Irish as bestial and untrustworthy. One critic sums up the thrust of Giraldus' work as 'his unqualified vilification of the religion and customs of the Irish and his justification of the invasion [by Henry] on the grounds of its civilising influence upon Ireland'.[52] Giraldus, who is one source for Molyneux's argument that the Irish willingly accepted Henry, wrote elsewhere of the Irish 'This is a filthy people, wallowing in vice. Of all peoples it is the least instructed in the rudiments of the Faith.'[53] Molyneux takes from Giraldus what suits his analysis and ignores what does not.

A second example of partiality is Molyneux's silence on Henry's motives for coming to Ireland. He says that at the time of Dermot's expedition Henry had

---

48 Ibid., p. 29 (and nearly all the Irish leaders). 49 Ibid., pp 30-1. 50 Ibid., p. 31. 51 Ibid., p. 25. 52 Ned Lebow, 'British Historians and Irish History', *Eire – Ireland* 8, no. 4 (1973), p. 6. Giraldus had visited Ireland in 1185-6 and gave a disparaging view of the Irish and their culture (see Elizabeth L. Rambo, *Colonial Ireland in Medieval English Literature*, London, 1994). 53 Giraldus Cambrensis, *The History and Topography of Ireland* (1187), trans. John O'Meara (Mountrath, 1982), p. 106. Giraldus defends his account with the remark, 'The austere discipline of history spares neither truth nor modesty' (ibid., p. 110).

no intention of visiting Ireland, and then simply that he came and received homage. There is no allusion to his argument with the archbishop of Canterbury as to whether Ireland should be incorporated into the English realm in order to gain control of the Irish church, or of Henry's response to Pope Adrian IV's grant of Ireland if he subjected it to Peter's pence, nor Henry's attitude to the Anglo-Normans in Ireland.[54] He sets all these issues aside, most of which would prejudice his case, to make a single and relatively narrow point: Henry did not design to nor in fact did he conquer Ireland.

A third instance is that Molyneux makes sparing reference to those commentators who argued that Henry did conquer Ireland. He claims in his 'Preface to the Reader' that he is a disinterested observer arguing a principle rather than entering into a debate.[55] He is silent on the several writers in the wake of Giraldus who had no doubt that Henry had 'subjugated' Ireland and regarded that conquest as a benefit to an otherwise uncivilised people.[56] Sir Richard Cox, an uncompromising supporter of William in Ireland, had written as recently as 1689,

> As by God's Providence and Appointment, Ireland is now become subject, and under the King of England; so the same should take from thence the Order, Rule and Manner how to Reform themselves, and to live in better Order: For whatever Good Thing is befallen to the Church and Realm of Ireland, they owe the same to the King of England, and are to be thankful unto him for the same: For before his coming into the Land of Ireland, many and all sorts of Wickedness, in Times past, flowed and reigned among them; all which, now by his Authority and Goodness are abolish'd.[57]

Molyneux's claim to impartiality is a subterfuge for highly selective evidence that the English meant well towards Ireland from the start – that there was no conquest. This strategy was necessary for a work whose aim was to reconstruct the relationship between Protestant Ireland and Westminster. Hence, as Simms notes, 'The historical basis for Molyneux's argument is mythical.'[58]

Another way in which Molyneux gives an impression of impartiality is to raise the argument from a level of historical analysis to moral principle. It suits his purpose not to enter the contentious area of detailed events and motivations, but rather to focus attention on principles on the understanding that these transcend historical circumstance. As Denis Donoghue puts it,

---

54 See Curtis, *A History of Ireland*, pp 52-7.   55 *Case of Ireland*, pp 21-2.   56 Giraldus, *History and Topography of Ireland*, p. 124.   57 Sir Richard Cox, *Hibernia Anglicana: or, the History of Ireland from the Conquest thereof by the English to this Present Time* (London, 1689), p. 24.   58 Simms, *Colonial Nationalism*, p. 30.

Ostensibly, Molyneux is stating a case, marshalling his evidence, but his typical procedure is to transcend evidence; giving it as a weary necessity, but transcending it by appeal to the deepest and truest nature of man.[59]

Ireland, Locke and liberty

The second phase of the *Case* contends that even if Henry had conquered Ireland conquest would give him or England very few rights. In this section dealing with the moral consequences of conquest, Molyneux takes much of his argument and some of his detailed examples from Locke's *Second Treatise of Civil Government*. Locke's approach to conquest is particularly rationalist in that he makes no concession to historical contextualisation. He is arguing about principles. Similarly Molyneux does not refer to precedents, political motivations or the wider international scene. Only occasionally is there an allusion which reminds the reader that these principles are to apply to England and Ireland. Molyneux asks what rights does conquest give – be it unjust or just. The answer is, Virtually none. Repeating Locke verbatim at several points he argues that conquest gives rights only over the persons of those who actively resisted, but not over their property or their descendants. There may be an argument from 'Public Safety' for touching the latter, but only in exceptional circumstances. The argument had few supporters in a nation whose dream of Westminster as the seat of a global empire was soon to be so lucidly expressed by Pope,

> There mighty Nations shall enquire their Doom,
> The World's great Oracle in Times to come;
> There Kings shall sue, and suppliant States be seen
> Once more to bend before a British QUEEN.[60]

Locke had a different view. The fact of conquest, he said, did not remove people's rights. Following Locke, Molyneux concludes,

> From what has been said, I presume it pretty clearly appears that an *Unjust* Conquest gives *no Title* at all; That a *Just* Conquest gives Power only over the *Lives* and *Liberties* of the *Actual Opposers*, but not over their *Posterity* or *Estates*, otherwise than as before is mentioned; and not at all over those that did *not Concur* in the Opposition.[61]

Whether Ireland was conquered or not England has no right to 'intermeddle with the Affairs of Ireland, and Bind us up by Laws made in their House'.[62] As

59 Denis Donoghue, Afterword, *Case of Ireland*, p. 135. 60 Alexander Pope, *Windsor Forest* (1713), ll. 381-4. 61 *Case of Ireland*, p. 39; cf. Locke, 'Of Civil Government', in *The Works of John Locke*, 9 vols (London, 1824), iv, sect. 175, p. 443 and sect. 180, pp 446-7. 62 *Case of Ireland*, p. 25.

Locke says, 'the conqueror, even in a just war, hath by his conquest no right of dominion'.[63] England had no rights over the people or estates of Ireland even a generation later than Henry's landing, much less in the last years of the seventeenth century. This part of Molyneux's *Case* rests on the principle enunciated in the opening pages – 'Liberty seems the Inherent Right of all Mankind'[64] – and leads on to a European, then universal application of the same principle:

> No one or more Men, can by *Nature* challenge any *Right, Liberty* or *Freedom* … which all other Men have not an *Equally Just Claim to*. Is *England* a *Free People*? So ought *France* to be. Is *Poland* so? *Turkey* likewise, and all the *Eastern Dominions*, ought to be so: And the same runs throughout the whole *Race of Mankind*.[65]

Molyneux is the first to invoke the theory of Locke in defence of the colonised against the coloniser, a brave and radical move given that Locke's theory of rights and conquest was not generally accepted. But it could also be regarded as politically naive because, as Caroline Robbins notes, it 'struck at the whole basis of regulation of the economic life of colonies and plantations by England, and at the mercantilist theories of the time'.[66] Molyneux could hardly expect his English readers to accept so radical an argument and one which recent history did not validate. On the contrary, the British, like the Dutch, the Spaniards, the Portuguese and the French were in frequent competition for conquests in the Far East and the Americas and the liberty of those peoples had no place on their agenda. Conquests were, as Gulliver noted with disapproval, a matter of acquisition and national pride. The practice of conquest was to subject by force and then 'to convert and civilise an idolatrous and barbarous people'.[67] Gulliver saw it as a ruthless and exploitative exercise which he wanted nothing to do with, but ironically by that stage of his travels he speaks as a deranged Houyhnhnm. Molyneux was not unaware that his own line of argument ran against current practices: repeating Locke he writes,

> It must be confess'd that the Practice of the World is otherwise, and we commonly see the Conqueror (whether Just or Unjust) by the Force he has over the Conquer'd, compels them with a Sword at their Brest to stoop to his Conditions, and to submit to such a Government as he pleases to Afford them.[68]

---

63 Locke, 'Of Civil Government', sect. 185, p. 450. Patrick Kelly argues that Molyneux was the first to make use of Locke as a major political authority ('Perceptions of Locke in Eighteenth-Century Ireland', *Proceedings of the Royal Irish Academy*, 89, Sect. C (1989), 17-35). 64 *Case of Ireland*, p. 24. 65 Ibid., p. 119. 66 Caroline Robbins, *The Eighteenth-Century Commonwealthman* (London, 1959), p. 141. 67 Swift, *Gulliver's Travels* , p. 315. 68 *Case of Ireland*, p. 38; see Locke, 'Of Civil Government', sect. 175-6, pp 443-4.

Undeterred Molyneux insists that the principle is what matters: 'We Enquire not now, what is the Practice, but what Right there is to do so.'[69] Realising perhaps that reason and morality are the only weapons left to Ireland he attacks the fundamental *modus operandi* of the British empire. Of the several theories of conquest available to an Irishman speaking to Westminster he chose the one most advantageous to his case, but the least likely to impress those 'Men of Great Wisdom, Honour and Justice' in Westminster.

Rhetorical strategies of reconciliation

It is tempting therefore to dismiss Molyneux's *Case* as politically inept. The argument was so out of tune with the thinking of Westminster that the question arises as to what he thought he might achieve.[70] Like Swift's Injured Lady, he knew he was right but had no bargaining power to do anything about it.

Whatever the rhetorical strategies, the omissions, and the selectivity of argument the most striking feature of the *Case* is the language and tone of reconciliation. There is no word of anger or recrimination. It is a peaceable if at times aggrieved book. From the outset Molyneux foregrounds the goodwill of both Henry II and the Irish, in particular the Anglo-Norman Irish, who, Molyneux argues, because they co-operated with Henry, were not therefore conquered and remained free. An important facet of the myth which Simms refers to is its temperance: the English and the Irish respect one another. Henry II by the willing co-operation of the Irish introduced 'an Original Compact' between the king and people of Ireland, 'That they should Enjoy the like Liberties and Immunities, and be Govern'd by the same Mild Laws, both Civil and Ecclesiastical, as the People of England'.[71] Words like 'enjoy' and 'mild' establish the mood which permeates the myth and which Molyneux would like to see in the debates about Ireland in the 1690s. This compact is the product of what Molyneux believed in theory, if not in practice, about 'the strict Justice of the Parliament of England'. Whatever particular events or individuals may have conspired to destroy the myth, they could not invalidate it. The obverse and unspoken presumption of this vision was that Protestant Ireland could not envisage a future without it. Molyneux's main task therefore was to reconcile England to that image of itself which the myth provided.

The apparent ambiguity of writing an anti-colonial text in order to reconcile the coloniser with the colonised falls away if one recalls that Molyneux sees his English readers' problem as one of misinformation, even ignorance.[72] Reconciliation is the main thrust of the *Case*. This is apparent in the very structure of

---

69 *Case of Ireland*, p. 38. 70 Dickson notes that the *Case* 'was regarded as badly mis-timed and highly embarrassing by leading politicians in Dublin, including Molyneux's friends' (*New Foundations*, p. 48). 71 *Case of Ireland*, p. 46. 72 Ibid., p. 23.

the argument and in features of the text which may look impartial or merely functional. For example, much of the text is given to an historical account of Ireland's relation with England, and this is repeatedly interrupted by comments on and interpretations of the evidence. The historical passages are worth looking at in detail because they seem on the surface to be the least contentious part of the text. Yet as critics such as Hayden White have long argued, the driest historical account is never innocent. Structure and emplotment guide the reader to understand the events in one way rather than another. Historical discourse, says White, invites the reader 'to assume a certain attitude toward the facts and the interpretation of them offered on the manifest level of discourse.'[73] Molyneux's *Case* is designed to persuade his English readers to understand their historical relation with Ireland in a particular way, and I want now to examine a section of the *Case* to see whether the notion of reconciliation is sustainable at the level of narrative structure.

I have chosen the following passages as typical of Molyneux's descriptions of historical events. Other sections of the text would serve equally well. These passages give an account of Ireland under John and Henry III and, as frequently happens in the text, the story is interrupted from time to time by discussion.[74] But the narrative keeps returning to its main course which is to describe the events leading to the grant of Magna Carta to Ireland by Henry III:

> About the Twenty-third year of *Henry* the Second, (which was within Five years after his Return from *Ireland*) he created his younger Son John, King of Ireland, at a Parliament held at *Oxford*. Soon after *King John* being then about Twelve years of Age, came into *Ireland*, from *Milford* to *Waterford*, as his Father had formerly done. The *Irish* Nobility and Gentry immediately repaired to him; but being Received by him and his Retinue with some Scorn and Derision, by reason of their long rude Beards, *quas more Patrio grandes habebant & prolixas*, (says *Giraldus Cambrensis, Hib. Expug. Cap.* 35.) they took such Offence thereat, that they departed in much Discontent; which was the occasion of the young King's staying so short a time in *Ireland*, as he did this his first time of being here …
>
> After both Crowns [of England and Ireland] were united, on the death of *Richard* the First without Issue, in the Royal Person of King *John*: He, about the Twelfth Year of his Reign of *England*, went again into *Ireland*, viz. the Twenty Eighth day of *June*, 1210. and *Math. Paris* tells us, pag. 220. *Cum Venisset ad Dublinensem Civitatem Occurrerunt ei ibidem plus quam 20 Reguli illius Regionis qui omnes Timore maximo perterriti homagium ei & Fidelitatem fecerunt. Fecit quoque Rex ibidem,* Construere Leges

73 Hayden White, *Tropics of Discourse: Essays in Cultural Criticism* (Baltimore, 1978), p. 107. 74 *Case of Ireland*, pp 47-52.

& Consuetudines Anglicanas, *ponens Vicecomites aliosque Ministros, qui populum Regni illius* juxta Leges Anglicanas Judicarent.[75]

His Son King *Henry* the Third came to the Crown the Nineteenth of *October* 1216. and in *November* following he Granted to *Ireland* a *Magna Charta*, Dated at *Bristol* 12 *November*, the First Year of his Reign. 'Tis Prefaced, *that for the Honour of God, and Advancement of Holy Church, by the Advice of his Council of England*, (whose names are particularly recited) He makes the following *Grant to Ireland*; And then goes on Exactly Agreeable to the *Magna Charta* which he granted to *England*; only in ours we have *Civitas Dublin, & Avenliffee*, instead of *Civitas London*, and *Thamesis* with other Alterations of the like kind where Needful ...

In *February* following in the First Year likewise of his Reign, by Advice of all his Faithful Counsellors in *England*, to gratify the *Irish* (says (a) *Pryn*) for their eminent Loyalty to his Father and Him,[76] he granted them out of his *Special Grace*, that they and their Heirs for ever should enjoy the *Liberties* granted by his Father and Himself to the Realm of *England*; which he reduced into Writing, and sent Seal'd thither under the Seal of the Pope's Legat, and W. Earl Marshal his Governour, because he had then no Seal of his own ...

This factual information relates to three main events, John's first visit to Ireland, his second visit, and the grant of Magna Carta by Henry III. The information can be summarised as follows,

- Henry II made his younger son John, aged about twelve, King of Ireland at a parliament at Oxford;
- John came to Ireland;
- The Irish nobility and gentry came to him;
- He received them with scorn and derision because of their beards;
- They took offence and departed; John left after a short time.
- After Richard I's death John visited Ireland again;
- The Irish paid him homage;
- John established an administration in Ireland;
- Henry III granted Ireland Magna Carta in the first year of his reign;
- He wrote out a grant of liberties as a reward for their loyalty and sent it to Ireland under the papal seal.

75 Ibid., p. 50: 'When he had reached Dublin more than twenty chiefs of that region hurried to him there. Moved by the utmost fear they all paid him homage and fealty. The king for his part immediately established the English system of law, appointing officials and other administrators to govern the people of that kingdom according to English law.' 76 Molyneux has the note, ' Pryn against the 4th Inst. c. 76. p. 250.'

Molyneux organises the plot of his narrative so that it starts with the youthful misunderstanding of John, moves to a more mature relationship when he establishes an Irish administration, and that in turn leads to the grant of Magna Carta. What started unhappily ended up well; scorn and derision turned into generosity. Molyneux's emplotment belongs to what White calls a 'generic story type', in this case comedy, which arranges its materials in such a way as to achieve an optimistic vision.[77] Initial problems and difficulties are resolved. A misunderstanding – far from leading to destructive consequences – has been reversed. Patience and trust lead to positive benefits.

The main player in this comic story is England. England, in the person of John makes the initial mistake, learns better and ends up as the generous giver of Magna Carta. Ireland features only as the wronged party, the passive receiver, first of contempt, then of liberty. England is the one who has to change, and does so handsomely. Molyneux's narrative therefore uncovers a pattern of meaning in Anglo-Irish history by which England learns from its mistakes and goes on to play an enlightened and generous role.

Molyneux passes over an aspect of this story which other writers available to him usually included. He makes no mention of the turbulent state of Ireland at the time of John's second visit. Edmund Campion for instance writes,

> To settle the Realme of Ireland, King John brought thither a maine Armye, banished the Lacyes, subdued the remanents, tooke pledges, punished malefactours, established the execution of English Lawes, coyned money of like value currant sterling in both Realmes.[78]

Hanmer's *Chronicle of Ireland* gives an even more disturbed picture of the situation as John found it and, by implication, suggests a quite different purpose for his visit to that implied by Molyneux. John arrived on his second visit, 'with a huge army, marvellous well appointed to pacify that rebellious people, that were universally revolted, burning, spoyling, preying, and massacring the English'.[79] John came to quell the unruly Irish, to restore order, receive homage, and set up his laws. The violence with which he imposed the English presence comes across in words like 'banished', 'subdued', 'punished', 'pacify'. Molyneux's response to the English bias of such accounts is not to offer an alternative version, but to pass over them in silence. In other words he refuses to confront that colonial discourse which he knew was so righteous and so disparaging about Ireland. In the structure of Molyneux's narrative John's visit was but a phase in the ongoing attempt by England to do justice to Ireland. Campion and Hanmer have a quite differ-

77 White, *Tropics of Discourse*, p. 110.   78 Edmund Campion, *A History of Ireland, written in the Yeare 1571* (Dublin, 1633; Dublin, 1809), p. 109.   79 *The Chronicle of Ireland, collected by Meredith Hanmer in 1571* (Dublin, 1633; Dublin, 1809), p. 372.

ent view of what that justice implies. In their view justice means English control, and this needs 'a huge army' because the Irish are so troublesome. Molyneux's silence on this aspect, taken with his kindly reading of Henry II's involvement with Ireland in 1171, indicates his underlying concern to put the engagement of the two peoples on a footing of untroubled interaction. To introduce the power struggle in Ireland between the Welsh Norman barons and Henry would considerably weaken his case because it would necessitate a much modified image of both the English and the Irish. The fact that the Irish people, their kings and chiefs, had seen their country and political structures reduced at the hands of a Norman-English struggle for power has no place in a narrative that is generically comic.

Instead, Molyneux's narrative directs the reader's understanding towards a benevolent, even admirable image of the English. This is all the more apparent if we compare it with a twentieth-century account:

> In 1199 John succeeded to the English throne, and the Lordship of Ireland was merged for good in the Crown of England. John had learned that the Monarchy, as reconstructed by his father, and the Baronage were natural enemies. Whatever his fortunes in the struggle were in England, in Ireland at least he succeeded in depressing the feudal interest and exalting the royal authority, by the policy of raising up against the old a new and more limited baronage and favouring the Irish chiefs as a counter-balance to the Norman conquistadors.[80]

Here John's concerns with Ireland are less to do with improving Anglo-Irish relations than with consolidating his position as monarch. The word 'struggle' leads on to opposing words like 'depressing' and 'exalting' and then 'counter-balance', all of which give the sense that John was involved in a power-play in Ireland which was but part of the wider problem he faced. This dimension too is absent from Molyneux, and would if admitted make the tone of reconciliation as well as the myth of equality impossible.

The myth and its uses

Molyneux does not fashion his image just to flatter the English. He has a serious political intent which becomes clear later in the *Case* where he complains that in the 1690s the comic vision he has built up has been disrupted. Since the accession of William an inherent contradiction has established itself at the centre of Anglo-Irish politics. He writes,

80 Curtis, *History of Ireland*, p. 66.

> I am sorry to reflect, That since the late Revolution in these Kingdoms, when the Subjects of *England* have more strenuously than ever Asserted their own *Rights*, and the *Liberty* of Parliaments, it has pleased them to bear harder on their Poor Neighbours, than has ever yet been done in many Ages foregoing.[81]

This gently ironic rebuke of the English reveals the contradiction at the heart of their relation with Ireland. Liberty and oppression are uncomfortable bed-fellows. Molyneux, in spite of this awareness and against all the evidence, restates his confidence in 'that Wise and Just Body of Senators'. That is central to the myth. The blame he says lies on a minority group, 'some Men', who have abused Ireland for their own purposes.[82] The ensuing arguments, particularly about the need for the consent of the people – 'I have no other Notion of Slavery, but being Bound by a Law to which I do not Consent'[83] – are debated in a mood of trust that wisdom will prevail, England will return to its mythical character, a caring and benevolent nation. His closing exhortation, while acknowledging a world of seemingly tragic possibilities, ends on a note of optimism that Ireland and England can unite in preserving liberty:

> The *Rights of Parliament* should be preserved *Sacred* and *Inviolable*, wherever they are found. This kind of Government, once so *Universal* all over *Europe*, is now almost *Vanished* from amongst the Nations thereof. Our King's Dominions are the only Supporters of this noble *Gothick Constitution*, save only what little remains may be found thereof in *Poland*. We should not therefore make so light of that sort of Legislature, and as it were Abolish it in One Kingdom of the Three, wherein it appears; but rather Cherish and Encourage it wherever we meet it.[84]

The repeated use of 'we' is a reminder of the common purpose incumbent on Irish Protestants and the English. They have a shared responsibility to preserve the tradition of liberty which his *Case* has outlined. The words 'our' and 'we' consolidate the rhetoric of reconciliation, but they also subvert England's understanding of its superior relationship with Ireland.

This subtle strategy of praise and blame serves to image the English as the last hope for the preservation of liberty in Europe. The proof would be that the rights of parliament are acknowledged in Ireland. That challenge is perhaps what later writers like Swift and Grattan, and more recently Yeats, had in mind when they invoked the spirit of Molyneux. Yet they addressed the English in a quite different temper to Molyneux. Far from reiterating Molyneux's conciliatory, even laudatory tone towards the English, they castigated them. Molyneux's

81 *Case of Ireland*, p. 89.   82 Ibid.   83 Ibid., p. 129.   84 Ibid., p. 132.

followers admired his insistence on Irish liberties, not his deferential if double-edged praise. In their writings his ironic image of the English as wise upholders of liberty becomes a whipping boy. From Swift's image of England as an unscrupulous and hard hearted gentleman, a cunning horse-jockey, through to Grattan and Curran the dominant tropes are contemptuous and derisive. What so frequently angers Curran later in the century is England's duplicitous confusion of liberty with force. He tells the jury in the trial of Patrick Finney for treason in 1798, 'You are called upon in defiance of shame, of truth, of honour to deny the sufferings under which you groan and to flatter the persecution that tramples you under foot.'[85] That was not Molyneux's style. What he provided was the myth. England's repeated failure to measure up to that during the ensuing century gave later Irish writers a licence to castigate, lampoon, abuse and ridicule her.

At each moment of crisis in Anglo-Irish relations during the century the feeling of outrage goes back to Molyneux's myth. If England had but fulfilled the expectations of that image, Ireland would be a happy and prosperous nation. But England repeatedly failed to live up to Molyneux's vision. The Woollen Act of 1699, the negative response to England's union with Scotland (1707), the Declaratory Act of 1720 and the attempt to impose Wood's half-pence in the 1720s were but some instances of the betrayal. At each crisis the vilification of the English takes its moral confidence from the discrepancy between the image which Molyneux had given and actual practice.

What Irish protesters would not acknowledge was that the myth itself had proved sterile. Without it the Protestants in Ireland had nowhere to turn. Beckett traces their predicament back to one of the invidious dualisms of Irish history: as Maurice fitz Gerald is reputed to have said in 1171: 'just as we are English so far as the Irish are concerned, likewise to the English we are Irish'.[86] The settlers' constantly shifting identity was compounded by the ambiguity of their role. They were agents and beneficiaries of England's power, yet they considered themselves Irish. However, they were at odds with the native Irish in every significant sphere – religion, politics, culture. They could only be strangers in their adopted country. Hence they put their hope in Westminster and insisted on the repeated resurrection of Molyneux's myth even as far into the eighteenth century as Grattan's parliament in 1782. Its beguiling attraction was that it gave such a clear and favourable moral framework in which to campaign for Ireland's legislative independence and their own security. It set Ireland in an historical and humane context which was readily acceptable in theory to the English because so flattering and so seemingly just. The notions of equity and liberty

85 *Speeches of John Philpot Curran* (Dublin, 1805), pp 264-5; the unnamed editor acknowledges that the text may be 'inaccurate' (pp iii-iv). 86 J.C. Beckett, 'Literature in English, 1691-1800', *New History of Ireland*, iv, 425.

handed down from Magna Carta and discussed so learnedly at universities by Blackstone in Oxford and Sullivan in Dublin in the mid-century were points of appeal which England could not but recognise as fundamental to the British constitution.

The pain for Irish Protestants was that when their interests conflicted with England's the English were more ready to forget principles and follow age-old prejudices than to listen to plaudits of their legal heritage. An Irish pamphleteer of the 1720s, John Browne, argued that the difficulties which eighteenth-century Protestants had with England dated back to the old Irish. Deeply ingrained animosities remained since those times. Nevertheless Irish history had to move forward into a different phase:

> Our Predecessors have been in perpetual Wars and Enmity with the old Irish, who inhabited this Island: There were here frequent Rebellions and bloody Massacres, and in the last Struggles for their expiring Liberties, nothing was left undone which a desperate People could undertake, in Defence of the most valuable Blessings; this laid a strong and lasting Foundation for Hatred and ill Blood, between the contending Parties, and it has taken so deep a Root in England, that they even forget how that People are no more, how we are here no longer their Enemies, but their Sons and their Brethren, and how we must ever be studious to support the Glory of that People, from whom we are every one of us descended, and from whom we derive the most valuable of our Rights and Possessions.[87]

The 'Hatred and ill Blood' in England's attitude to the Irish must be put away. Echoing the spirit of Molyneux, Browne's phrase 'we must ever be studious to support the Glory of that People' sums up the positive agenda which Molyneux had set in motion. However, such sentiments leave the Irish Protestants in no less an ambivalent position as settlers. Molyneux's myth, together with Browne, encourages them to find their identity in links across the Irish sea, yet those help to reinforce rather than ameliorate their differences from the majority of the people of Ireland.

Molyneux's myth seemed at last to have assumed tangible form with the grant of legislative independence by England to Grattan's parliament in 1782. However, it did not take long from then onwards, as we shall see, for the Irish to realise that the myth had been hollow all along. In the final analysis Molyneux

---

87 John Browne, *Reflections upon the Present unhappy Circumstances of Ireland* ... (Dublin, 1731) in *Miscellanies in Prose*, ed. Andrew Carpenter, Irish Writings from the Age of Swift series (1972), i. 25-6. Browne (d. 1762), a Protestant landowner, ran a small ironworks in Co. Mayo. He was attacked by Swift for supporting Wood's plan to coin money for Ireland, but later was reconciled to him and erected a monument to honour Swift.

was an ambiguous blessing in Ireland's struggle for independence. On the one hand he established an image of the English as preservers of liberty, a wise and conscientious people, respecters of ancient precedents, defenders of the principle of laws by popular consent. This was the myth against which the English parliament would be measured and so often found wanting. Molyneux became a major rallying point for the Irish patriots, and particularly Swift, Lucas, Flood, Grattan and Curran. On the other hand, as Wolfe Tone implied in the 1790s, perhaps Molyneux did more to harm than help Ireland because the image he framed so monopolised Irish thinking that it forestalled any other initiative than a clamour for its realisation. When after 1782 the English continued to presume control of Irish trade, the Irish realised that legislative independence made little substantial change to their powers to determine their own affairs. In 1785 the English proposed that, if Ireland would contribute financially to the empire's defence, England would grant commercial equality. The ensuing debate in the Irish parliament reflects the same outrage as was voiced before 1782. The initial delay in providing the necessary documents was read as 'evidence of a very incapable or very idle minister;' the attorney-general was criticised for the 'air of *hauteur* with which that right honourable gentleman frequently treats this assembly'.[88] William Brownlow attacked Thomas Orde, the proposer,

> Does the right honourable gentleman mean that we should become a tributary nation? Is this the boasted extension of our commerce? Is this the reciprocal advantage we were to enjoy? Sir, I reject the gift, and I hurl it back with scorn. I never will consent to be a slave, nor to pay tribute.[89]

Grattan said the proposals were 'subversive of the liberties of Ireland'; he reminded parliament that 'if others are to make laws to bind us, we are slaves, even though our own parliament registers these laws'.[90] These are the arguments and the sentiments heard frequently before England granted legislative independence. Molyneux's myth was as unrealistic as ever. It had no substance. The consequences were disillusion, a polarisation of political agendas, and the rebellion of 1798 followed by the Union.

Molyneux's mistake was to believe that an appeal to English probity and the principles of Locke would change the direction of England's colonial agenda towards Ireland. That naïveté separates his anti-colonialist stance from that of later Irish writers. Yet his crucial contribution was his insistence on liberty which Swift was to pick up. Swift's indignation stems not least from the conviction that English presumptions about Ireland deserved only ridicule and contempt. He

---

88 Isaac Corry, *The Parliamentary Register* (Dublin, 1785), iv, 87-8 (4 Feb. 1785). 89 Ibid., iv, 125 (7 Feb. 1785). 90 Ibid., iv, 316 (2 Aug. 1785).

kept to Molyneux's philosophical principles but turned Irish postcolonial writing into a satirical channel. He turned from Molyneux's subtle ironies to ridicule; his versatility in derision and his fertile array of abuse introduced a note of self-confidence which was as important to later Irish writing in the century as all that Molyneux had said.

CHAPTER THREE

Jonathan Swift and the 'proud oppressor's hand'

The epitaph on Jonathan Swift's grave in St Patrick's Cathedral, Dublin, reads,

> Here lies the body of Jonathan Swift of this cathedral church dean where savage indignation cannot lacerate his heart anymore. Traveller, go, and imitate if you can his strenuous vindication of man's liberty.

The tribute is evidenced in virtually everything Swift wrote and yet it hides complex and difficult issues. Swift's denunciations of colonialism are among the most vicious in the English language, and yet, like Molyneux, he did not accept that Ireland was a colony. When he championed liberty for the Irish, his concern was not for the nation at large, including the 'wild Irish Papists',[1] but for middle-class Protestants. Much of his feeling about Ireland, the land of his birth, was summed up in a verse he wrote in 1727 while waiting to cross from Holyhead to Dublin to see his dying Stella: 'I never was in hast before/ To reach that hateful slavish shore.'[2] The hatred is as much for the hapless Irish and what the English had reduced them to as for the distance between him in Dublin and his friends at Moor Park, the seat of Sir William Temple, or in London. He loved and yet he hated England. He loved it for what it could give him and Ireland, and hated it for its several abuses of Ireland – Ireland's woollens trade, its commerce, its pensions list and its offices so often given to appointees from England. As Deane notes, whatever name this oppression goes by, if not colonialism, Swift recognised the extensive human suffering it caused.[3] Swift's hatred engendered a clarity of mind and feeling which railed against its every manifestation.

---

1 Letter VI, *Drapier's Letters* in *Prose Works of Swift*, x, 103.   2 'Holyhead. Sept. 25 1727', ll.19-20, *Poems of Jonathan Swift*, ed. Harold Williams, 3 vols, 2nd edn (Oxford, 1958), ii. 420.   3 Seamus Deane, *A Short History of Irish Literature* (London, 1986), p. 48.

Ireland: the injured lady

To turn from Molyneux to Swift entails a shift from the gentleness of reconcili-ation to the savagery of abuse. Swift's ambivalence has an energy and extravagant imaginative range absent in Molyneux's lucid measured prose. While supporting Molyneux's myth, Swift projects the English as untrustworthy, devious, unscrupulous. The new tenor of protest is evident in a short piece, 'The Story of an Injured Lady', together with 'The Answer to the Injured Lady', based on Ireland's predicament at the start of the eighteenth century.[4] In the early years of Queen Anne's reign there was much talk about a possible union between England and Ireland and England and Scotland. Irish politicians were arguing their way towards a new legislative programme that included plans to reduce the inheritance rights of Catholics and the possibility of abolishing the Irish parlia-ment. By 1703 arguments in Ireland for a union with England had gathered suf-ficient support for an address to be made to Queen Anne asking that Westminster either guarantee the rights of the Irish parliament or agree to a union of the two kingdoms. The request went unattended. Delays and neglect by the English, together with a declining economy, meant no decision was taken. Gradually the suspicion grew that this was a deliberate policy to impoverish Ireland. Meanwhile England's negotiations with Scotland made progress and that Union was finalised in 1707.

In Swift's allegory of these events the lady (Ireland) writes for advice to an unnamed male friend because she feels betrayed by her gentleman lover (England) who, after seducing her, has decided to marry her 'poor and beggarly' rival (Scotland).[5] She describes how the gentleman living across the river wooed her and then seduced her. He then started to criticise her for the way she ran her estate, imposed his own steward and later his servants upon her. He made her sell her goods at his market and placed 'an hundred other Hardships' on her.[6] All this time he was courting her rival whom he planned to marry. The lady, fraught with confusion and uncertainty, writes for advice as to how to safeguard herself from further exploitation and to protect her liberty and fortune.

Much of the dramatic power in this allegory of courtship and marriage rests on the sense of betrayal. England has deceived Ireland, married her rival and then treated her as a subservient cast-off. The two-timing English gentleman is as duplicitous as the beaux in Restoration comedy, only more sinister because so ruthless. In addition his masculinity along with his exploitative agenda suggests a combination of power and design beyond the defences of the lady. This is an unequal encounter. Swift, unlike Molyneux, acknowledges that power lies with

4 The pamphlet was written in 1707 but not published until 1746. Swift was afraid the pamphlet 'might prejudice negotiations with England by which the church of Ireland hoped to obtain the remission of Crown taxes known as "first fruits"': Oliver W. Ferguson, *Jonathan Swift and Ireland* (Urbana, 1962), pp 30-1. 5 'The Story of an Injured Lady', *Prose Works of Swift*, ix, 3. 6 Ibid., 6.

the gentleman, and it is no surprise that the lady has been outwitted. She has been marginalised and her voice now comes from no recognised centre of power.

Swift, by handing over the narration to a female voice, dissociates himself from the masculine role of domination (England) and foregrounds the 'other', the female. Her opening remarks indicate her plight,

> Sir,
> Being ruined by the Inconstancy and Unkindness of a Lover, I hope, a true and plain Relation of my Misfortunes may be of Use and Warning to credulous Maids, never to put too much Trust in deceitful Men.[7]

The male-female metaphor enables Swift to highlight England's characteristics as a cavalier lover, a man of promises, deceit and arrogance. By having the woman tell the story he also draws attention to the effects on her. This is not an argumentative text; it dwells rather on her anger and jealousy, her disappointment, indignation, her desperate hopes for a reconciliation. 'Nothwithstanding all that had passed, and without binding him to any conditions in my own favour, I would stand by him against her [Scotland] and all the world, while I had a penny in my purse, or a petticoat to pawn.'[8] This marriage, which the lady sounds desperate for, yet another sign of the fluctuating relationship between the two countries, would make Molyneux's image of Ireland as a separate kingdom redundant. In the new arrangement Ireland would complement England, but in so doing surrender her individual identity. The strengths of the woman are her capacity to love, to reconcile, to be faithful – qualities lacking in the gentleman. His strengths are persuasion, organisation, entrepreneurial skill, trade – which Ireland has little experience of. But her gender differences are quickly exploited by the gentleman as weaknesses. The lady makes Molyneux's mistake of thinking she is negotiating on equal terms. The gentleman knows otherwise. Like Molyneux she complains, but the fact is that in England's eyes Ireland is no more than a weak neighbour there to be exploited.

Swift's choice of the familiar letter as his medium of protest subverts the more formal modes of argument between the two countries. The more intimate mode gives it a tone of private complaint, even of powerlessness. The familiar letter had gained considerable popularity with the English reading public at the time as a medium for love affairs. Robert Beaumont writes, 'Letters are the engines of Love'.[9] In the late seventeenth century the particular vogue was for letters by forsaken lovers. Sir Roger L'Estrange's translation in 1678 of *Les Lettres Portugaises* (1669), 'Five love letters from a nun to a cavalier', had a number of imitations in which 'the mourning, forsaken, letter-writing lover, developed into

---

7 Ibid., 3. 8 Ibid., 7. 9 Robert Beaumont, 'Address to the Reader', *Missives to Virtue* (1660), cited by Robert Adams Day, *Told in Letters: Epistolary Fiction before Richardson* (Ann Arbor, 1966), p. 56.

a stock fictional figure'.[10] However, Swift's lady is different from her predecessors in the convention. A lonely figure she lacks the support which many letter-writers could count on from their parents, sisters or aunts. Private and personal as her letter is, her predicament affects everyone on her estate. She is a public figure in keeping with the woman Ireland who had appeared in several political allegories, often as England's younger sister.[11] What Swift does not do is make her a nationalist figure in the tradition of the woman Ireland in the visionary or 'aisling' poems of Gaelic literature. That figure was sorrowful, waiting for the return of her lover from exile who would liberate her from foreign masters:[12]

> Oh, my misery, my woe, my sorrow and my anguish
> My bitter source of dolour is evermore that she,
> The loveliest of the lovely, should thus be left to languish
> Amid a ruffian horde till the Heroes cross the sea.[13]

Swift's lady has no such heroes to hope for. She is a landowner and a business woman and apart from her good looks has no affinity with either her Gaelic counterpart or the young English women of the English convention which produced Pamela and Clarissa. She is an Anglo-Irish creation, the singular product of the Irish Protestant imagination which adapts the English and Gaelic conventions to a new political purpose.[14] The ploy of her letter not only helps emphasise her helplessness but highlights England as deceitful, insensitive and unreasonably demanding. The allegory conveys in embryo almost all that Swift was later to say on Anglo-Irish relations.[15] The colonised woman sees her coloniser first as seducer, then as tyrant.

Although the lady does not dwell on her seduction, the metaphor itself gives further definition to the colonising process. The gentleman achieved his conquest, she says, 'half by force and half by consent, after solemn vows and protestations of marriage.' The consequent transformation in her life is the opposite of what she hoped for. He then began 'to act like a Conqueror.'[16] The allegory alludes to those debates among historians about the character of Ireland's first encounter with Henry II in 1171. Like Molyneux the lady sees her English gen-

---

10 *The Novel in Letters: Epistolary Fiction in the Early English Novel, 1678-1740*, ed. Natascha Wurzbach (London, 1969), p. 3. 11 See Ferguson, *Jonathan Swift and Ireland*, p. 6. A later example is the elder and younger sisters in Richard Cox's satire, *The Life of Betty Ireland*, London, 1753. 12 See Brian Ó Cuiv, 'Irish Language and Literature, 1691-1845', *New History of Ireland*, iv, 406. 13 O'Rathaille trans. James Clarence Mangan in Daniel Corkery, *The Hidden Ireland: A Study of Gaelic Munster in the Eighteenth Century* (1924; Dublin, 1967), p. 177. 14 See R.A. Breatnach, 'The Lady and the King: a Theme of Irish Literature', *Studies* 42 (1953), 321-36. P.J. Corish suggests that Queen Sive of the Gaelic tradition was imaged during the Whiteboy disturbances of 1761-5 as seeking marriage with George III (*The Catholic Community in the Seventeenth and Eighteenth Centuries* (Dublin, 1981), p. 126). 15 J.C.Beckett, 'Literature in English, 1691-1800', *New History of Ireland*, iv, 433. 16 'Injured Lady', *Prose Works of Swift*, ix, 5.

tleman as a worthy partner. He, like Henry, would secure laws and liberties, not conquest. According to Molyneux, none of the English kings 'established those Laws in Ireland by any Power of the Parliament of England, but by the free Consent, Allowance and Acceptance of the People of Ireland.'[17] Likewise the Injured Lady expects that her relationship will bring marriage as well as security and prosperity. What she finds is abuse and deprivation. This was the image fostered by Burke in that description of Henry crossing the Irish sea 'with a fleet of four hundred sail, at once to secure the conquest, and the allegiance of the conquerors.'[18] The lady has been grievously deceived.

Her account of her gentleman after the seduction emphasises his obsession to control her estate. His irrational and unsubtle design to dominate and then reduce her contrasts with her patient acquiescence so that her protest reads like the uncomprehending confusion of a well-intentioned but helpless woman: 'to reward my Love, Constancy, and Generosity, he hath bestowed on me the Office of being Semptstress to his Grooms and Footmen, which I am forced to accept or starve'.[19] The image offers no way out. In political terms Ireland is trapped into colonial subservience, and that was the predicament which many a Protestant Irish writer after Swift complained of. Their only recourse was to appeal to England's sense of justice. Any other solution such as the radical breakaway attempted by Wolfe Tone at the end of the century was here inconceivable. Protestants in Ireland were bonded to England by history, religion and blood; hence the solution can only lie within a shared system of values, a common discourse in which words like love, constancy and generosity are agreed markers of conduct.

Answer to the lady

The lady's letter draws a reply from a male confidant who chides her for not playing a smarter political game and for listening to 'the pernicious Counsels of some about you'.[20] That old Irish fault of squabbling among themselves has only weakened her. She should have joined forces with her rival against the gentleman or at least said nothing against her which would have made the gentleman wary. She was foolish to give herself to him and then expect him to honour her original demands. Sluts are wiser than that. The relationship between coloniser and colonised operates like a sexual relationship in which institutional power rests with the man. That is the reality she has to live with. The lady is right to complain of his abuses, but she must recognise his power. Ireland has to accept that fact. The lady must learn – as do Defoe's heroines – that a woman survives not by righteousness but by accommodation and guile. The lady's confidant duly

17 Molyneux, *The Case of Ireland*, p. 56. 18 Burke, 'Abridgment of English History', *Writings and Speeches of Edmund Burke*, i, 513. 19 'Injured Lady', *Prose Works of Swift*, ix, 7-8. 20 Ibid., 11.

advises her to work for a mutual agreement about the management of her estates, to insist on her independence in marketing her produce, to ask that her leases are respected. Such 'just and reasonable Offers' should effect a reconciliation.[21] It should be noted, however, that this ameliorative advice at the close of the confidant's letter baulks at the more radical undercurrent of much else he has said. His letter carries radical insinuations that politics, like sex, is a game, and the lady might be better off not marrying at all.

The answer takes us back to the problematics of Swift's view of Ireland as a separate kingdom. History suggests it was that only in name. The Declaratory Act of 1720 settled the issue with the pronouncement that Ireland was 'subordinate unto and dependent upon the imperial crown of Great Britain'.[22] But, as the confidant seems to realise, an improvement in Ireland's fortunes depends on a change of heart in England. That is the lynch-pin of protest by followers of Molyneux until the 1760s. By imaging that relationship in male/female terms Swift unwittingly acknowledges that in eighteenth-century terms the woman is at the mercy of the man and consequently she is indeed what Swift so often denied, a dependent.

The dilemma facing the injured lady is endemic to whatever Swift wrote about England's exploitation of Ireland. The difference between him and the lady is that he expressed the injury he felt not in perplexed complaints but in angry contempt. He berated, ridiculed and lampooned English administrators, politicians and bishops as well as those Protestant Irish who aped their English counterparts and colluded in Ireland's subservience. His inveterate scepticism about men in public office is summed up in his remark, 'The two Maxims of any great Man at Court are, always to keep his Countenance, and never to keep his Word.'[23] He criticised bishops sent over from England. They,

> Came but to plunder and enslave us;
> Nor ever owned a Pow'r Divine,
> But Mammon, and the German Line.[24]

Swift finds Ireland's own politicians, whom he castigates in 'The Legion Club' (1736), just as culpable. His bold confrontational protest sets the tone for decades to come. For instance, Curran told parliament in 1787 that the church of Ireland 'had been in the hands of strangers' for centuries, 'inclined naturally to oppress us, to hate us, and to defame us'.[25] Swift's 'The Legion Club' was a poem written against the Irish Commons for an attempt to deprive the clergy of their tithes

---

21 Ibid., 12. 22 *Irish Historical Documents*, p. 186. 23 'Thoughts on Various Subjects', *Prose Works of Swift*, iv, 252. 24 'On Dr Rundle', *Poems of Jonathan Swift*, iii, 819-21. 25 Cited by a Member of the Bar, *Irish Eloquence: the Speeches of the Celebrated Irish Orators, Philips, Curran and Grattan* (Philadelphia, 1836), p. 357.

from pasture lands.[26] He imagines first the devil wreaking God's punishment on 'the Den of Thieves' (28); then he sees the Irish House of Commons severally as Bedlam, as a cage of monkeys, and as Hell populated by 'Phantoms, bodiless and vane,/ Empty Visions of the Brain' (101-2). Like Aeneas in the underworld, Swift sees the many 'heroes' (136) of the place, including Sir John Bingham who 'sleeps the whole Debate' (165) but remains 'firm in his Vocation/ For the Court against the Nation' (171-2). A major trope of the poem is bestiality at its foul-smelling and noisy worst,

> three hundred Brutes
> All involv'd in wild Disputes;
> Roaring till their lungs were spent,
> Privilege of Parliament. (113-16)

The Irish parliament thus becomes a grotesque mad-house echoing with the nonsensical rhetoric of its inmates. Yet these are the people who presume to govern Ireland. 'The Legion Club', like 'The Story of the Injured Lady', images masters who care for nothing but their own power. They deny Ireland her separate identity and substitute instead a master/slave relationship which in 'The Legion Club' turns into the bizarre image of beasts ruling the people.

   The satirical voice situates Swift at a point outside the axis of Westminster and the Irish administration from where he looks in upon the roaring brutes and the contradictions of their situation with a knowing contempt. The humour mingles with a disturbing undercurrent of despair that this bestial degradation is Ireland's waking nightmare.

Writing back: The Drapier's Letters

A more subtle and devastating example of Swift striking back at the centre is his series of pamphlets published as *The Drapier's Letters*. Posing as a humble and assiduous drapier writing 'from my shop in St. Frances' Street', he takes up a cause already broached by Dublin's Archbishop King against an English manufacturer, William Wood, who had obtained a patent from the king's mistress, the duchess of Kendal, in 1722 to coin one hundred and eighty thousand pounds worth of small money for use in Ireland. Ireland had no mint of its own and depended for its coinage on England and its trading partners.[27] Wood was granted a fourteen-year contract that allowed him to manufacture the coins at a lower rate of value to weight of copper than that pertaining in England. The

---

26 'The Legion Club', *Poems of Jonathan Swift*, iii. 829-39.   27 For a perceptive analysis of the crisis see Patrick McNally, 'Wood's Halfpence, Carteret, and the government of Ireland, 1723-6', *IHS* 30, no. 119 (May 1997), 354-76.

curious feature about copper farthings and halfpence, which were in fact brass, was that they were a convenience and not strictly legal tender in either England or Ireland; hence no one was obliged to use them.[28] Swift transforms this local wrangle to a contest between the power of the metropole and the liberty of Ireland.

The debate at one level is between the simple common sense of the Drapier, arguing by 'plain Reason, unassisted by Art, Cunning or Eloquence',[29] and Wood's 'impudence, villainy and folly'.[30] Swift thus reverses the good and bad characteristics of the disputants as usually understood by the English. The Dublin Drapier comes to speak for the whole of Ireland against 'one obscure ironmonger',[31] who in turn epitomises the presumptuous scheming English. The argument – whether between drapier and ironmonger, or Ireland and England – is not in Swift's view between master and servant:

> Were not the People of Ireland born as free as those of England? How have they forfeited their Freedom? Is not their Parliament as fair a Representative of the People, as that of England? And hath not their Privy Council as great, or a greater Share in the Administration of pub-lick Affairs? Are they not Subject of the same King? Does not the same Sun shine over them? And have they not the same God for their Protector? Am I a Free man in England, and do I become a Slave in six Hours by crossing the Channel?[32]

The point rings like an echo in the fourth letter where he reminds the people of Ireland that they are free to choose whether they want Wood's copper coin or not: 'You *are* and you *ought to* be as *free* a people as your brethren in England': the imposition of Wood's coinage would be an assault on that liberty because, says Swift echoing Molyneux, 'all Government without the Consent of the Governed, is the very Definition of Slavery'.[33]

What was a dispute between a lady and a gentleman in the 'Injured Lady' here takes on the guise of a David and Goliath confrontation. The Drapier plays humorously with the biblical resonances concluding that Goliath 'was like Mr Wood, all over brass'. But if the Drapier triumphs he promises that Goliath 'shall never be a Servant of mine; for I do not think him fit to be trusted in any honest Man's Shop'.[34] The Drapier's scorn counters the ironmonger's hauteur, but he does pay Wood the backhanded compliment that he presumably knew something about Ireland which is more than most Englishmen do about their dependencies,

---

28 Irwin Ehrenpreis, *Swift, the Man, His Works, and the Age*, 3 vols (London), iii (1983), 187-94.   29 Letter III, *Drapier's Letters* in *Prose Works of Swift*, x, 29.   30 Letter II, ibid., 19.   31 Letter IV, ibid., 54.   32 Letter III, ibid., 31.   33 Letter IV, ibid., 63; cf. Molyneux, *The Case of Ireland*, p. 129: 'I have no other Notion of *Slavery, but being Bound by a Law to which I do not Consent.*'   34 Letter III, *Drapier's Letters* in *Prose Works of Swift*, x, 48; cf. 1 *Samuel*, 17. 5-6.

As to Ireland, they know little more than they do of Mexico; further than that it is a Country subject to the King of England, full of Boggs, inhabited by wild Irish Papists; who are kept in Awe by mercenary Troops sent from thence: And their general Opinion is, that it were better for England if this whole Island were sunk into the Sea.[35]

Ireland, like Mexico, has no more substance than a word, a name for some far away place in the speeches of politicians. The consequences of such ignorance are a macabre travesty of the imperial vision as expressed for example by Pope, 'Earth's distant Ends our Glory shall behold,/ And the new World launch forth to see the Old.'[36] The Drapier gives a comical twist to Pope's imperial optimism. He contemplates Ireland as Wood might have it,

> I reflected with some Pleasure what a Jolly Crew it would bring over among us of Lords and Squires, and Pensioners of Both Sexes, and Officers Civil and Military; where we should live together as merry and sociable as Beggars; only with this one Abatement, that we should neither have Meat to feed, nor Manufactures to Cloath us; unless we could be content to Prance about in Coats of Mail; or eat Brass as Ostritches do Iron.[37]

The sour glee of such writing carries a moral confidence which is untouched by the Drapier's awareness that Wood has political power on his side. The Drapier likens Wood to a rat, then a horse-dealer.[38] Wood's attempt on Ireland reminds the Drapier of the dumb boy who finds his tongue when he sees the murderer's knife at his father's throat:

> This may lessen the Wonder, that a Tradesman hid in Privacy and Silence should cry out when the Life and Being of his Political Mother are attempted before his Face; and by so infamous a Hand.[39]

The image of a murderous Englishman reads like a later episode in the relation between the injured lady and her gentleman.

Despite the Drapier's ridicule in the earlier letters he dwells on the more sombre point that this incident is but the culmination of a long history of oppression. Whether the term colony is used or not, Ireland's experience of British rule is a record of degradation which has robbed her even of the benefits of belonging to the empire. The Protestant Irish,

> have been rewarded with a worse Climate, the Privilege of being governed by Laws to which we do not consent; a ruined Trade, a House of Peers

---

35 Letter VI, ibid., 103. 36 Pope, 'Windsor Forest' (1713), ll. 401-2. 37 Letter IV, *Drapier's Letters* in *Prose Works of Swift*, x, 59. 38 Letter II, ibid., 20; Letter III, ibid., 45. 39 Letter V, ibid., 89.

without Jurisdiction; almost an Incapacity for all Employments, and the Dread of Wood's Half-pence.[40]

Such impositions have become a way of life and Ireland, with nothing to show to her advantage, is like the ass in the fable beaten beyond caring by her master who,

> entreated his Ass to fly for Fear of being taken by the Enemy; but the Ass refused to give himself that Trouble; and upon a very wise Reason; because he could not possibly change his present Master for a worse: The Enemy could not make him fare harder; beat him more cruelly; nor load him with heavier Burthens.[41]

This stark analogy is supported by the Drapier's account of the many ways in which the Irish revenue has been drained to serve absentee landlords, pensions, the army, the revenue commissioners. Wood stands ready for the final blow – 'and now the Branches are all cut off, he stands ready with his Ax at the Root'.[42] The threat of final ruin is depicted without a trace of irony or humour. Like the flying island of Laputa, it is too imminent to be a fanciful joke.

The imaginative energy of this writing runs counter to everything the English thought of themselves as promoters of empire and a civilisation marked by liberty and prosperity. Swift's friend Joseph Addison expressed the widely held English view that 'Riches and Plenty are the natural Fruits of Liberty, and where these abound, Learning and all the Liberal Arts will immediately lift up their Heads and flourish.'[43] Against such imperial images the Drapier depicts England as a rapacious bird of prey waiting to swoop: 'Nature hath instructed even a Brood of Goslings to stick together while the Kite is hovering over their Heads.'[44]

Swift as paternalist

The Drapier's triumph came in August 1725 when the news arrived in Dublin that Wood's patent had been cancelled.[45] A poem 'On the Drapier' typifies Ireland's gratitude to the Drapier. Swift was hailed as Ireland's liberator.

> UNDONE by Fools at home, abroad by Knaves,
> The Isle of Saints became the land of Slaves,

40 Letter IV, ibid., 55.   41 Letter VII, ibid., 122-3.   42 Letter VII, ibid., 129.   43 *Spectator*, no. 287 [29 Jan. 1712] in *The Spectator*, ed. Donald F. Bond, 5 vols (Oxford, 1965), iii, 21.   44 Letter VII, *Drapier's Letters* in *Prose Works of Swift*, x, 134; cf. *Luke*, 13. 34: 'I have gathered thy children together, as a hen doth gather her brood under her wings.'   45 See David Noakes, *Jonathan Swift, A Hypocrite Reversed: A Critical Biography* (Oxford, 1987), p. 294.

Trembling beneath her proud oppressor's hand;
But, when thy reason thunder'd through the land,
Then all the public spirit breath'd in thee,
And all, except the sons of guilt, were free.
Blest Isle, blest Patriot, ever-glorious strife!
You gave her Freedom as she gave thee Life.
Thus Cato fought, whom Brutus copy'd well,
And with those rights, for which you stand, he fell.[46]

The anti-colonial protest rings out in Ireland's transformation from saints to slaves and later in the assertion that the language of protest had made Ireland free. Yet in this time of triumph it is easy, as David Noakes points out, to overlook the point that Swift was not writing to or for 'the whole people of Ireland', but for the merchants and shopkeepers who would be affected by the coinage and to a circumscribed political circle, in particular Lord Lieutenant Carteret and Walpole.[47] The excited rhetoric of 'On the Drapier', culminating in a closing trope that equates the Drapier to Cato and Brutus in ancient Rome signifies that the Drapier is being metamorphosed by his supporters into a classical figure of resistance, a typological hero in the ever recurring struggle between tyranny and liberty.

The implied reader of this kind of political discourse as well as of *The Drapier's Letters* was a smaller community than the phrase 'the whole people of Ireland' suggests. Certainly it would include Protestant Anglo-Irish readers like Swift who read Faulkner's *Dublin Journal*, frequented Dublin's coffee houses, followed the proceedings of parliament and celebrated the battle of the Boyne. This readership constituted but one of what Anderson calls the 'imagined communities' in Ireland.[48] But the language repeatedly attempts to transcend this limited sense of the Irish community by using inclusive terms. A phrase in the poem like 'The Isle of Saints' and the repeated use of 'all' suggests the wider community of Catholics and Dissenters, in fact all Irish people. Yet, as we shall see, that wider community had a very different sense of what tyranny and liberty meant.

Whereas later in the century Burke and Tone speak up for the marginalised Catholic majority, Swift's voice conceals an ambiguous relation with Ireland. A champion against the oppressor, he neglects much more obvious and immediate examples of oppression. His is an Irish voice, but minority Irish. His target here is England's political mismanagement and neglect of Irish Protestant interests; it has nothing to say about the way England treats the Catholic majority. When

---

46 'On the Drapier', *Miscellanies in Verse*, ed. Andrew Carpenter, Irish Writings from the Age of Swift series, (Dublin, 1973), p. 25. Carpenter notes that some of the poems in praise of the Drapier were written by Swift himself. 47 Noakes, *Jonathan Swift*, pp 295-6; for a contrary view see Carole Fabricant, *Swift's Landscape* (London, 1982), p. 253. 48 See Benedict Anderson, *Imagined Communities: Reflections on the Origin and Spread of Nationalism*, London, 1993.

the Drapier turns in the last letter to 'the poorer sort of our natives', his advice reads like the report of a colonial governor on the uncivilised natives. He speaks one kind of language when facing the English across the Irish sea, but when he looks westwards into Ireland the 'blest Patriot' sounds very different. For example, referring to Ireland's Catholics, he advises,

> That some effectual Methods may be taken to civilize the poorer Sort of our Natives, in all those Parts of this Kingdom where the Irish abound; by introducing among them our Language and Customs; for want of which they live in the utmost Ignorance, Barbarity and Poverty; giving themselves wholly up to Idleness, Nastyness and Thievery.[49]

The paternalism of 'our natives' and the ensuing attack on their 'Barbarity', their 'Idleness, Nastyness and Thievery' are features of colonial discourse going back to Spenser.[50] The English made several attempts to incorporate the Irish into their notion of civilisation, but like Prospero they found their savage Caliban recalcitrant and ungrateful. Spenser likened the Irish to unbridled colts. They were,

> at first well handled and wisely brought to acknowledge allegiance to the kings of England, but being straight left unto themselves and their own inordinate life and manners, they eftsones forgot what before they were taught, and so soon as they were out of sight by themselves shook off their bridles and began to colt anew, more licentiously than before.[51]

Swift's argument for the civilising effects of English ways is a reminder that he occupies that adversarial space between the metropole and the native Irish. He is patriot and liberator *vis-à-vis* Ireland's legislative independence, but the liberty he fights for is also a liberty to promote English and Protestant culture, to reform the Irish from their barbarism and assimilate them into the ideology of the metropole. This is not a contradiction in Swift, because, as all the eighteenth-century patriots were to argue, the liberties enshrined in Magna Carta not only provided against autocratic power but generated the climate in which English laws, constitution, customs and arts could flourish. There is no place in such a climate for oppression, slavery or injustice, because the moral ethos is monoculturally English or, as the English think, universal.[52] Swift protests at the absence of that kind of liberty. His concern to civilise the native Irish puts him back on the side of the colonisers whose agenda is religious and cultural orthodoxy.

---

49 Letter VII, *Drapier's Letters* in *Prose Works of Swift*, x, 139. 50 E.g. Spenser, *A View of the Present State of Ireland*, pp 52, 72, 83. 51 Ibid., p. 6. 52 Cf. *The Empire Writes Back*, pp 188-9: 'In the evaluation of post-colonial literature it is the centre which imposes its criteria as universal, and dictates an order in terms of which the cultural margins must always see themselves as disorder and chaos.'

The same civilising mission informs much other writing of the day such as William Phillips' play, *Hibernia Freed*, about the expulsion of the Vikings from Ireland in 1014. A Gaelic bard Eugenius prophesies that another race will conquer Ireland,

> Another Nation, famous through the World,
> For martial Deeds, for Strength and Skill in Arms,
> Belov'd and blest for their Humanity ...
> They shall succeed, invited to our Aid,
> And mix their Blood with ours; one People grow,
> Polish our Manners, and improve our Minds.[53]

Again the language insists that this transformation will be to Ireland's benefit. Ireland will be assimilated into a superior culture.

Gulliver colonised

Cultural assimilation and the problems involved are at the centre of Swift's major satire *Gulliver's Travels* (1726). Allegorical readings of the work are often difficult to sustain in detail and as F.P. Lock shows with respect to Laputa in Book III it is as easy to erect new allegorical readings as it is to demolish old ones.[54] Nevertheless *Gulliver's Travels* exhibits several traits of that fundamental aspect of colonialism, cultural assimilation and the colonising of the mind. What the book deals with at one level is the alienating experience of a person moving from the securities of his own culture into another culture. The process follows a similar pattern in each book and one familiar to Irish people going to England or colonised peoples in the twentieth century moving from their rural home to the city or to Europe. Gulliver experiences severe cultural shock on each voyage. As the stranger, the outsider, he has to adjust from his own to the new culture. For his physical and mental survival he has first to learn the language of his masters and then understand their conventions and manners so that he does not offend against their value systems. The more successfully he achieves these goals the more ready are the strangers to take him seriously. Only then does he begin to ask for his liberty. If he shows the slightest sign of threatening them, as among the Lilliputians and Houyhnhnms, they retaliate. As the process develops, Gulliver has occasion to compare his own with his masters' culture, and particularly in Brobdingnag and Houyhnhnmland he experiences a conflict between his own and his masters' way of thinking. This dislocation is the start of his mental colonisation which shows itself most acutely at the end of Book IV, where he

---

53 William Phillips, *Hibernia Freed* (? Dublin, c.1723), Act V, p. 61. 54 F.P. Lock, *The Politics of Gulliver's Travels* (Oxford, 1980), pp 89-122.

rejects the company of his wife and family, preferring to talk to his horses. He now sees his countrymen as Yahoos whom he resolves to reform. He has become an agent for a task the Houyhnhnms found impossible.

Colonisers sometimes find the natives intransigent, and, as critics have noted, the savage Yahoos may be an ironic image of the Irish. Anne Kelly argues that the Houynhnhnms' treatment of the Yahoos has similarities with England's government of Ireland.[55] Afraid of and ignorant about the Yahoos, the Houynhnhnms so bestialise them that they behave like brutes and thus confirm their masters' suspicions that they are inferior and incapable of being civilised. Kelly writes, 'To view the oppressed as irrational, or lacking in humanity, is a perfect excuse for treating him as a chattel slave.'[56] In postcolonial terms the Yahoos fulfil the essentialist and static image conferred on them by their Houynhnhnm masters. England comes through this analogical reading as both authoritarian and anxiously afraid of its colony's natives.

Another colonial inference in the text is that although Gulliver so admires the Houyhnhnms he remains a second-class citizen among them. Their self-confidence in their culture allows nothing more than scorn for his. Gulliver's attempts to convince the king of Brobdingnag of the splendours, for example, of English politics, the legislature and the church are met with laughter and scorn. Like Addison Gulliver presumes of his own culture that it is 'an unspeakable Blessing to be born in those Parts of the World where Wisdom and Knowledge flourish'.[57] Yet after close discussion he finds that the king of Brobdingnag thinks 'the bulk of your natives, to be the most pernicious race of little odious vermin that nature ever suffered to crawl upon the surface of the earth'.[58] For all Gulliver's enthusiasm for his own culture and the questioning of his masters, he remains but an object of curiosity, an outsider in his new and unfamiliar environment.

The way in which Swift establishes this alienation is worth looking at in detail. In his first encounter with strange peoples Gulliver is always at a disadvantage: the Lilliputians pin him to the ground, the Brobdingnagian farmer holds him up between forefinger and thumb the better to scrutinise him, he shouts for help to the people on the flying island, he is set upon by Yahoos who clamber up the tree 'to discharge their excrements on my head'.[59] Briefly he tries to make sense of his situation in his own terms, but his cultural perceptions are inadequate. As he moves from the margins to the centre of each society he becomes submissive and accepts the terms of the strange society. On the shore at

55 Anne Cline Kelly, 'Swift's Explorations of Slavery in Houyhnhnmland and Ireland', *PMLA* 91 (1976), 846-55; also C.H. Firth, 'The Political Significance of *Gulliver's Travels*', in *Essays Historical and Literary* (Oxford, 1938), pp 228-31 and D.T. Torchiana, 'Jonathan Swift, the Irish and the Yahoos: the Case Reconsidered', *Philological Quarterly* 54 (1975), 195-212. 56 Kelly, 'Swift's Explorations of Slavery', *PMLA* 91, 854. 57 *Spectator*, no. 215 (6 November 1711), *The Spectator*, ii, 340. 58 Swift, *Gulliver's Travels*, p. 140. 59 Ibid., p. 238.

Lilliput he thinks for a moment of fighting free but decides not to 'because of the promise of honour I made them' and 'the laws of hospitality'.[60] In this instance the few norms he can think of serve ironically but to consolidate his subjection. He tells the Lilliputians 'they might do with me what they pleased'.[61]

Physical confinement is but the forerunner to a more serious problem, his inability to comprehend. His physical restriction in all but Book III signifies something of his mental confinement. He cannot engage with, let alone comprehend, his new context, so he has to acquire the language, first to communicate his needs and then to relate to the strange society. Like Caliban he is dependent on his masters' language for acceptance and as a security against humiliation, if not suffering. Often his newly acquired language only brings disillusionment, be it with politicians in Lilliput or with scientific projects in Balnibarbi. But language, especially in Brobdingnag and Houyhnhnmland, serves the additional functions of holding up Gulliver's society to scrutiny and confirming his inferiority to the masters. The Houyhnhnm family were eager to teach him, 'for they looked upon it as a prodigy, that a brute animal should discover such marks of a rational creature'.[62] Gulliver is presumed to be a savage like the Yahoos incapable of the intelligence, skills or conduct of a Houyhnhnm. All the more reason for Gulliver to learn the language so that he can explain himself, defend himself from this presumption and demonstrate his equality in terms comprehensible to his master. The task is necessary to his self-esteem, and yet futile. In his discussions with the king of Brobdingnag and his master Houyhnhnm Gulliver himself often escapes censure, but not his society. His species are seen as inferior and despicably so. In Houyhnhnmland he struggles to insist he is not a Yahoo, claiming to be as horrified by the filthy creatures as his master is 'convinced that the hatred I bore these brutes would never suffer me to be corrupted by them'.[63] But his rejection of this image leads him to take his identity instead from the Houynhnhnms. He becomes enslaved to them just when he thinks he has been liberated.

> I freely confess, that all the little knowledge I have of any value, was acquired by the lectures I received from my master, and from hearing the discourses of him and his friends; to which I should be prouder to listen, than to dictate to the greatest and wisest assembly in Europe. I admired the strength, comeliness and speed of the inhabitants; and such a constellation of virtues in such amiable persons, produced in me the highest veneration. At first, indeed, I did not feel that natural awe, which the Yahoos and all the other animals, bear towards them; but it grew upon me by degrees, much sooner than I imagined.[64]

The only allusion to Gulliver's own background, 'the greatest and wisest assembly in Europe', is brushed aside as of no consequence. Gulliver's hyperboles far

60 Ibid., p. 19. 61 Ibid., p. 20. 62 Ibid., p. 249. 63 Ibid., p. 283. 64 Ibid., pp 297-8.

from convincing the reader stir suspicions that he has lost his critical bearings. The colonised parvenu filled with 'the highest veneration' and 'natural awe' – an ironic pun suggesting the normalcy of his response – yearns for acceptance by his masters. He hopes 'that they would condescend to distinguish me from the rest of my species'.[65] This rejection of self completes his mental colonisation. As Fanon writes, 'In the colonial context the settler only ends his work of breaking in the native when the latter admits loudly and intelligently the supremacy of the white man's values.'[66]

In the light of the above, Gulliver's outburst against colonialism in the closing pages of the last voyage is all the more ironic. 'It was whispered to me,' he writes, 'that I was bound in duty as a subject of England, to have given in a memorial to a Secretary of State … because whatever lands are discovered by a subject, belong to the Crown.'[67] He dismisses any suggestion that England should colonise the lands he has visited, least of all Brobdingnag and Houyhnhnmland,[68] and he proceeds to condemn colonisation. Sounding more like the king of Brobdingnag than an empire man he argues that colonisation is characterised by torture, lust and blood; it is brutal and demeaning. But the patriot in Gulliver then surfaces to exonerate the British from such barbarous behaviour. Their colonies are different: they are planted with 'care, wisdom and justice.' Even so, the lands he visited 'were by no means proper objects of our zeal, or valour, or our interest.'[69]

Gulliver ends up a conglomerate contradiction of Houyhnhnm and English patriot. Incapable of settling his identity in either culture, he returns home a confused, alienated and pathetic figure. His mind still obsessed with the differences between Houyhnhnms and Yahoos, he carries them into his own home adulating his horses and disgusted by his Yahoo wife. Unable to make meaningful contact with either or assimilate the virtues of one with the other, he experiences that cultural disintegration which so many colonised people have known, for example, in Africa, India and the Caribbean in the last two centuries.

The point is not without its personal ironies for Swift who at times so lamented his posting to Ireland that eight years after he became dean of St Patrick's he could still be riled to be reminded by his friend John Gay of the cultural and intellectual life he was missing in England. Only malice, he says, could prompt Gay to wake him from his 'Scurvy Sleep':

> My Business, my Diversions my Conversations are all entirely changed for the Worse, and So are my studyes and my Amusements in writing; Yet after all, this humdrum way of Life might be passable enough if you would let me alone. I shall not be able to relish my Wine, my Parsons, my

65 Ibid., p. 298. 66 Frantz Fanon, *The Wretched of the Earth*, trans. Constance Farrington (London, 1965), p. 35. 67 *Gulliver's Travels*, p. 314. 68 Ibid., p. 315. 69 Ibid., p. 316.

Horses nor my Garden for three months, till the Spirit you have raised
Shall be dispossessed.[70]

At times Swift shared Gulliver's yearning for a society so much more admirable
than what the Yahoos offered him.

This reading of the colonisation and disorientation of Gulliver's mind reinforces rather than detracts from the wider satirical thrusts of the book against
human pride, political corruption, projectors and travel literature itself. Gulliver's
attack on colonialism at the end draws the reader's attention back to England
and English administrators as a major target in the book. His panegyric on the
way the British, as opposed to other unscrupulous nations, conduct their colonies
builds with typically Swiftian craft to a litany of national virtues. The fluent
rhetoric of the encomium might easily distract the reader from remembering
what Swift had said elsewhere about England's treatment of Ireland. Suddenly
the British are exempt from his murderous description of colonialism, which he
says,

> doth by no means affect the British nation, who may be an example to the
> whole world for their wisdom, care, and justice in planting colonies the
> liberal endowments for the advancement of religion and learning; their
> choice of devout and able pastors to propagate Christianity; their caution
> in stocking their provinces with people of sober lives and conversations
> from this the mother kingdom; their strict regard to the distribution of
> justice, in supplying the civil administration through all their colonies
> with officers of the greatest abilities, utter strangers to corruption: and to
> crown all, by sending the most vigilant and virtuous governors, who have
> no other view than the happiness of the people over whom they preside,
> and the honour of the king their master.[71]

This mock patriotic fervour is designed partly to puff the British at the expense
of other colonisers like the Portuguese, the Dutch and the French, but its main
purpose is to tease the reader to measure the imperial myth against the facts.
Several English governors in the early colonies were the very opposite of what
Gulliver claims. Francis Nicholson, the able but fiery-tempered governor of
Virginia from 1698 to 1705, fell foul of the colonists, whose long list of complaints
led to his recall to England.[72] They accused him of a 'vast number of instances of
his injustice, oppression, and insolence'. For example, he controlled the revenue

---

70 Swift to Gay, 8 Jan. 1723, *The Correspondence of Jonathan Swift*, ed. Harold Williams, 5 vols
(Oxford, 1963-5), ii, 442.   71 *Gulliver's Travels*, p. 316.   72 See 'A Memorial Concerning the
Maladministrations of His Excellency Francis Nicholson ...', *English Historical Documents*, ix,
'American Colonial Documents to 1776', ed. Merrill Jensen (London, 1955), 254-60.

'without the knowledge and consent of the Council'. The colonists spoke of his 'abusive way of browbeating, discouraging, and threatening all that speak anything contrary to his opinions or designs'. He encouraged sycophants and was guilty of 'many gross immoralities and pranks of lewdness'. Colonel Peake, a less competent governor of Barbados, was 'wounded in the rebellion which followed his attempts on the planters' wives ... was stripped and left to die in the open in the heat'.[73]

Gulliver's claims strike a particularly hollow note when applied to Ireland. Spenser was embarrassed and appalled,

> to see Her Majesty so much abused by some whom they put in special trust of those great affairs, of which some being martial men will not do always what they may, for quieting of things, but will rather wink at some faults, and suffer them unpunished.

The cunning and unpredictable behaviour of governors in Ireland is 'the wretchedness of that fatal kingdom'.[74]

In the early eighteenth century about half Ireland's Protestant bishops had been sent over from England. Swift is reported to have told a story about them in which he says the monarch had selected good men, 'but they were murdered by a parcel of highwaymen between Chester and London, who slipping on their gowns and cassocks here pretend to pass for bishops'.[75] Swift's attack on the Englishman Bishop Josiah Hort well illustrates how vapid is Gulliver's praise for 'devout and able pastors'. Hort, educated in a Nonconformist school, had no university degree. He had been chaplain in Ireland to Lord Wharton, lord lieutenant from 1709 to 1711, and was made bishop of Kilmore and Armagh and later archbishop of Tuam.

> Would you rise in the Church, be Stupid and Dull,
> Be empty of Learning, of Insolence full:
> Be Lewd and Immoral, be Formal and Grave,
> In Flatt'ry an Artist, in Fawning a Slave,
> No Merit, no Science, no Virtue is wanting
> In him that's accomplish'd in Cringing and Canting:
> Be studious to practice true Meanness of Spirit;
> For who but Lord Bolton was mitred for Merit?
> Wou'd you wish to be wrap'd in a Rochet – In short.
> Be as Pox'd and Profane as Fanatical H[ort].[76]

73 John Bowle, *The Imperial Achievement: the Rise and Transformation of the British Empire* (London, 1974), p. 123, n. 29. 74 Spenser, *A View of the Present State of Ireand*, pp 91-2. 75 Attributed to Lord Egmont by Ehrenpreis, *Swift*, iii, 167-8. 76 'Advice to a Parson, An Epigram' (1732), *Poems of*

Gulliver's praise for 'the most vigilant and virtuous governors' could hardly include Sunderland, appointed lord lieutenant in 1714, nor his successor Townshend, both of whom failed to visit Ireland during their tenure.[77] Swift called the next lord lieutenant, Lord Bolton, 'a great Booby' whereas the antiquarian Thomas Hearne said he was lewd, lying and bibulous.[78] Only Swift's long-standing friend Lord Carteret, lord lieutenant from 1724 to 1730, escaped Swift's contempt. As Ehrenpreis observes Swift's praise of Carteret 'sometimes echoes Gulliver's remarks on the King of the Giants'.[79] Carteret like the king of Brobdingnag was an exception.

Gulliver's eulogy on the British colonies could also be read as a reminder of how colonialism should operate, and thus could stand as a measure of transgression. The fact that Wood's halfpence, for example, demonstrated that Westminster had come to accept transgression as the norm is not an argument against colonialism but against its abuse. In Edward Said's terms, if Swift's satire is a mode of transgressing British decorum so is British decorum a mode of transgressing Ireland's liberty.[80]

Although Gulliver's travels start as trading ventures to the East or the South Seas, they become voyages of discovery. Gulliver's account subverts the very *raison d'être* of such voyages which was to broaden the mind, contribute to knowledge and extend the frontiers of understanding. What draws Gulliver's outburst against colonialism is that travel, be it, as he tells his Houyhnhnm master, 'to get riches'[81] or to explore, had an underlying political agenda which was to expand the empire. Gulliver's voyages brought him intellectual derangement and cultural alienation, the opposite to what was anticipated. Whereas his English readers expected Gulliver to be a coloniser, he comes to hate his own kind and himself becomes colonised. The book is a mockery of the imperial enterprise transforming it from the triumphant into the macabre. As Said points out with regard to *The Drapier's Letters*, Swift displaces what he sees as British fictions about politics in Ireland with alternative fictions:

> An imaginative event and, by extension, writing that involved imaginative projections, comically displaced real events; thus Swift's mind remained faithful to the presence of events, if only by mocking merely verbal fictions of reality, like Wood's scheme, with alternative schemes.[82]

Gulliver's voyage to the Houyhnhnms is just such another imaginative projection that displaces the actual politics of the way the English treated the Irish. Gulliver

Jonathan Swift, iii, 807-8; for other poems on the bishops see 'Judas' (1731/2) and 'On the Irish Bishops' (1732). Swift was later reconciled to Hort.   77 Charles Viscount Townshend was appointed in February 1717 and succeeded by Charles Paulet, Duke of Bolton, in April 1717.   78 Ehrenpreis, *Swift*, ii, 40.   79 Ibid., iii, 224.   80 See Edward W. Said, 'Swift's Tory Anarchy', *Eighteenth-Century Studies* 3 (1969), 65-6; also, Ehrenpreis, 'Swift on Liberty', *Swift: Modern Judgements*, ed. A. Norman Jeffares (London, 1968), pp 59-73.   81 *Gulliver's Travels*, p. 259.   82 Said, 'Swift's Tory Anarchy', *Eighteenth-Century Studies* 3 (1969), 57-8.

acknowledges as much when he first visits a Houyhnhnm house: 'I rubbed mine eyes often but the same objects still occurred. I pinched my arms and sides to awake myself, hoping I might be in a dream.'[83] A reality that seems unthinkable is transmuted into fiction where it acquires substance. The possibility of analogy between the fiction and reality then recoils with ridiculous force on English prejudices about the Irish. Colonial government thus becomes yet another of England's 'verbal fictions of reality.'

Both fictions, be they Gulliver's trauma in Houyhnhnmland, where he ends up disgusted with himself as a Yahoo, or colonialism itself, transgress the notion of liberty which Swift yearned for Ireland. At the end of *Gulliver's Travels* the Council of Houyhnhnms decides that Gulliver must either live and work like the rest of the Yahoos or leave the country. Their basic fear was that Gulliver with his 'rudiments of reason' might start a rebellion.[84] The 'clever native' of so much subsequent colonial history has to be suppressed or sent into exile. What he must not have is liberty. That would threaten the metropolitan power. The Irish like the injured lady and the Yahoos have to be subjected to the central authority, be it by 'Inconstancy and Unkindness' as in her case[85] or by political power as Gulliver so often witnesses on his travels.

For Swift that liberty is Ireland's right and is obtainable within the existing constitutional framework. The stumbling block is corrupt politicians and administrators. One of the many ironies about Gulliver as an English traveller is that so much of the satire implicitly is directed at the Protestant Irish, particularly the politicians. Reflecting on his happiness among the Houyhnhnms, he thinks of the catalogue of evils in England he has escaped. It starts with precisely the fault of the gentleman who seduced the injured lady – treachery:

> I did not feel the treachery or inconstancy of a friend, nor the injuries of a secret or open enemy. I had no occasion of bribing, flattering or pimping, to procure the favour of any great man, or of his minion. I wanted no fence against fraud or oppression ...[86]

Gulliver charges his fellow English with the faults Swift elsewhere raged against. Like Gulliver, Swift longs for the alternative virtues which he presumes are universal and therefore transcend national and religious differences. They are consonant with loyalty to the British crown and his conception of Ireland within the empire. In the 'Verses on the Death of Dr Swift' he writes, 'His Satyr points at no Defect, /But what all Mortals may correct.'[87] But this faith is so often undermined by the corrupting forces within Anglo-Irish politics. His images of the English keep returning to the deceit of the gentleman in 'The Story of the

---

83 *Gulliver's Travels*, p. 243.   84 Ibid., p. 299.   85 'Injured Lady', *Prose Works of Swift*, ix, 3.   86 *Gulliver's Travels*, pp 295-6.   87 'Verses on the Death of Dr Swift', ll. 463-4, *Poems of Jonathan Swift*, ii, 571.

Injured Lady'. Yet Swift, like the lady, sees no way out of Ireland's predicament as a *de facto* colonised subordinate state. That was the paradox for the Anglo-Irish for much of the eighteenth century. The partnership with England, a *de jure* relationship of equality under the crown and ratified by legal history, as Molyneux had argued, was characterised on England's side by deception and on Ireland's side by incompetence and fear. What is curious in terms of postcolonial writing is that in this contest between English 'knaves' and Irish 'fools' Swift never conceives of liberty in other terms than those produced by England. To do so would have been as unthinkable as the Council of Houyhnhms debating whether to set the Yahoos free.

Stripping the colonial mask

What distinguishes Swift from other eighteenth-century Anglo-Irish protesters, indeed from all postcolonial writers is the sustained savagery of his satire, and nowhere is this more clearly evident than in his pamphlet published in 1729, *A Modest Proposal for Preventing the Children of Poor People from being a Burthen to their Parents or Country, and for Making them Beneficial to the Public.* His pose as a concerned patriot is the platform for devastating ironies aimed at those who claim to be Ireland's benefactors but are in fact her worst enemies. What prompts the proposal is the shocking poverty he sees on the streets of Dublin and elsewhere in Ireland:

> It is a melancholly Object to those, who walk through this great Town, or travel in the Country, when they see the Streets, the Roads, and Cabbin-doors, crowded with Beggars of the Female Sex, followed by three, four, or six Children, all in Rags, and importuning every Passenger for an Alms.[88]

To alleviate this situation the persona proposes that the poor fatten up their babies until they are a year old; they could then sell them as a delicacy for the table of the upper classes. The benefits to the 'Beggars of the Female Sex' would be money in their hand, no more expenses providing for their children through years of degrading poverty, and no more abortions or infanticide. In addition the number of Catholics in Ireland would be significantly reduced, an argument that echoes Gullliver's suggestion that the Houyhnhms castrate the younger Yahoos which 'would in an age, put an end to the whole species'.[89]

As if this proposal were not shocking enough, the projector goes into calm and careful calculations as to the details of his proposal – how many children could be disposed of in this way and how many kept to propagate the species to

88 *A Modest Proposal* in *Prose Works of Swift*, xii, 109. 89 *Gulliver's Travels*, p. 291.

ensure a future supply. The economics of the project preclude any moral sense and thus the Irish are transformed from human beings into a commodity on a par with 'Sheep, black Cattle, or Swine'.[90] The projector's aside that children of the Irish poor 'are seldom the fruits of marriage' leads not just to the patronising remark that 'our savages' show little concern for marriage, but allows him to think of them as animals and apply farmyard economics to their propagation and control.

The point is extended by an acquaintance of the projector who adds the macabre refinement that unemployed youngsters could likewise supply the recent shortage of venison:

> He said, that many Gentlemen of this Kingdom, having of late destroyed their Deer; he conceived, that the Want of Venison might be well supplied by the Bodies of young Lads and Maidens, not exceeding fourteen Years of Age, nor under twelve; so great a Number of both Sexes in every County being now ready to starve, for Want of Work and Service.[91]

The projector decides against this refinement, partly because the meat of the boys would be tough and partly because he wouldn't want to be thought cruel to the girls. This twinge of sensitivity simply emphasises its harrowing absence throughout the proposal. Phrases like 'A very worthy Person, a true Lover of his Country' take on a sinister ambiguity. Irony transforms the projector who poses as Ireland's benefactor into one of the most ghoulish characters in anti-colonial literature.

In terms of postcolonial discourse the projector reflects the desire of the dominant ideology to write the peasant people as a commodity and thereby transform them from people into disposable goods for the economic improvement of Ireland. The bland voice of the opening leads the reader into presuming that only the coloniser knows how to dispose of Ireland's surplus population and thus ease her economic difficulties. The Irish poor remain a silent presence throughout. This mimicry of the colonising voice in effect subverts it while seeming to give it a central place in the text. Swift ironically displaces its authority, and as in his other satires he establishes an alternative moral authority for himself well beyond the control of the metropole.

In the closing pages the projector dismisses all previous proposals such as taxing absentee landlords, supporting Irish woollens, calling a halt to rackrenting, and 'of putting a Spirit of Honesty, Industry, and Skill' into Ireland's shopkeepers.[92] Ironically Swift had had a hand in many of these schemes. The problem for the projector, as for the administration, is to find a useful niche for the 'savages' in the economic order, a problem that was to recur throughout the empire in the

90 *Modest Proposal* in *Prose Works of Swift*, xii, 111. 91 Ibid., 113. 92 Ibid., 116.

nineteenth and twentieth centuries. The final solution is for the children of the Catholic poor to be served up to their masters, a metaphor that vividly captures the process of degradation which is at the heart of Ireland's postcolonial predicament. It touches a raw truth about England's wish 'to bind the kingdom and the people of Ireland'.[93]

One of the disturbing ambiguities of the *Modest Proposal* is the benevolent and courteous inhumanity towards the Catholics. This proposal to reduce their number is a radical alternative to that allowed for by the legislation which aimed to persuade them away from their religion into the Church of Ireland. Either way, Protestant discourse was inclined to refer to Catholics as though they constituted a discrete and homogenous group in Ireland. That was an important fiction that helped Irish Protestants define themselves as different from the Catholics. In their arguments with England about liberty and legislative independence it was perhaps inevitable that they would ignore the emergence of a much more complex Catholic presence than their essentialist view acknowledged. But as the century moved on, that new and often divided Catholic presence made itself felt. That in turn meant the emergence of new kinds of discourse in eighteenth-century Irish writing among both Protestants and Catholics.

93 Declaratory Act, *Irish Historical Documents, 1172-1922*, p. 186.

CHAPTER FOUR

Catholic voices
in mid eighteenth-century Ireland

RELIGION AND NATION

Ireland's problems with self-definition kept coming back to the Catholics. The tendency of Swift's projector to lump the 'papists' together continued through much of the century. When Dr Johnson complained of the severity with which Protestants treated the Catholics in Ireland, he implied that in English eyes one Irish Catholic was much the same as another.[1] In terms of the penal laws he was right, because those laws were designed to punish any and every Catholic without discrimination. The Catholics were thus an easily identifiable and large group of the people of Ireland. In the light of this it is surprising that they did not have the confidence to protest at both the laws and the oversimplification with one voice. During the first half of the century some Catholics did contest the penal laws, not publicly but through conventional political and diplomatic channels: petitions to parliament in Dublin and London were presented by legal counsel;[2] individual bishops approached their counterparts in Catholic Europe, or Rome, to voice objections; ambassadors of Catholic powers in London were asked to use their influence to have the laws modified or rejected. What these tactics implied was that the majority of Catholics had been not only marginalised, but effectively silenced. Not until mid-century was there a significant change.

Yet those same penal laws were slowly prompting initiatives, causing differences and achieving fragmentation among the Catholics. As their relationship

1 'There is no instance, even in the ten persecutions, of such severity as that which the Protestants of Ireland have exercised against the Catholicks': Boswell, *Life of Johnson*, ed. R.W. Chapman, corr. J.D. Fleeman (London, 1970), p. 544. 2 E.g. a petition to the Irish Lords against further penal laws by Lord Mountgarrett, John Nugent, Robert French and Nicholas Weldon 'on behalf of themselves and the other Roman Catholics of Ireland': 30 March 1748, *Journals of the House of Lords*, 8 vols (Dublin, 1784), iii, 703. I am grateful to Patrick Fagan for this information.

with the land and institutions shifted, so they had to negotiate new ways of surviving and speaking up. As a result the Catholic voice gradually becomes much more diverse in its politics, culture, economic standing, education, protest and class than ever the Protestant voice was.

The tension between a singular view of the Irish Catholics and a more diverse view had been present in Irish history for centuries. The singular view is evident in the Irish Jacobite tradition which identified Irish Catholics as the nation of Ireland. 'I call the Irish Catholics *the Nation of Ireland,* because the Protestants therein are deemed generally but intruders and newcomers.'[3] The argument had been made by Keating, who was one of the first to elaborate on Ireland's claim to be a Catholic kingdom, albeit under the English crown.[4] Apart from the political strategy inherent in this claim, with its attendant millennial hopes, it also suggests that because pre-conquest Ireland was Catholic, so only Catholics can be the genuine postcolonial Irish. But this is an essentialist voice which prefers religious to more complex historical and national criteria, and it raises the obvious problem that Henry and the early settlers were also Catholics. The pre-Reformation Statutes of Kilkenny in 1366 emphasise only differences of culture and political power, not religion. To claim that Catholics are the authentic Irish raises the question as to which Catholics – settler or pre-settler stock? Even when that question is answered, we are still left with the point Spenser makes that Ireland's first inhabitants were not homogeneous but included Scythians, Gauls, Spaniards and Britons.[5]

The penal laws allowed for no diversity and made the simple presumption that the Catholics were a community of believers whose single qualification for notice, irrespective of differences among them, was their religion. These laws thus enforced a sense of community. As Wolfe Tone was to note in 1791, 'Persecution bound the Irish Papist to his Priest, and the Priest to the Pope; the bond of union is drawn tighter by oppression.'[6] Shared grievances gave Catholics a strong bond of identity. Reduced from owners to tenants on their own land and denied any meaningful role in the life-stream of their country, Catholics realised that at one level their religion rather than the land or culture or class now linked them to one another and to their history. This was what distinguished them from the English and provided consoling bonds with Catholic Europe. The force of this, as Whelan notes, 'lay more in the emotional and symbolic ... than in the actual

---

3 Anonymous pamphlet written between *c.*1696 and 1712, cited by Breandán Ó Buachalla, 'Irish Jacobitism and Irish nationalism', *Nations and Nationalisms,* p. 110.   4 Brendan Bradshaw, 'Geoffrey Keating: Apologist of Irish Ireland', *Representing Ireland: Literature and the Origins of Conflict, 1534–1660,* eds Brendan Bradshaw, Andrew Hadfield and Willy Maley (Cambridge, 1993), p. 186.   5 Spenser, *A View of the Present State of Ireland,* pp 46-7.   6 *An Argument on behalf of the Catholics of Ireland, in which the Present Political State of that Country, and the Necessity of a Parliamentary Reform, are Considered. Addressed to the People, and more particularly to the Protestants of Ireland. 1791.* I am indebted to C.J. Woods for the text as it will appear in *The Writings of Theobald Wolfe Tone,* 3 vols, eds T.W. Moody, R.B. McDowell and C.J. Woods (Oxford, in press), i, 121-2.

realm'.⁷ Thus they became in Protestant and English eyes the 'other' Ireland to that which the administration was empowered to create. The fact that Catholics comprised over two-thirds of Ireland's population, a sizeable and dangerous majority, gave the fiction respectability in Protestant eyes because it isolated the Catholic religion as the major cause of their own lack of success in creating a new Ireland.

Seen from a Gaelic Catholic perspective this 'other' Ireland is united too in the misery brought on by the penal laws. Brian Merriman for example in his rumbustuous satirical poem *The Midnight Court* says 'Ireland's bandjaxed',

> Farms are bankrupt, freedom banned,
> No law or leader in the land;
> Our country's raped and Luck, the coward,
> Shuns a virgin that's deflowered –
> Far afield our men are shipped
> While by grabbing hands she's stripped.⁸

Such catalogues of suffering were but one way in which Catholics countered the stereotype image fabricated by Protestants. That image began to crumble from the mid-century onwards as Catholics started to voice a counter-discourse which was at once varied and yet increasingly insistent in its demands for relief and a place in the Irish nation.

Catholics: predicament and responses

Estimates of the population of Ireland in the eighteenth century while not entirely reliable indicate that by the 1730s the figure was over two million. Of these, about 70 per cent were Catholic. About two-thirds of Ireland's population spoke Gaelic as their first language.⁹ The largest city, Dublin, had a population in the early part of the century of about 50,000 rising to 150,000 or more by 1776, with only Cork and Limerick registering any appreciable size.¹⁰ The majority of people lived away from the cities and the concentration of Catholics increased the further west one went. Connaught was about 90 per cent Catholic. This demographic picture is not reflected, however, in the figures for Catholic owner-

---

7 Kevin Whelan, 'The Catholic Church in County Tipperary 1700-1900', *Tipperary: History and Society*, ed. William Nolan (Dublin, 1985), p. 218. 8 Brian Merriman, *The Midnight Court*, trans. David Marcus (Dublin, 1966), p. 11. 9 J.L. McCracken, 'The Social Structure and Social Life, 1714-60', *New History of Ireland*, iv, 37; Brian Ó Cuiv, 'Irish Language and Literature, 1691-1845', *New History of Ireland*, iv, 383. L.M. Cullen has reservations about population figures given by K.H. Connell, which are 2.8 million in 1712 and 3.2 million in 1754 (L.M. Cullen 'Economic Development, 1750-1800', *New History of Ireland*, iv, 161). 10 J.L. McCracken, *New History of Ireland*, iv, 31. The figure for Dublin in 1776 is taken from Peter Somerville-Large, *Dublin* (1979; London, 1981), p. 194.

ship of land which show a decline to less than 10 per cent by 1776.[11] In Connaught less than half the land was owned by Catholics.[12] For many, the dispossession was yet another source of grievance and emotional bonding. Some Catholic families retained their lands; some, like the O'Shaughlins in *Castle Rackrent*, kept them by conforming to the Church of Ireland.

A marked characteristic of Irish Catholics was the diversity of initiative, wealth and occupation among them – from itinerants, labourers and cottiers through to tenant farmers, middlemen, traders in wine, woollens and beef, to millers and clothiers. Relatively few remained as landholders. Some sought education on the continent, some had no education at all. Some enjoyed an income and life-style commensurate with those of the Protestant gentry. The family of Gillo, a substantial Catholic tenant farmer, described in the poem *Hesperi-Neso-Graphia*, enjoyed a life-style of ease and plenty:

> Now listen well and you shall hear,
> With what vast prodigious Chear,
> And with what Heaps of various Meat,
> His Friends and Neighbours he did treat.[13]

At the other end of the economic scale, as Swift often noticed, less fortunate Catholics walked the streets of Dublin or Cork, a prey to poverty and violence. On the other hand it was not uncommon for a son to go abroad to be educated for the priesthood in one of the several Irish Colleges in France or Spain, or to enlist in an Irish regiment on the continent. At the battle of Fontenoy six regiments of Irish foot-soldiers helped France to a victory over the English,

> Through shattered ranks, and severed files, and trampled flags they tore;
> The English strove with desperate strength, paused, rallied, staggered,
> fled —[14]

Some families had a network of trading contacts with brothers or cousins in Nantes or Bordeaux. Several thousand Catholics and Protestants emigrated to America, particularly in years of poor harvest.[15]

Families were sometimes divided by religion. The penal laws could be said to have encouraged such division by making conformity attractive to Catholics.

11 J.L. McCracken, 'The Social Structure and Social Life, 1714-60', *New History of Ireland*, iv, 34, and Bartlett, *The Fall and Rise of the Irish Nation*, p. 47. See also Connolly, *Religion, Law and Power* on these figures (pp 147, 309-10) and for a map of the distribution of Catholic households in 1732, p. 146. 12 J.G. Simms, 'Protestant Ascendancy, 1691-1714', *New History of Ireland*, iv, 13. 13 *Verse in English from Eighteenth-Century Ireland*, ed. Andrew Carpenter (Cork, 1998), p. 120. 14 Thomas Davis, *Battle of Fontenoy (1745)* in *The Poems of Thomas Davis*, ed. John Mitchel (New York, n.d.), p. 168. 15 J.L. McCracken, *New History of Ireland*, iv, 32. Protestant families also witnessed divided loyalties; e.g. Tone's brother William served for a time in the British army while another brother Matthew tried to join the French army.

When a Catholic landowner died, the land had to be shared equally among the surviving sons, but if one conformed to the Church of Ireland he inherited the lot. Burke's father conformed in order to practise as an attorney. In spite of moving from Cork to Dublin, where the sons were brought up as Protestants, the family kept close ties with their maternal Catholic relations, the Nagles, in Munster. Burke's brother Garrett, and later Burke himself, acted as landlord to the Nagle estate at Clogher in a complicated family ruse to circumvent the law.[16] It could be argued that it would be easier to conform and inherit the land than it would be for later generations to repossess it. By 1771 at least 4,000 Catholics had conformed to the established religion, many of them gentry or near gentry stock who had something to gain.[17]

This diversity among Catholics took several decades to develop as did the confidence of Catholics to engage in public debates. In the immediate wake of the treaty of Limerick in 1691 Catholic Ireland went through one of the most depressed moments of its history. Its leaders had either fled or were dispossessed, much of their land had been confiscated and they faced a series of new laws which were to exclude them from any meaningful role in government at national and local levels until late into the eighteenth century. They felt betrayed by the English after the treaty. Resistance was a lost cause. What hope for change they had lay with the defeated James II and the Stuart cause now in exile in France.[18] This sense of defeat helps explain the slow and cautious emergence of a Catholic voice during the century. Henry Grattan recognised as much in his famous speech on Ireland's attainment of legislative independence in 1782,

> I found Ireland on her knees, I watched over her with a paternal solicitude; I have traced her progress from injuries to arms, and from arms to liberty. Spirit of Swift! spirit of Molyneux! your genius has prevailed! Ireland is now a nation![19]

In the fifty years following the treaty of Limerick it is difficult to find written evidence of how Catholics responded to their desperate situation. The earliest but short-lived source is historical writing about the war against William in

16 *The Correspondence of Burke*, i, 217, n. 1. 17 Dickson, *New Foundations*, p. 74; Whelan, 'The Catholic Church in County Tipperary 1700-1900', p. 219. The Convert Rolls give a figure of 5,797 who filed certificates between 1703 and 1800; Thomas P. Power discusses the reliability of this figure in 'Converts', *Endurance and Emergence*, pp 101-27. 18 Catholics had accepted the legitimacy of the Stuarts since James I who was regarded as a direct descendant of Fergus, king of Ireland (Breandan Ó Buachalla, 'Irish Jacobitism and Irish nationalism: the literary evidence', *Nations and Nationalisms*, pp 104-16. 19 'Triumph of Irish Independence' (16 April 1782), *Speeches of the Right Hon. Henry Grattan*, ed. Daniel Owen Madden, 2nd edn (Dublin, 1861), p.70. Gerard O'Brien argues that these words are part of a substantially reworked version of the speech written by Grattan shortly before his death: 'The Grattan Mystique', *Eighteenth-Century Ireland* 1 (1986), 194.

Ireland, but much of this material is unpublished. According to Kelly, 'The sole major statement of the catholic view to appear in print between 1691 and the middle of the eighteenth century was the anonymous *Ireland's case briefly stated* of 1695.'[20] Among the unpublished writings is a manuscript by Nicholas Plunkett known as *A Light to the Blind*, a Jacobite reading of the previous hundred years of Ireland's relation with England leading up to the reign of William.[21] Plunkett takes the view that Ireland's colonial bonds with England are too strong to expect change, not least because the bloods have been mixed:

> The Heads of the ancient Irish Septs are so linkt in flesh and blood with those ould English, and so train'd up in their manners especially since the reign of James the first; that they roul in the same sphere of Inclination and Interest.[22]

England's ties with the 'ould English' settlers provide 'motives of flesh to keep Ireland under'.[23] He castigates the English settlers for sticking to their Protestant faith at the expense of Ireland and accuses them of having 'demean'd themselves like cannibals to their Kings and their Adherents.' He adds with acerbic humour, 'We cannot admire at it, since lyeing hath ever been the prime Talent of Hereticks'.[24] Plunkett's 'we' is Catholic Ireland, not the Ireland of the Molyneux tradition. This is the Ireland he refers to in another work addressed to English Protestant readers as 'an oppress'd Nation' laid open to the 'perfidiousness of a People, that think themselves by their practise, to be above your vindicative Reach, tho' your Power be revered by the Extremes of the Earth'.[25] Such abuse and anger are all that is left to the Catholic Irish as their hopes for a Jacobite restoration recede. This is what conquest and colonisation have reduced them to. Even this rhetorical resistance was soon to die away until the mid-century.

Another source of Catholic sentiment in the early decades of the eighteenth century is Gaelic poetry. In their hopeless condition the Catholics nevertheless held on to their spiritual and cultural inheritance, their religion and their poetry: poets continued their prophetic yearnings. But, as Leerssen notes, 'the future foretold often seems more a return to the past'.[26] Much of this poetry grieves as it looks back to better days,

> The heart within my breast tonight is wild with grief
> Because of all the haughty men who ruled this place,

20 Patrick Kelly, '"A Light to the Blind": The Voice of the Dispossessed Elite in the Generation after the Defeat at Limerick', *IHS* 24, no. 96 (1985), 432; Kelly says the piece is probably by Hugh Reily, a Catholic lawyer. 21 This is analysed in detail by Kelly, '"A Light to the Blind" ...', *IHS* 24, 431-62. 22 Bodleian Library, Oxford, MS Carte 229, 'The Improvement of Ireland' (n.d.), f. 1-2. 23 Ibid., f. 1. 24 Ibid., f. 2. 25 'A Speech before Justice' (1704), MS Carte 229, f. 114. 26 Leerssen *Mere Irish and Fior-Ghael*, p. 238; changes in the Gaelic poetic tradition in the eighteenth century, brought about by political and social upheaval, included a self-conscious commitment to the Irish language (see ibid.,

North Munster and South Munster to the wave beneath,
None lives, and where they lived lives now an alien race.[27]

A famous recurring motif in the poetry is the image of Ireland as a distressed woman. Sometimes she is waiting for the return of her husband, as O'Rahilly puts it, 'to the place which is his by kingly descent'.[28] She must be patient, says the poet,

O my sickness, my misfortune, my fall, my sorrow, my loss!
The bright, fond, kind, fair, soft-lipped, gentle maiden,
Held by a horned, malicious, croaking, yellow clown, with a black troop!
While no relief can reach her until the heroes come back across the main.[29]

Hope for a restoration of the old order, however forlorn, is still alive, as is the abuse of English overlords which continues in angry and despairing phrases like 'wicked, alien boars', 'that wicked race'.[30] The resistance in such poetry lies more in spirit than in action; its well-springs are resentment and wishful thinking, not serious political plotting.[31] So long as the Jacobite cause had a flicker of promise so long did the dream and the bitter vilification continue. Yet in those same years O'Rahilly's poetry reflects a despair at the mutilation and demise of his own culture brought about by his own people.[32] The Gaelic poets had lost their patrons together with the old aristocratic framework which had given them a respected place in Irish society. They knew perhaps more acutely than most that fundamental changes were at work.

Civilising the natives

The Catholic majority in Ireland had long been a problem for the English administration in several ways. Tensions ran particularly high after the 1641 rebellion, in which, according to Clarendon, Catholics massacred 150,000 Protestants.[33] William's victory at the Boyne in 1690 was a victory, not just of one monarch over his rival, but of Protestants over Catholics in a contest of religions which had much of Europe as its backdrop. As Leighton puts it,

The Irish Jacobite threat which they faced was in the view of seventeenth and eighteenth-century Protestants, merely a particular manifestation of the universal Catholic threat.[34]

pp 229-38). 27 From Egan ORahilly, 'A Sleepless Night', trans. Frank O'Connor, *The Penguin Book of Irish Verse*, p. 74. 28 'Gile na Gile', *Poems of Egan O'Rahilly*, ed. Patrick S. Dinneen and Tadhg O'Donoghue, 2nd edn (London, 1911), p. 19. 29 Ibid., p. 21. 30 Ibid., pp 5, 167. 31 L.M. Cullen, 'The Blackwater Catholics and County Cork Society and Politics in the Eighteenth Century', *Cork History and Society*, eds Patrick Flanagan and Cornelius Buttimer (Dublin, 1993), pp 560-1. 32 Seamus Deane, *A Short History of Irish Literature*, p. 22. 33 Cited by Henry Brooke in *The Tryal of the Roman Catholics of Ireland* (Dublin, 1761; London, 1767), p. 5. 34 Leighton, *Catholicism in a*

This wider threat was one reason for the punishing anti-Catholic legislation that followed William's victory, but was prompted also by worried Protestant gentry in the Irish parliament 'in a desire to avenge past humiliations as well as to prevent future threats to their economic and social ascendancy'.[35] William's answer to a speech by the Anglican bishop of Meath in 1690 sets the tone for decades to come:

> I am come hither to deliver you from the Tyranny of Popery and Slavery, to Protect the Protestant Religion, and restore you in your Liberties and Properties; and you may depend upon it.[36]

His promise was fulfilled in the penal laws which from 1695 through to the 1720s curtailed every aspect of Irish Catholic life from religion to land to the value of the horse they could ride. To interpret this response as colonialist would be a mistake in so far as it would distract attention from the particular causes of animosity and from Protestant anxieties about Catholic Europe. Protestants in Ireland were well aware that the large majority of the people they governed not only opposed them in religion but had the sympathy of France and the pope. Many of their leaders were in exile on the continent, serving in European armies. Clandestine recruitment from Ireland continued well into the century.[37]

Yet the penal laws played a part in the colonising strategy. They were feasible only because of conquest and Ireland's subjugation. The particular anxieties of Ireland's Protestant gentry and the parliamentary action they took to protect their interests can be construed as a local colonial agenda within England's wider European concerns. That was how many Catholics perceived the letter of the penal laws, a view made explicit by Irish exiles in Bordeaux. The fact that the laws were not enforced with either vigour or consistency was no reason for complacency. For instance, by mid-century Catholic parish clergy were often looked to by Protestant gentry to ensure peace in the community and to root out trouble-makers.[38] This trust disappeared as soon as there was a suspicion of political subversion or Jacobite infiltration. In these uncertain circumstances the priest's role in the community was particularly vulnerable. For example, at the time of the Whiteboy agrarian disturbances in Munster in the early 1760s five priests along with several Catholic gentry were arrested under the penal laws. One of the priests, Fr Nicholas Sheehy, was indicted in Tipperary on charges of rebellion and treason. He was sentenced to death on highly contentious grounds along

Protestant Kingdom, p. 6. 35 J.G. Simms, 'The Establishment of Protestant Ascendancy, 1691-1714', *New History of Ireland*, iv, 16. 36 *Miscellanies in Prose*, ed. Andrew Carpenter, Irish Writings from the Age of Swift, 10 vols (Dublin, 1972), i, 46. 37 See my article, 'A Crisis for the Irish in Bordeaux: 1756', *Nations and Nationalisms*, p. 136. 38 Dickson, *New Foundations*, p. 74.

with four others in 1766. The administration carried out the hangings to exemplify their determination to stamp out Catholic opposition. Burke put the incident in perspective in an angry letter to his friend Charles O'Hara, a member of the Irish parliament. Referring to the administration he wrote,

> Their unmeaning Senseless malice is insatiable … I am told, that these miserable wretches whom they have hanged, died with one Voice declaring their innocence: but truly for my part, I want no man dying, or risen from the dead, to tell me, that lies are lies, and nonsense is nonsense. I wish your absurdity was less mischievous, and less bloody.[39]

The case illustrates the latent power of the penal laws.

Much more common among Protestant gentry however was the sense not that the Catholics were a threat but a nuisance and a scandal. The attitude is framed in terms that have the patronising ring of a colonial overlord. Catholics were seen by many, Swift and Berkeley among them, as an indolent, dirty, populous people, cowed by their church and unwilling to contribute to their own or Ireland's welfare. The several campaigns to persuade Catholics to renounce their religion for the Church of Ireland were driven not least by a conviction that Protestants, and indeed England, offered a superior moral and cultural ethos. In 1689 Chief Justice Sir Richard Cox explains at the start of his significantly titled *Hibernia Anglicana* that England has brought Ireland both civilisation and happiness.

> What I aim at is to show, That the Irish did continue in their Barbarity, Poverty, and Ignorance until the English conquest; and that all the Improvement themselves or this Country received, and their great difference between their Manners and Condition now and then, is to be ascribed to the English Government, under which they have lived far happier than ever they did under the Tyranny of their own Lords.[40]

Swift makes a similar point in gentler but no less patronising terms. Sensitive to the sufferings of Catholics he wrote boldly for their relief, but the remedies have the sure touch of a Protestant reformer. The wretched condition of Dublin's poor leads him to propose the establishment of schools in every parish where 'the meaner and poorer' children could learn to speak and read English:

> This would, in Time, abolish that Part of Barbarity and Ignorance, for which our Natives are so despised by all Foreigners; this would bring them to think and act according to the Rules of Reason, by which a Spirit of Industry, and Thrift, and Honesty, would be introduced among them.[41]

39 Burke to O'Hara, 24 [May, 1766], *Correspondence of Burke*, i, 256. 40 Sir Richard Cox, *Hibernia Anglicana; or, the History of Ireland* (London, pt i, 1689; pt ii, 1690), p. *m*; see ch 6 note 63. 41 Swift,

The give-away word, as elsewhere in Swift, is 'our' – 'our Natives'. Swift looks forward to an Ireland where all the people speak English, respect English customs, and are industrious and truthful in the mould of the Protestant work ethic. In their present state the Catholic peasantry are Yahoos with nothing to offer.

In a sense Protestants were patronising because they were patriotic. An anti-Catholic writer like Samuel Madden was inventive and energetic in trying to improve industry and agriculture for the betterment of Ireland. The country would prosper all the more if only Catholics would throw off their indolence and participate in the economy. Many Protestants believed that Catholics needed to be liberated from the totalitarian strictures of their religion, from a spiritual servitude that denied them their individuality and a motivation to self-improvement. Those Houyhnhnm qualities with which Gulliver wanted to civilise Europe are much the same as Protestant Irish wanted for the Catholics – 'honour, justice, truth, temperance, public spirit, fortitude, chastity, friendship, benevolence, and fidelity'.[42] In terms of Hogarth's well-known print series, 'Industry and Idleness' (1747), the virtues of industry were what the Protestant Irish saw so glaringly absent in the Catholic majority. Without such virtues there was no hope that the peasant Catholic Irish would improve or indeed be civilised.

As the second half of the century progressed and England became embroiled in the war of American independence these colonial attitudes yielded to the pressing need to enable and then persuade Irish Catholics to enlist in the army.[43] As Bartlett remarks, 'It was no coincidence that the major catholic relief acts of the late eighteenth century were put through in time of war'.[44]

The language question: English/Irish

The question therefore arose as how best to inculcate Catholics into the Church of Ireland and Protestant ways. Debates in the early decades of the century about how best to proselytise Catholics ran into considerable disagreement about what language to use. The Statutes of Kilkenny in 1366 had attempted to assert the English language and manners. They failed in that respect, and Irish resistance was evident through the centuries, despite considerable attrition, until the eighteenth century. What one post-colonial critic calls 'a process of deracination and disruption' caused by the imposition of English on the colonised people was less evident in Ireland six centuries after the arrival of the Anglo-Normans than in

'Sermon on the Causes of the Wretched Condition of Ireland', *Prose Works of Swift*, ix, 202. **42** *Gulliver's Travels*, p. 343. One of the paradoxes of colonialism is that people of the governing élite often show considerable kindness to the lower orders. Further on this in Ireland see Connolly, *Religion, Law and Power*, pp 128-43. **43** For Lord North's strategy on this relief and Burke's support for the plan see Robert K. Donovan, 'The Military Origins of the Roman Catholic Relief Programme of 1778', *Historical Journal* 28 (1985), 87-9. **44** Thomas Bartlett, 'The Origin and Progress of the Catholic Question in Ireland', *Endurance and Emergence*, p. 8.

many more recent British colonies.[45] With the majority of Irish people excluded from the English- speaking institutions of political power, from corporations and guilds, the Irish language continued to be spoken throughout the country as the preferred language of most people. It is thought that in the early 1730s about two-thirds of Ireland's population used Irish as their everyday language,[46] and in 1781 the *Hibernian Journal* noted that 'above a Million and a half of the common People speak nothing but Irish'.[47] The same tendency did not apply to the book trade where 'less than a hundred works in Irish were printed in the entire century'.[48] Yet it is estimated that by the 1780s 52 per cent of Ireland's population could read English, a figure that suggests that economic and political changes in the second half of the century led also to a wider spread of English.[49]

At the start of the century Protestant zealots argued that Irish was the way into the Catholic mind. For a time catechisms and bibles were produced in Irish. In 1710 the Irish parliament passed a resolution that a certain number of Protestant clerics should instruct and conduct services in the Irish language. Swift like many others held the opposite view: 'It would be a noble achievement to abolish the Irish language in the kingdom, so far at least as to oblige all the natives to speak only English on every occasion of business, in shops, markets, fairs, and other places of dealing.' This would, said Swift, 'in a great measure, civilize the most barbarous among them'.[50]

The Protestant response to the language issue soon settled for a position much the same as in many later colonial situations where the indigenous language and culture were regarded as a hindrance to progress and probably worthless. English became the language for evangelisation. By the 1750s it was also accepted by Gaelic-speaking Catholics as the language of political debate. By the 1740s Gaelic had no place as a medium for public political argument be it in the market place or in that other important arena the writing of history.[51]

The climate of debate

The penal laws were effectively an inscription not just of Protestant power but of anxieties and aspirations. The purpose of the laws, argues Kelly, was 'to put it beyond the capacity of Catholics ever again to challenge the colonists' hegemony

45 Stephen Slemon, 'Reading for Resistance in the Post-Colonial Literatures' in *A Shaping of Connections*, eds Hena Maes-Jelinal, K.H. Petersen, Anna Rutherford (Sydney, 1989), p. 103.   46 Brian Ó Cuiv, 'Irish Language and Literature, 1691-1845', *New History of Ireland*, iv. 383.   47 Cited by M. Pollard, *Dublin's Trade in Books 1550-1800*, Lyell Lectures, 1986-1987 (Oxford, 1989), pp 211-12.   48 Ibid., p. 211, n. 113.   49 Ibid., p. 214. Carpenter draws attention to poems in the latter half of the century 'written partly in Irish and partly in English', a phenomenon that presupposes an audience 'able to understand both languages' (*Verse in English from Eighteenth-Century Ireland*, p. 22).   50 'An Answer to Several Letters sent to me from unknown Hands' (1729), *Prose Works, of Swift*, xii. 89.   51 The Irish Lords passed a bill on 18 February 1738 'that all Proceedings in Courts of Justice within the Kingdom, shall be in the English Language' (*Journals of the House of Lords*, iii, 402).

in Ireland'.[52] The laws helped focus resistance, channel resentment and provide the materials for counter-argument. One of the early eighteenth-century Catholic voices to enter the contest was a priest, Cornelius Nary (1658-1738). A native of Kildare he was ordained in 1682 and obtained doctorates in canon and civil law in Paris. When he returned to Dublin at the turn of the century, he was probably the best equipped Catholic in Ireland to debate with Protestants on those issues which Protestants found most objectionable about the Catholic religion – the mass, transubstantiation, purgatory, the supremacy of the pope, the authority of the church. Nary's books and pamphlets contesting Protestant views on such topics were a significant kind of resistance because they challenged the doctrinal basis of Protestant antagonism towards Catholics. The political implications are considerable because, as Boyce notes, Protestant nationalism was not only to do with physical place, Ireland, 'it was also a nationalism of faith. Because the nation was Protestant, the Anglican church constituted a kind of national church'.[53]

In his arguments with prominent clergymen like the bishop of Tuam and his son Edward Synge, the prebendary of St Patrick's cathedral, Nary was not afraid to point up the political consequences for Ireland of the Protestant position. His pamphlet, *The Case of the Roman Catholics* (1724), published anonymously when legislation against the Catholics was at its most severe, attacked a proposal to prohibit priests from saying mass unless they had sworn an oath of abjuration.[54] The oath, disputed even by Protestants, denied King James any claim to the English crown and required explicit acceptance of the Protestant succession. Nary argued against this on principle and for practical reasons. It would deny Catholics the service of their priests and drive many of them abroad. Since an increasing number of Catholics were merchants and traders Ireland could ill afford to lose them. Besides Catholics wanted to participate in the affairs of their country and therefore,

> Be pleased most excellent Lords and noble Senators, to give us the same liberty and freedom as our fellow subjects have to use our industry and enjoy the fruits thereof. Let no distinction be made but of good and bad, and I will engage the Government will have our hearts, our Affections, and our Hands.[55]

Ironically the appeal, from a Catholic to his Protestant countrymen, has the same conciliatory tone as Molyneux pleading with Westminster twenty-five years earlier.

52 Patrick Kelly, 'Ireland and the Glorious Revolution: From Kingdom to Colony' in *The Revolutions of 1688*, ed. Robert Beddard (Oxford, 1991), p. 186.   53 Boyce, *Nationalism in Ireland*, p. 106.   54 Patrick Fagan, *Dublin's Turbulent Priest: Cornelius Nary (1658-1738)*, p. 114   55 Cited in ibid., p. 119.

As events turned out the disputed legislation was dropped, more as a result of international pressure than of Nary's pamphlet. Nevertheless Nary as much by his learning and his manner gave the lie to the stereotype Catholic who according to the oath of abjuration was a victim of superstition, idolatry and equivocation.[56] A man of European learning, respectful and well-informed in debate, Nary offered a quite different reading of Catholicism to that backward, superstitious and authoritarian religion that so preoccupied the Protestants. Within a couple of decades that prejudiced view was on the wane and by mid-century Catholics not only contested it but took the debate into more secular issues.

Of the many reasons for this shift two deserve mention – the development of extra-parliamentary debates and the redundancy of the old anti-Catholic rhetoric. The first was assisted by the emergence of an anti-establishment press as was evident in the Lucas affair of the 1740s and 1750s.[57] Lucas was no supporter of the Catholics, but his political activities in the 1740s shocked the Dublin public into a new kind of popular political debate. Lucas was a Dublin apothecary and pamphleteer, an outspoken admirer of Molyneux and Swift. He first came to public notice as a member of the Dublin corporation in 1741, was later dismissed and stood for parliament in 1749. He ran an energetic campaign for reform of Dublin's corporation and was a vociferous campaigner for Ireland's parliamentary independence in his anti-government paper *The Censor*. His journalistic abuse of those in power gave a new edge to popular rhetoric taking the ideas of Molyneux onto the streets of Dublin and injecting political debate with a fresh brusqueness. As Hill points out, Lucas 'called into being a civic Patriot movement that was influential down to the French revolutionary era'.[58] He blamed the ruin of Ireland on the flow of self-seeking English noblemen, prelates and judges into high office:

> The Infection came industriously wrapped in *Ermine, Purple*, and *Lawn*; and unhappily found a Climate, not unprepared to receive and nourish the baneful Weed. *Sham-Patriots* were employed to explane away your Rights ... and *mercenary, corrupt Judges*, refined *sacred* RIGHT into *Expediency*, or *Conveniency*, or substituted their own *perverse Will.*[59]

Such virulent criticism stirred up a considerable pamphlet war,[60] polarised the city and prompted an action against him in parliament for scandalous libel. He had to leave Ireland before the election took place.

56 The oath is given in *Irish Historical Documents, 1172-1922*, p. 192. 57 Extra-parliamentary debate was given further impetus in the 1750s by Henry Boyle's handling of the money bill dispute (see Bartlett, 'The Origins and Progress of the Catholic Question in Ireland', *Endurance and Emergence*, pp 6-7). 58 Jacqueline Hill, *From Patriots to Unionists*, p, 112. 59 *Censor*, V [1 July 1749] in *The Political Constitutions of Great Britain and Ireland* (1751), ii, 475. 60 Over 150 pamphlets were published during the election (Dickson, *New Foundations*, p. 88).

Lucas carried political issues like the constitution, the powers of the administration and the rights of the electorate into extra-parliamentary bodies such as
as the guilds and corporations. In spite of his vilification by the administration
Lucas had shown that controversy involved the people, not just those in power.
He made the striking point that an anti-government press could make a considerable impact. It is unlikely that Lucas was responsible for the emergence of
hitherto silent voices in Irish politics, but his Wilkes-like style and his rhetorical
daring, twenty years before Wilkes, introduced a new climate to political debate
in Ireland. He opened up a discursive space between people and parliament
where myths and prejudices could be contested and argued out. This makes the
contentious climate of debate in the 1750s less surprising.

Lucas's arguments turn a blind eye to the Catholic point of view. As with
many a political crisis in the first half of the century the debate carried on as if
the majority of the Irish people had nothing to say. Lucas for obvious reasons
had no place in his political agenda for the Catholics.[61] In the early 1750s it was
still common for Irish Protestant writers to look Janus-like with scorn across the
Channel at the English and with contempt inland at the Irish Catholics. The
point is illustrated in a mock dialogue between two Cork Protestants published
in 1751.[62] They sit over a drink discussing a forthcoming election. Simon has
promised his vote to an Englishman: he sees no point in having a parliament in
Ireland when England has the power anyway to bind Ireland by its own acts of
parliament. Jack argues that England is cynical enough to require that the Irish
be seen to go through the motions of parliamentary debate:

> When we must learn to pay Money without having Liberty to earn it, 'tis
> then the Work must be done by our Parliament: All this must appear to
> the World to be our own Act and Deed, and that no arbitrary Power was
> exerted by an English Ministry to procure it.[63]

Simon's vote for an Englishman, says Jack, simply consolidates a system of heartless exploitation by 'a Sett of Thieves and Pirates'.[64] It is not possible for an
English candidate, whose property, friends and benefactors are in England to
have any regard for Ireland 'where he is only in the Nature of a Factor'.[65] But in
the closing stages of the conversation Jack falls back into conventional patriotic
terms made familiar by Lucas: the English as a race are not inherently wicked;
Ireland has much to be grateful for from their presence. Protestant values have
redeemed the Irish from their native weaknesses. The English, says Jack,

---

61 Some argue that Lucas was decidedly anti-Catholic, cf. Leighton, *Catholicism in a Protestant
Kingdom*, pp 77-83. 62 *A Dialogue between Jack Cane and Simon Curtin, Freemen of Cork concerning
Parliamentary Men*, Cork, 1751. 63 Ibid., p. 6. 64 Ibid., p. 10. 65 Ibid., p. 11.

relieved us from the vilest Subjection; taught us Industry, Trades, and Science, and made as many of us happy as can be reclaimed from our native Vices, from Sloth, Treachery and Cowardice.[66]

Swift and Berkeley had helped to consolidate the view that these vices were peculiar to the Catholics and were engendered by their Roman faith. Protestants could argue their way around English duplicity but not the wickedness of the Catholics. During the 1750s changes in this attitude came to the surface. The old anti-Catholic rhetoric began to sound out of date. There were exceptional moments, as in the dispute over tithes in the 1780s when the more conservative element among Protestants showed a renewed righteousness.[67] But the bulk of the evidence suggests that the former determined policy of Protestants 'to uproot and destroy the rival and defeated culture' had lost its impetus.[68]

Catholic merchants

Among the many interlinking factors contributing to these changes was the growing commercial significance of Catholic merchants. Their success, which parliament made no attempt to curtail, was built on a close network of trading contacts both within Ireland and with Irish exiles on the continent and in the Americas.[69] In spite of the penal laws Catholics did become rich.[70] Nary claimed in 1724 that Catholics were responsible for half of Ireland's trade. Many of these were 'old' English stock or Catholics who had lost their lands and had turned to trade instead.[71] As one observer noted in 1737, 'From the mutual kindness of all men under oppression and a natural hatred of their oppressors, they deal with, and always employ one another.'[72] Their influence had been slow to establish itself. They were disadvantaged in terms of property, warehousing, access to finance and eligibility to government contracts.[73] However their integration into Ireland's trade and commerce is marked from the 1750s onwards. A Catholic merchant in Cork took a case to the court of the king's bench challenging the long-standing practice by Protestant businessmen of compelling Catholic master

66 Ibid., p. 13.   67 James Kelly, 'Relations between the Protestant Church of Ireland and the Presbyterian Church in Late Eighteenth-Century Ireland', *Eire-Ireland* 23 (1988), 52.   68 R.B. McDowell, *Irish Public Opinion, 1750-1800* (London, 1944), p. 9. For an extensive view of the Catholics and Anglo-Irish politics see Thomas Bartlett, *The Fall and Rise of the Irish Nation: the Catholic Question*, Dublin,1992.   69 Cf. Maureen Wall, 'The Rise of a Catholic Middle-Class in Eighteenth-Century Ireland', *IHS* 11, 42 (1958), 91-115; J.L. McCracken, 'The Social Structure and Social Life, 1714-60', *New History of Ireland*, iv, 38-9.   70 Wall, 'The Rise of a Catholic Middle-Class', 94.   71 Fagan, *Dublin's Turbulent Priest*, pp 119-20. This is not to suggest that most Catholics moved off the land to commerce. From the 1750s onwards Catholic lease-hold farmers contributed in large measure to the upturn in Ireland's agricultural production (see L.M. Cullen, 'Catholic Social Classes under the Penal Laws' in *Endurance and Emergence*, pp 57-84).   72 Cited by Wall, 'The Rise of a Catholic Middle-Class', *IHS* 11, 113.   73 David Dickson, 'Catholics and Trade in Eighteenth-Century Ireland: An Old Debate Revisited' in *Endurance and Emergence*, pp 85-100.

craftsmen and traders to pay a fee or quarterage for quasi membership of the appropriate guilds. Such membership meant a general encouragement of their business but none of the civic or political privileges enjoyed by Protestant guild members. The court decided there was no legal basis for the compulsion and found in favour of the Catholics. The guilds were worried that the Catholic merchants were becoming too influential and in the following ten years several attempts were made to have legislation passed that would reverse the effect of the judgement, but to no avail.[74] Catholics continued to grow as a prospering merchant presence and were admitted by Protestant merchants to their committees in the 1770s. Catholics were major employers in the silk, cotton and sugar industries in the latter part of the century.[75] By the 1780s a third of Dublin's merchants were Catholics and when the Bank of Ireland was formed in 1783 about ten per cent of the founding capital came from Catholics.[76]

The guilds case illustrates that Catholics could contest a powerful Protestant interest and win, but this could not have happened without a gradual change of attitude towards them which had been happening over the years in several undramatic ways, such as in the printing trade. Under the penal laws Catholics had been forbidden to publish or sell Catholic books, and printers had been jailed in the early years of the century.[77] The only loop-hole, as indicated above, was for Catholics to be admitted to the guild which was controlled by Protestants. Their membership was on a quarterly basis and they had no say in the deliberations of the guild.[78] A few Catholics made a successful living this way. Luke Dowling, for instance, was registered as a printer and bookseller in Dublin in 1698, and James Hoey in 1726 who had a hand with George Faulkner in two newspapers and a number of almanacs. Ignatius Kelly printed devotional books and Patrick Lord became notorious for his pro-Catholic tracts.[79] A few Catholic printers had set up in the provinces, for example James O'Connor in Drogheda in 1728 and Jeremiah Calwell in Waterford in 1738.[80] Because of the scarcity of specifically Catholic books the Dublin booksellers took in much other stock and, along with the Quakers, were largely responsible for the supply of reading matter to rural Ireland.[81]

Gradually the law against Catholic publishers and printers was disregarded and by the 1750s the practice was quite different. Catholic printers were providing books of religious interest such as sermons and service-books. Catholic

---

74 Cf. Dickson, *New Foundations*, p. 136. 75 Dickson, 'Catholics and Trade' in *Endurance and Emergence*, pp 97-8. 76 Sarah Foster, 'Buying Irish – Consumer Nationalism in 18th-Century Dublin', *History Today* 47, no. 6 (1997), 48. 77 Hugh Fenning, 'The Catholic press in Munster in the eighteenth century', *Books beyond the Pale: Aspects of the provincial book trade in Ireland before 1850*, ed. Gerard Long (Dublin, 1996), p. 19. 78 James W. Phillips, *Printing and Bookselling in Dublin, 1670-1800: a Bibliographical Enquiry* (Dublin, 1998), pp 7-10. 79 Robert Munter, *A Dictionary of the Print Trade in Ireland 1550-1775* (New York, 1988), pp 134-5, 154, 170. 80 For O'Connor see Joanna Finegan, 'Georgian Drogheda and the printed word', *Books beyond the Pale*, p. 38. 81 Pollard, *Dublin's Trade in Books*, p. 190.

churches and schools had become a tacitly accepted part of Dublin city life. These had been growing in number over the previous decades. In 1731 the city had 45 Catholic schools, however small;[82] many of them were set up by Catholic bishops to counteract the work of the Protestant charter schools.[83] After the collapse of the floor in an overcrowded chapel in Dublin in 1745, incurring the deaths of several people, the lord lieutenant Lord Chesterfield gave permission for more solid structures to be built.[84]

Clerical rhetoric

By the 1750s the Protestants had come to accept that they had failed to convert or conciliate the Catholic majority.[85] Although the penal laws were a serious threat on paper they had long been ineffective. Two decades earlier in 1731 the Protestant bishop of Clonfert questioned whether the laws were working:

> They are all either Evaded, or not Executed: So that, however severe and coercive the laws may be in themselves, the real Effects of them, upon the State of the Papists among us have been very inconsiderable, I had almost said none at all.[86]

So long as Catholics and their clergy did not encroach on Protestant interests – a priest was transported in 1742 for converting a Protestant girl[87] – the Protestants turned a blind eye to the penal laws and on occasion made overtures to ease old tensions. For example, the Protestant vicar-general of Dublin cautioned his flock against bigotry towards Catholics. After reminding those in public office that whatever power they had, 'they are, by the Laws of the Gospel, no more than mere Trustees'; he advises a spirit of goodwill 'to Christians of all Denominations'.[88] Despite his own prejudices towards the Catholics he calls for a new spirit of compassion towards them:

> Even those, whose Subjection to a foreign Jurisdiction renders them, in some Degree, Enemies to the State; but whose miserable Delusion by a System of Priest-Craft, most artfully continued to aggrandise the Wealth and Power of their Clergy at the Expence of the very Morals of the

82 Report on the State of Popery in Ireland (1731), cited by Peter Somerville-Large, *Dublin* (London, 1979), p. 176. 83 J.L. McCracken, 'The Ecclesiastical Structure, 1714-60', *New History of Ireland*, iv, 95. 84 Somerville-Large, *Dublin*, p. 178. About this time Dublin had nine public Catholic chapels (Wall, *The Penal Laws*, p. 45). 85 Patrick J. Corish, *The Catholic Community in the Seventeenth and Eighteenth Centuries* (Dublin, 1981), p. 80. 86 Edward Synge, *A Sermon Preached at Christ-Church, Dublin on Saturday 23rd of October 1731 Being the Anniversary of the Irish Rebellion* (Dublin, 1731), p. 17. 87 Wall, *The Penal Laws*, p. 55. 88 *A Charge given by the Vicar-General of Dublin, on the Triennial Visitation of that Province ... Published at the Request of the Clergy* (Dublin, 1760), p. 10.

People, renders them Objects of real Compassion, not of bigotted Resentment.[89]

The subtext of this exhortation could be an old theme – if Protestants treat
Catholics with compassion there is more likelihood that Catholics will see the
virtues of the Church of Ireland and conform. 'Bigotry,' he says, 'is highly detrimental to the Protestant interest'.[90]

The vicar-general puts away the old rhetoric for a new tone of conciliation.
Bishop Berkeley had given a precedent for this more open if patronising
approach in his *Word to the Wise* in 1749 where he urged the Catholic clergy to
persuade their flock to contribute more positively to the welfare of the country.
Noblemen and gentry were said to distribute the pamphlet to their tenants and
labourers, 'to spirit them up to Cleanliness, Industry, Honesty, and Riches'.[91] A
priest in Lucan read it to his congregation, 'which was very well received'.[92]
Dublin's Catholic clergy thanked Berkeley for his advice. During the Seven
Years' War Catholics held prayers for the king after Mass on Sundays.[93] Another
example of the changing climate is the playwright and poet Henry Brooke who
in a series of pamphlets during the Jacobite scare in 1745 had warned Protestants
of the dangers of trusting Catholics, but by 1761 he writes publicly for a relaxation
of the penal laws.[94] Such writings demonstrate a gradual willingness to accept
that the Catholics were an entity to reckon with and that they might well have a
place in the welfare of Ireland, albeit on terms that reflect Protestant values.

It could be argued that at least a sector of Catholic opinion had made itself
felt long before the 1750s in public statements such as addresses of loyalty to the
Hanoverian kings, but these were not always accepted as trustworthy by either
the Protestant establishment or other Catholics. On the death of George I in
1727 for instance some twenty or more Catholic lords and gentlemen drew up an
address on behalf of Irish Catholics expressing grief at the death of the king, 'the
Goodness and Unity of whose Government we are deeply sensible of';[95] they
congratulated George II on coming to the throne and assured him of allegiance,
an assurance prompted by 'a Religious Duty'.[96]

Edward Synge did not believe that this address expressed the true feelings of
Irish Catholics whom he regarded as 'Enemies to the Protestant Government'.[97]
The address had also annoyed certain Catholic clergy because they had not been
consulted beforehand. They called it 'precipitate, passionate and presumptuous';

---

89 *A Charge given by the Vicar-General*, p. 10. 90 Ibid., p. 11. 91 *Dublin Journal*, 18-21 November, 1749,
p. 1. 92 Ibid., 28 November-2 December, 1749, p. 1. 93 Corish, *The Catholic Community*, pp 118-19.
94 Henry Brooke, *The Farmer's Six Letters to the Protestants of Ireland*, Dublin, 1745; *The Trial of the
Cause of the Roman Catholics*, Dublin, 1761. 95 'The Most Humble Address of the Roman Catholics
of Ireland', Appendix to Edward Synge, *A Sermon Preached at Christ-Church, Dublin ... 1731*, p. 21. 96
Ibid. 97 *A Sermon Preached at Christ-Church, Dublin ... 1731*, p. 17. For the Synges' part in Protestant
controversies about the Catholics see for example T.C.Barnard, 'The Uses of 23 October 1641 and
Irish Protestant Celebrations', *English Historical Review* 106, no. 421 (1991), 902-3.

[105]

they questioned whether the language would not 'wipe away our tears without removing the Cause', whether some of the phrasing 'may not be understood to be vile and nauseous Flattery', whether certain parts did not offend against conscience, even defy comprehension.[98] It would have been better to present 'an humble Petition ... and a Remonstrance of our Grievances'.[99] This radical line from the clergy suggests a flock divided on how to tackle their own problems. Many agreed with their remark that the penal laws made it 'natural for us to complain',[100] but there was no consensus on how to do this. Part of the difficulty may have been that there was no agenda for reconstituting their relation with the Protestants to accompany the complaint. The dispute among themselves was to resurface again and again through the century.

Despite these differences it was the rhetoric of official statements from Catholic lords and gentlemen and officials in the church which predominated into the 1750s. The Dublin clergy, responding to the conciliatory tones of Berkeley and the vicar-general, echo the 'nauseous Flattery' of their predecessors. In the *Exhortation of the Roman Catholic Clergy of Dublin, read from their Altars on the Second of October 1757*[101] they thank God for relief in recent times of scarcity, and add, 'We ought especially to be most earnest in our thanks to the chief governors and magistrates of the kingdom'.[102] Thanks is best expressed through obedience. Although they admit persecution took place in the past they seem intent to image the English administration under George II as considerate and mild:

> A series of more than sixty years, spent with a pious resignation under the hardships of very severe Penal Laws and with the greatest thankfulness for the lenity and consideration with which they were executed ever since the accession of the present royal family, is certainly a fact which must outweigh ... any misconceived opinions of the doctrine and tenets of our holy church.[103]

This awkward balance between protest at past severities and gratitude for the government's present leniency, between loyalty to the royal family and to 'our holy church' leads to an uneasy closing prayer in which the Dublin Catholic clergy ask God to bless the administration,

> to aid their councils in such a manner, that, whilst they intend to assist us, like kind benefactors, they may not, contrary to their intentions, by mistaking the means, most irretrievably destroy us.[104]

98 Thirteen Catholic Queries, cited by Fagan, *Dublin's Turbulent Priest*, pp 130-1. 99 Ibid. 100 Fagan, *Dublin's Turbulent Priest*, p. 130. 101 Appendix to Nicholas Taaffe, *Observations on Affairs in Ireland* (London, 1766), pp 33-6. 102 *Exhortation of the Roman Catholic Clergy*, p. 33. 103 Ibid., p. 34. 104 Ibid., p. 35.

The rhetorical ploy of this address is to so praise the administration as to persuade them not to be swayed by anti-Catholic prejudices. They acknowledge where power lies, that the Hanoverians are here to stay, but the image which comes through is of an administration that works by whim rather than principle. Catholics had reason to object to such 'nauseous Flattery' but the Catholic clergy of Dublin, without disagreeing over the grievances done to their people, preferred the politics of insinuation to that of confrontation. It is thus not surprising that the clergy absent themselves from public debates with the administration and the parliamentary patriots. Their attitude is markedly different from that of say the Catholic merchants. Certainly there were divisions of temper and aspirations at several levels of Catholic society.

The Catholic Committee

The example of the Dublin clergy's acquiescence stands in contrast to the more combative mood of other Catholic interests, not least the newly formed Catholic Committee as well as Catholic historians. The Catholic Committee, following the Catholic Association formed in 1756, was started early in 1760 by Catholic gentlemen and traders including the antiquarian and historian Charles O'Conor and the Dublin physician and historian Dr John Curry.[105] Its aim was to press for relief from the penal laws. The time was right, thought O'Conor, to reassess both the penal laws and relations between Catholics and government. The politicians who introduced the laws had passed on. The period of confiscations and violence was past:

> Time gave at last the security which force gave at first, and what was once a lawless possession, as well as government, is by prescription become both valid and legal. The posterity of both parties is now in a different situation; and difference of situation will undoubtably more or less beget a
> · difference of principles and dispose consequently to a difference of conduct.[106]

In keeping with such conviction that the laws were redundant, detrimental to the Irish economy and prevented the participation of Catholics in Ireland's development, some Catholics presented an address to King George III on his accession expressing their commitment to Ireland's welfare and prosperity. This initiative

105 Catholics returning to Ireland from medical training on the Continent were permitted to practise their profession. For a disparaging view of the Committee see Thomas Bartlett, '"A Weapon of War yet Untried": Irish Catholics and the Armed Forces of the Crown, 1760-1830', *Men, Women and War*, eds T.B. Fraser and Keith Taffery, Historical Studies series, xviii (Dublin, 1993), p. 66: 'this committee was a byword for internal division and rivalry.' 106 O'Conor to Curry, 20 August 1756 in *The Letters of Charles O'Conor of Belanagare*, eds Catherine C. Ward and Robert Ward, 2 vols (Ann Arbor, 1980), i, 21.

has to be weighed against a more guarded address by Catholic gentlemen and nobility from Meath and Westmeath, another indicator of disagreement about tactics and agendas. Bartlett says the difference in the two addresses shows 'in the most public and emphatic way the separate courses that Catholic politics would pursue over the next thirty years or more'.[107] The Catholic Committee, despite early dissensions, wanted to discard that image of subservience acquired, for example, during the Jacobite rebellion in Scotland in 1745. Their members were to play a significant role in the 1780s and 1790s in the Catholics' campaign for emancipation.

Catholics and the writing of history

As will be seen in a later chapter written versions of Irish history had long been a contentious issue between the Irish and the English, Catholics and Protestants. Hugh Reily, the Jacobite lawyer who accompanied James II to France, had written his *Impartial History of Ireland* (1690) stressing that Catholics' rights had been disregarded by the English. This was answered by the Protestant Nathaniel Crouch. He dismissed Reily's claims in his *History of the Kingdom of Ireland* (1693) and blamed Catholic clergy for encouraging rebellion.[108] Written histories play a key role in postcolonial societies not least because colonised people resent being written into history as subordinate objects of another nation's history. John Lynch had said as much in his rebuttal of Giraldus: national history, he said, was the business of 'citizens residing in that nation, to the exclusion of foreigners from beyond the seas'.[109] Most published histories of Ireland in English before the mid-century were written by Englishmen. Ironically much of the documentary material on Irish history had been collected by these same writers, notably Thomas Carte.[110] By mid-century Catholic historians, O'Conor and Curry, had begun a fresh assault on English and Irish Protestant readings of Irish history as a story of barbarism, superstition and rebellion. Scholarly debates were difficult in a climate charged with religious and national prejudice. O'Conor told Curry he found Dublin Protestant historian Walter Harris' recent work malicious: 'Did you not observe how he has sacrificed common sense to his malice ...? Were it worth the while, he ought to be gutted up and gibbeted for the good of the public.'[111]

The rebellion of 1641 was central to the contest in that the massacre of Protestants in October 1641 was a principal argument by Protestants to prove the

107 Bartlett, *The Fall and Rise of the Irish Nation*, p. 63. 108 Reily's work was 'the principal statement of history from a Catholic point of view' in the early eighteenth century: Niall O'Ciosain, *Print and Popular Culture in Ireland, 1750–1850* (London, 1997), p. 103; both works were frequently reissued during the century. 109 John Lynch, 'Dedication', *Cambrensis Eversus* (1662), ed. and trans. Matthew Kelly, 3 vols (Dublin, 1848), i. 11. 110 See J.C. Beckett, 'Introduction, Eighteenth-Century Ireland', *New History of Ireland*, iv, pp lxii–lxiii. 111 *Letters of Charles O'Conor*, i, 15 [2 June 1756].

treachery and cruelty of Irish Catholics and helped justify the land confiscations that followed and the consolidation of Protestant power in the late seventeenth century.[112] From the start Protestant literature had often been hysterial about what happened. A pamphleteer advocating the reconquest of Ireland in 1649 writes, 'Do not the screeches and cries of those slaughtered men, women and children fill your ears, their sprawlings and gaspings appear in your eyes, while you hinder the just vengeance upon those barbarous murtherers?'[113] Such sentiments continued through most of the eighteenth century in anniversary sermons preached in Dublin on 23 October every year thanking God for rescuing Protestants during the rebellion and pointing to the Catholics as 'dangerous, unreasonable and uncivilised.'[114] As late as the 1780s a Protestant pamphleteer could write, 'The bloody standard is about to be erected and a renovation of the massacre of 1641 will be added if you do not keep the nails and claws of Presbyterians and Papists clipped.'[115] The 1641 rebellion took on mythic proportions in the Protestant mind and became prime evidence for keeping the penal laws. Curry in particular focused on sources for the history of the rebellion which had been portrayed particularly by Sir John Temple as savage and unprovoked.[116] Adopting the persona of a Protestant Curry in 1747 revisited much of the Protestant evidence pointing up its inconsistencies in *A brief account from the most authentic protestant writers of the causes, motives, and mischiefs, of the Irish rebellion ... 1641.*[117]

Burke was one of the few Protestant voices to agree with Curry in questioning the evidence. The rebellion, he wrote, 'has been extremely and most absurdly misrepresented.'[118] Writing his unpublished *Tracts Relating to Popery Laws* in the early 1760s he put his finger on the ideological issue behind English histories of the rebellion which are 'generally full of passion and of error',

> But there is an interior History of Ireland, the genuine voice of its records and monuments, which speaks a very different language from these histories, from Temple and from Clarendon, these restore Nature to its just rights, and policy to its proper order. For they even now show to those

---

112 Corish, *The Catholic Community*, p. 48. Curry and O'Conor tried to persuade Hume to change his anti-Catholic account of the massacre in his *History*. He modified some phrases in the 1770 edition: David Berman, 'David Hume on the 1641 Rebellion in Ireland', *Studies* 65 (Summer, 1976), 101-12. 113 'Walwyns Wiles: or The Manifestors Manifested', *The Leveller Tracts, 1647-1653*, eds William Haller and Godfrey Davies (Gloucester, Mass., 1964), p. 315. 114 T.C. Barnard, 'The Uses of 23 October 1641 and Irish Protestant Celebrations', *English Historical Review* 106, no. 421 (1991), 901 *et passim*. 115 Patrick Duigenan, *A Letter to Amyas Griffith* (Dublin, 1787), cited by James Kelly, 'Relations between the Protestant Church of Ireland and the Presbyterian Church in late Eighteenth Century Ireland', *Eire-Ireland* 23 (1988), 45. 116 Sir John Temple, *The Irish Rebellion: or, an history of the general rebellion raised with the kingdom of Ireland ... together with the barbarous cruelties and bloody massacre which ensued thereupon* (London, 1646). The work had been reprinted in 1679, 1713, 1724 and 1746. 117 Curry's later and important work on the subject was *An Historical and Critical Review of the Civil Wars in Ireland*, Dublin, 1775. 118 *Correspondence of Burke*, ii, 285.

who havè been at the pains to examine them, and they may show one day to all the world, that these rebellions were not produced by toleration, but by persecution; that they arose not from just and mild government, but from the most unparalleled oppression.[119]

When Catholic historians like Reily, O'Conor and Curry argued that the rebellion was the result of English provocation they too rejected the English myth that trouble in Ireland was always the result of recalcitrant natives wanting to overthrow their wise and just English masters. The argument not only presents the English as blind to their worst prejudices, but implies what Nary and others had already said that the penal laws are based on a false perception of the Irish Catholics.

Arguing against prejudice: finding a voice

The debate about the 1641 rebellion stemmed from English prejudices which were entwined with more general Protestant suspicions about Catholics, and these were still evident in certain quarters in the 1750s. This underlying prejudice comes to the surface in a debate started by O'Conor's provocative *The Case of the Roman Catholics of Ireland* (1755) in which he points out that before the sixteenth century 'the Great Charter of Liberties was obtained, and the Constitution of the present Government was brought almost to its Perfection, in the Days of Popery'.[120] If the cornerstone of British liberties was laid by papists then Irish Catholics had good reason to expect those liberties to be granted them for their improvement.[121] This is beating the Protestants with their own stick. O'Conor carries the principle into recent history by contrasting Queen Anne with the Georges. Under Anne,

> The Sensation of *real* and the Prospect of perpetual Bondage, produced woeful Counter-Actions in the human Mind; exchanging every laudable and generous Principle, for an Indifference to all Events.[122]

Such heartless oppression was beyond the comprehension of Irish Catholics. It broke their spirit and put a 'universal Damp on Trade' and as a result, 'many Parts of the Kingdom became a perfect Desert'.[123] But the Hanoverians introduced 'the

119 Burke, 'Tracts Relating to Popery Laws', *Writings and Speeches of Edmund Burke*, ix, 479. 120 Charles O'Conor, *The Case of the Roman Catholics of Ireland. Wherein the Principles and Conduct of the Party are fully Explained and Vindicated* (Dublin, 1755), p. 19. O'Conor's printer Patrick Lord is said to have stopped the press for fear the book would offend the Catholic clergy. A Cork edition was banned (Munter, *A Dictionary of the Print Trade in Ireland*, p. 170). 121 *The Case of the Roman Catholics*, p. 34. 122 Ibid., p. 45. 123 Ibid., p. 46; this is not entirely exaggerated: for the volatile economics of Ireland during Queen Anne's reign see L.M.Cullen, 'Economic Development, 1691-1750',

German Spirit of Toleration'.[124] Catholics have proved themselves loyal and obedient, a point they made throughout the century, giving the lie to Protestant fears. The need therefore to repeal the penal laws and provide relief by liberalising trade is obvious. The obverse to this argument is that if relief is not forthcoming then Catholics will have grounds to suspect England's motives:

> Where no political Crime exists, active or intentional, Stripes are not wholesome Punishment, but Tyranny; not the cool and necessary Chastisement of Liberty, but the Glorification of private Revenge, and the Defiance of public Good.[125]

Voices from as disparate backgrounds as O'Conor, Lucas and Burke echo this moral condemnation of the English – tyranny, revenge, defiance of Ireland's interests, but for O'Conor the root cause of the problem was religious prejudice. This determined policy in Dublin and Westminster. In spite of the changing climate in the 1750s Protestants continued to draw attention to critical moments in history when they seemed most threatened by Catholics. In O'Conor's view, 'Prejudices against the Roman Catholic Religion, and consequently against the Professors of it, I am confident, run still very high.'[126]

O'Conor's pamphlet drew a reply from the more extreme quarters of Protestant thinking. The anonymous author of *Remarks on a late Pamphlet* (1755) starts by saying he knows of no legal wrongs done to Catholics, or 'that there have been any partial or illegal Proceedings in relation to any of their Affairs'.[127] This is followed by a number of hackneyed accusations such as that Catholics are 'constantly endeavouring to throw these Kingdoms back into their ancient State of Bondage', 'Can the Roman Catholics absolutely be relied on?' and would they not support a French landing?[128]

Catholic writers countered such ingenuous attitudes by recalling religious prejudices, questioning the need for the penal laws, and reaffirming their loyalty to the crown, all of which evidenced their desire to be recognised as fully fledged citizens of Ireland. These writers were usually middle-class Dublin Catholics whose political views and expression were not very different from those of many Protestant patriots. It is ironic that Lucas' remark, 'the English cannot make Us Slaves, without becoming Tyrants themselves', could well have been made by O'Conor, although for different reasons.[129]

New History of Ireland, iv, 142–3. **124** *The Case of the Roman Catholics,* p. 47. **125** Ibid., p. 50. **126** Ibid., p.77; for examples of Protestant fears see John Garnett, Bishop of Clogher, *A Sermon Preached in Christ-Church, Dublin on Monday, the 5th of November, 1753, being the Anniversary of the Gunpowder-plot ...,* Dublin, 1754, and Antoine Court, *An Historical Memorial of the most Remarkable Proceedings against the Protestants in France, from the Year 1744 to 1751,* translated from the French, Dublin, 1752. **127** *Remarks on a late Pamphlet, by a Protestant* (Dublin, 1755), p. 7. **128** Ibid., pp 16, 24. **129** Lucas, *Address XIX* (25 September 1749), *The Political Constitutions,* ii, 343.

The growing confidence of Catholic voices is evidenced in another pamphlet in the debate which sounds a warning to the English administration. *Remarks on a late Pamphlet* was answered by *A Vindication of a Pamphlet lately Published* (1755) which defends O'Conor's pamphlet as having being written to rescue Ireland 'from many incumbent, many inveterate, and many menacing Evils'.[130] Arguments are repeated about the loyalty to the crown, respect for the Constitution and admiration for the Hanoverians. The writer turns this last point to the Catholics' advantage: 'Why his Majesty's Roman-Catholic Subjects may not be rendered as useful in these Kingdoms, as they are in Lower Saxony, no good Reason, we think can be assigned.'[131] The contradiction is compounded to England's disadvantage by the fact that Ireland is still in 'a State of Dependency' upon England: this may in the future 'create Heart-burnings and Complaints in this Island'.[132] England's treatment of Ireland is creating problems for herself. The writer cleverly uses this ominous forecast to argue that in times of trouble it would be better for England to have loyal rather than disgruntled Catholics on her side.[133]

However, this challenging talk is not sustained, and slips back, as so often in Catholic discourse of the mid-century, into the paradox that in spite of oppression Catholics will remain loyal: 'Our Religion enforceth Civil Obedience to this, and every established Government.'[134] Yet in the very justification from scripture for this stance, a justification less frequently invoked than might be expected, comes a barbed analogy which is a sign of latent resentment. Catholics will accept the authority of government because they follow the example of Christ who gave obedience 'to the Tiberius's and Herods of his own Time'.[135]

Although the emerging Catholic voice of the 1750s is oblique, ironic and guarded, its varied and frequent presence gives a new dimension to public debate. O'Conor was not the first to write on the Catholic cause, but he was responsible for trying to disentangle political from theological issues,[136] and to rid the debates both of religious prejudice and traditional modes of thought. Like Nary he adopted a new mode of address to the Protestants seeking to allay their fears and encourage a rapprochement. O'Conor's approach is indicative of the mid-century climate in which both parties began to realise that the old attitudes were counter-productive. As Burke puts it to his friend Charles O'Hara, there was no future in the old attitudes:

> Mais cultivons Notre Jardin – ... party rage, ignorance, and bigotry – If we wait until these evils cease to be the lot of the best as well as the worst men, we shall have no Cabbages.[137]

130 *A Vindication of a Pamphlet lately Published* (Dublin, 1755), p. 5.   131 Ibid., p. 17.   132 Ibid., p. 32.
133 Ibid., p. 33.   134 Ibid., p. 49.   135 Ibid., p. 49.   136 Leighton, *Catholicism in a Protestant Kingdom*, p. 94.   137 'But let us work at our garden'; Burke to Charles O'Hara, 20 June, 1770; *Correspondence of Burke*, ii, 143.

New challenges, old attitudes

As prejudices became a topic for public debate so people on both sides began to question the old attitudes. But while recognising the need for change they were not clear what that change might entail. The Catholic voice does not provide a vision. But it does raise fundamental questions – were anti-Catholic prejudices not counter-productive to the administration's desire for a peaceful and more prosperous Ireland? What was the role of the Catholic majority in Ireland's development? Would greater legislative autonomy for Ireland benefit all the people of Ireland? And on the wider imperial scale how was England to encourage the Irish to enlist for military service in America if it continued to treat them as outcasts at home?

Recent studies have argued, as mentioned earlier, that the major reason why the Catholic question became so central in Irish politics in the latter half of the century was England's need to recruit soldiers for its armies.[138] The postcolonial observation that no colonial enterprise ever succeeded without the collaboration of the colonised takes an unusual turn in the latter part of the eighteenth century. In the early 1760s Protestants tacitly accepted that Catholics might be admitted in the defence of the empire and by the 1770s they were being recruited in larger numbers for service in India and America.[139] Colonial subjects from one part of the empire were thus recruited to assert the colonial presence in another, though not in positions of significant authority.[140] England's need for the troops and the Catholics' collaboration had the anomalous effect in the 1770s of rousing Protestant fears at home, pushing their sympathies towards the American colonists. The English became more amenable to exchange Catholic loyalty for Catholic relief. While collaboration was designed to tighten the bonds of empire abroad it helped loosen them across the Irish sea.

An interesting feature in this time of change is the mildness of the Catholic voice. Both O'Conor and Curry have their aggressive moments but there is no sustained argument that Ireland would be a better place without the Protestants or the English administrators, nothing to match the prophetic certainty in earlier Gaelic writers, such as, 'You will see in Ireland some time, there will be change there; the saints and the true clerics say that the Englishry will be destroyed.'[141] By mid-century there was tacit acceptance among Catholics that the Protestants were there to stay. The pamphlets are anti-English but nobody suggests the English should leave. Catholic bishops, clergy and middle-class

---

138 See Jacqueline Hill, '1641 and the Quest for Catholic Emancipation, 1691-1829', *Ulster 1641: Aspects of the Rising* (Belfast, 1993), ed. Brian Mac Cuarta, p. 165 and Bartlett, '"A Weapon of War yet Untried"', *Men, Women and War*, pp 66-85.   139 Ibid., pp 69-70.   140 A twentieth-century example of the same phenomenon is France's deployment of troops from Senegal to serve elsewhere in Africa. The Catholic Relief Act of 1793 allowed Catholics to take commissions in the army in Ireland, but not in England.   141 Cited by Ó Buachalla, 'Irish Jacobitism and Irish nationalism: the literary evidence', *Nations and Nationalisms*, p. 107.

merchants continued to express their loyalty to the king and his administration. Change would have to be within a modified version of the old settler order. This is not to say the silent majority in rural Ireland nor the exiles on the continent supported that vision. Many did not.

The easing of anti-Catholic prejudices in mid-century is but a trend and it by no means displaces the old attitudes. Underlying suspicions and grievances lingered on in private and in public. John Stratford asks his son Edward to look for a butler and have him interviewed: 'examine him, enquire into his character, and be sure he is a protestant'.[142] Public debates between Catholics and the administration remained polemical and fractious, rather than analytic. The visions and political goals of Catholics and Protestants were so different that they often paid little or no attention either to what one another were saying or to their common distrust and bitterness towards the English. Lord George Grenville noted when he was lord lieutenant that opposition groups, however hostile to one another, succeeded in 'agreeing in insulting the government'.[143] The patriots of the mid-century, preoccupied with Ireland's parliamentary interests, seem deaf to the arguments of a writer like O'Conor who asks them to concentrate on national rather than sectarian goals. This may have been because Protestants realised that O'Conor's arguments could lead to a very different political solution to the one they had in mind.[144] More obviously the patriots were speaking to a quite different audience which was more suspicious of Catholics than they were – the Irish parliament, the Castle, Westminster. These were the arenas of power where issues such as money bills were fought out, and within these the Catholics still had no place. Patriot perceptions of themselves in the 1750s were reflected for example in Dunn's *Universal Advertiser* which, according to Dickson,

> popularised the sense of a black-and-white political firmament, filled by virtuous patriots struggling against a venal Castle administration, corrupt placemen, and an English ministry intent on further subjugating the Irish parliament and draining the Irish treasury for non-Irish purposes.[145]

The Catholics whose interests were repeatedly championed by the patriots were excluded from and ignored in such debates: silence about the Catholics in the money-bill crises of the 1750s is evidence that in political circles they were still regarded as marginal to Ireland's self-determination. The Bishop of Cloyne argued in 1787 that Catholics should be allowed to practise their religion, but should be kept out of politics because Protestants must retain 'the power of con-

142 John Stratford to his son Edward, 25 March, 1753, in Ethel M.Richardson, *Long Forgotten Days* (London, 1928), p. 52. 143 Cited by J.C.D. Clark, 'Whig Tactics and Parliamentary Protest: the English Management of Irish Politics, 1754-1756', *Historical Journal* 21 (1978), 284. 144 Leighton, *Catholicism in a Protestant Kingdom*, p. 121. 145 Dickson, *New Foundations*, p. 93.

trol'. As the Protestant landholder looked to 'the Protestant ascendancy' for his security, so,

> The preservation of that ascendancy depends entirely on an indissoluble connexion between the Sister Kingdoms. But let him consult his own reason ... how these great points are to be secured. Is it by increasing the influence of Popery? The idea is revolting to common sense.[146]

Protestant interests had no doubts about their own role in these changing times to determine the character of Ireland. Whenever challenged and notably in the early 1790s, when the revitalised Catholic Committee and Wolfe Tone were establishing extra-parliamentary support, Protestant interests hit back in an uncompromising mood. The Dublin corporation announced in 1792,

> The Protestants of Ireland would not be compelled by any authority whatever to abandon the political situation which their forefathers had won with their swords and which is therefore their birthright, or to surrender their religion at the footstool of Popery.[147]

Such confidence was often the reverse side of a lingering unease. Old Protestant suspicions about Jacobite sympathies among the Catholics may have been on the wane, but they were easily roused, especially during the Seven Years' War. The Whiteboy disturbances in the early 1760s were immediately suspected by the administration as having Jacobite links.[148] In some quarters such suspicions lingered into the 1780s when, for example, Protestants took fright at the Rightboy disturbances in Munster.[149] The Catholic clergy were always open to suspicion. The Jacobite court continued to have a say in the appointment of Irish bishops until the death of James III in 1766;[150] the church's ties with the continent, with Rome, with the Irish Colleges in France and Spain, the bishops' journeys to and from the continent for the ordination of their priests, all these factors gave Protestants reason to question Catholic loyalties to the administration and the crown.

By the mid-century official attitudes towards the Catholics had begun to lag behind what was happening in trade, commerce and the intercourse of daily life. There was a mobility at that level which was quietly changing the face and temper of Ireland. Although there was no concensus among Catholics as to how to negotiate relief from the penal laws, much less to establish a more stable posi-

---

146 Richard Woodward, *The Present State of the Church of Ireland*, p. 18.   147 *Freeman's Journal*, 15 September, 1792 cited by Marianne Elliott, *Wolfe Tone, Prophet of Irish Independence* (London, 1989), p. 185.   148 For Burke's interest in these allegations see *Correspondence of Burke*, i, 147, n. 5.   149 Leighton gives an example from 1785 (*Catholicism in a Protestant Kingdom*, p. 173, n. 73).   150 Ibid., pp 56-7.

tion in the political and economic arenas, their voices were at last being heard in the market place. The fact that O'Conor, a Gaelic speaker of an old aristocratic Catholic family from Co. Sligo, could come to Dublin, befriend the librarian of Trinity College and do his research there, indicates a much more flexible climate of relations than the statutes and official pronouncements lead us to believe. As recent work on eighteenth-century translations of Keating has shown, 'there was much more interaction between Irish-language and English-language cultures and between catholics and protestants in Ireland than has been widely assumed'.[151] A key figure in this rapprochement of the two cultures is Charles O'Conor.

151 Diarmaid Ó Catháin, 'Dermot O'Connor, Translator of Keating', *Eighteenth-Century Ireland* 2 (1987), 86.

CHAPTER FIVE

Voices from abroad:
the Irish in Bordeaux[1]

One of the unusual bodies of Irish postcolonial writing in the eighteenth century is that by Irish Catholic exiles in Europe. Exiles from colonisation usually have to struggle for survival in their new surroundings; they encounter prejudice, live in ghettos and find themselves among the lower economic and social group in their new society. Such was the experience of blacks in America or England or France who had left their colonised country in search of relief. Some of these were emigrants to 'the imperial heartlands' and went there by choice rather than from direct political harassment.[2] Those who could claim to be political refugees were often better cared for by the host country than the rest. Irish exiles in France do not fall easily into any of these categories.

The Irish diaspora to Europe in the eighteenth century happened for one or more of three reasons all of which related in some way to religion – political subversion, or the penal laws, or military service in a European army. What this chapter examines is the case of the community of Irish in Bordeaux, most of whom blamed the penal laws for their exile, and yet who experienced none of the alienating effects found so frequently in diasporic history.

Bordeaux and the Irish

France's western seaports had long been an attractive haven to the Irish. Ports like La Rochelle, Nantes and Bordeaux were situated on the European seaboard closest to Ireland and their people shared with the Irish the same Catholic faith and a similar animosity to England. During the late seventeenth century small

1 An earlier version of this chapter was published as 'A Crisis for the Irish in Bordeaux: 1756' in *Nations and Nationalisms* , pp 129-45. 2 Childs and Williams, *An Introduction to Post-Colonial Theory*, p. 13

communities of Irish exiles grew up in La Rochelle and Nantes which became landing points for Irish recruits to the French army and for clerical students coming to study at the Irish colleges in France which had been established to ensure a continuing supply of Irish priests now that the penal laws forbade such education. The community in Bordeaux had even earlier origins. Forty Irish priests arrived there as refugees from Ireland in 1603 and an Irish seminary was established in 1654 which was the start of Bordeaux's Irish College. This and other Irish communities grew as further waves of refugees arrived in France, particularly the Jacobite exodus after the treaty of Limerick. In La Rochelle in 1692 the bishop and his clergy donated 600 livres 'for the relief of poor Irish families who were refugees in France after the reduction of Limerick'.[3] After King James had been defeated at the battle of the Boyne, the French king recognised and accommodated him and his court near Paris at St Germain en Laye and that had the effect of providing a focus for Irish refugee sentiment.

In the wake of the initial influx of Jacobite exiles to Bordeaux another group of Irish had arrived between 1720 and 1750, and by mid-century this small group of some 300 were making a significant contribution to Bordeaux's international trade.[4] Bordeaux situated near the mouth of the Gironde river was uniquely placed to take advantage of trade developments in southern France in the eighteenth century. It became a major port for France's transatlantic shipping and a regular stopping place for ships plying between northern and southern European ports. The Gironde river gave access to the hinterland of southern France, a link facilitated by the Midi canal which ran from the Gironde across to the Midi on the Mediterranean coast. Bordeaux was a major port for the export of wine from vineyards across the country as far as the Rhone. This access also meant the ready supply of goods and provisions such as Irish dairy and meat products to the French hinterland through Bordeaux.

Irish families who settled in Bordeaux included both Protestants and Catholics. The latter had invariably left Ireland, as we shall see, for political and religious reasons. They heard from family or friends already there of the security from persecution. They soon realised Bordeaux was a place where Catholics, far from being outlawed, were accepted as fellow-religionists. If anyone was being persecuted it was the Protestants. The Edict of Nantes which gave religious toleration to the Huguenots was revoked in 1685 and 200,000 Huguenots were expelled from France. Burke noted that 'the privileges which the Protestants of

---

3 Archives départementales de la Charente-Maritime, La Rochelle, MS G 146.f. 60. 4 P.Butel and J-P. Poussou, *La Vie Quotidienne à Bordeaux au XVIIIe Siècle* (Paris, 1980), p. 24; see also L.M. Cullen, 'The Irish Merchant Communities at Bordeaux, La Rochelle and Cognac in the Eighteenth Century', in L.M. Cullen and Paul Butel, *Négoce et Industrie en France et en Irlande aux XVIIIe et XIXe Siècles* (Paris, 1980), pp 51-64; the figure of 300 includes those at the seminary almost all of whom were from Munster (Cathaldus Giblin, 'The Irish Colleges on the Continent', *The Irish French Connection, 1578-1978*, ed. Liam Swords (Paris, 1978), p. 19.

that kingdom enjoyed precedent to this revocation, were far greater than the Roman Catholics of Ireland ever aspired to under a contrary establishment.'[5] Irish Catholics who crossed to France must have been struck, as Burke was, by the contradictions. Burke writes,

> I flatter myself that not a few will be found, who do not think that the names of Protestant and Papist can make any change in the nature of essential justice. Such men will not allow that to be proper treatment to the one of these denominations, which would be cruelty to the other; and which converts its very crime into the instrument of its defence: they will hardly persuade themselves, that what was bad policy in France, can be good in Ireland; or that what was intolerable injustice in an arbitrary Monarch, becomes, only by being more extended and more violent, an equitable procedure, in a Country professing to be governed by Law.[6]

In his reference to 'bad policy in France' Burke may well have been alluding to the persecution of Protestants in the region of Nimes, Montpellier and the Cevennes. For example, in 1724 an order from the king set down severe penalties for members of the Protestant Reformed churches: pastors faced execution, those who attended services faced either the galleys, if they were men, or life imprisonment for women. In 1730 Marie Durand, aged fifteen, was imprisoned at Aigues-Mortes and kept there until 1768. Her brother was executed in 1732.[7] This persecution of Reformed church Protestants had a frightening brutality.

The irony of Irish Catholics emigrating to France to escape similar prejudices and penalties struck Burke as an indictment of both systems, if not of human nature itself. The Edict of Nantes which gave freedom of worship to Protestants in France had been gradually ignored in favour of a policy of persecution. Finally in 1685 Louis XIV revoked the laws and Reformed Protestants were subjected to harassment and unprecedented penalties. Many fled, some of them to Ireland. Burke reflects on Irish Catholics seeking refuge in France while French Huguenots looked to Ireland for refuge:

> To transfer humanity from its natural basis, our legitimate and home-bred connections; to lose all feelings for those who have grown up by our sides, in our eyes, to the benefit of whose cares and labours we have partaken from our birth; and meretriciously to hunt abroad after foreign affections; is such a disarrangement of the whole system of our duties, that I do not know whether benevolence so displaced is not almost the same thing as

5 Burke, 'Tracts relating to the Popery Laws', *Writings and Speeches of Edmund Burke*, ix, 460. 6 Ibid., 461. 7 See Pierre Fanguin, *Textes et documents sur l'histoire du protestantisme dans le Gard*, Nimes: Archives départementales du Gard, 1986.

destroyed, or what effect bigotry could have produced that is more fatal to society. This no one can help observing, who has seen our doors kindly and bountifully thrown open to foreign sufferers for conscience, whilst through the same ports were issuing fugitives of our own, driven from their Country for a cause which to an indifferent person would seem to be exactly similar, while we stood by, without any sense of impropriety of this extraordinary scene, accusing, and practising injustice.[8]

The Irish fugitives found in France what they were denied in their own country. They could set up in business, mix and deal with Protestant Irish without prejudice and practise their religion without hindrance under the encouragement of the Irish College. In 1734 the archbishop of Bordeaux ordered priests at the College to preach Lenten sermons for the Irish merchant families. St Patrick's Day was celebrated with a high mass and a special panegyric on St Patrick.[9] Exiles have seldom enjoyed such a reversal.

But not all the Irish in Bordeaux would regard themselves as exiles. About half were Protestants who were there for the trade. The Black family for example, a prosperous Protestant family from the north of Ireland, worked an import/export business in wine, brandy and butter from Bordeaux with family and connections in Portugal, Belfast, Dublin, Edinburgh, Glasgow and Rotterdam. John Black (b. 1682) lived in the Chartrons, the area of the city favoured by the Irish and bordering on the river. His household included his married son and his wife, a Protestant priest from Cork, two Protestant servants and a Catholic bookkeeper.[10] Both he and his sons made frequent journeys to Ireland and kept in regular correspondence with their wide-spread family.

Catholic families – Mitchell, Meade, Gernon, Power, Coppinger, MacCarthy, Bonfield – had also established themselves in business. They started out as Catholic exiles and quickly found that their involvement in business more than compensated for their estrangement from Ireland. Many were from Munster, some from Dublin and Galway. They set up as entrepreneurs in the wine, beef and butter trade. Some had taken French citizenship, many had married into French families, purchased a house along the Quai des Chartrons and employed one or two Irish servants. Irish businessmen liked to have at least one Irish clerk or 'commis' who could converse in both English and French and he usually lived with the family. The Chartrons became the Irishtown of Bordeaux where Protestants and Catholics lived side by side and traded with one another, though they seldom went into partnership together. They employed one another's

8 'Tracts relating to Popery Laws', *Writings and Speeches of Edmund Burke*, ix, 461. 9 T.J. Walsh, *The Irish Continental College Movement: The Colleges at Bordeaux, Toulouse, and Lille* (Dublin, 1973), p. 106; priests and students at the College were entitled to French citizenship under a grant by Louis XIV in 1654 (ibid., p. 109). 10 McLoughlin, 'A Crisis for the Irish in Bordeaux: 1756', *Nations and Nationalisms*, p. 144.

dependants and were in frequent correspondence with the mother country.[11] Away from Ireland's penal laws they made a living, raised a family, practised their religion without interference and thus enjoyed a new liberty from the divisions and restrictions they had known in Ireland. By the 1750s their initiative had made them an integral part of Bordeaux's prosperity. For example, in the early decades of the century Bordeaux had to import its wine bottles at great expense from places like Montpellier on the Mediterranean, and it was the Irishman Pierre Mitchell who set up Bordeaux's first glass and bottle-making factory in the Chartrons in 1723.[12] He was appointed glass manufacturer to the king in 1738.[13] The contribution of the Irish far outweighed their small numbers.

The crisis of 1756 and the Irish response

In the first few weeks of 1756 Bordeaux, like the rest of France, was busily preparing itself for war with Great Britain. Bordeaux's parliament had agreed that money and resources should be spent on making further munitions, and according to reports received in Dublin frigates were being fitted out in Bordeaux, 'to cruize against the English'.[14] The archbishop had ordered public prayers, 'pour fléchir la colère divine' which he said was evidenced by Europe's current troubles. Impressed by this order the mayor of Bordeaux on 31 January 1756 issued a ban on public festivities, dances and carnivals, and forbade the selling, buying or wearing of masks during this period.[15] These sombre developments posed no particular threat to the Irish. The shock for them came on 19 February when the Marquis de Tourny, Intendant en la Généralité de Guienne, made it known that the king had ordered the expulsion from France of all subjects of George II by 15 March.[16] The order threatened to throw the Irish back into the political and religious world from which they presumed they had escaped. Their response to this crisis reveals much about their place in eighteenth-century Bordeaux – who they were, what they were doing, why they had come to Bordeaux in the first place. It also reveals their opinions about Ireland.

The expulsion order was served personally to individuals concerned, but it allowed pleas for exemption and many Irish took advantage of this. Tourny it seems had the power to reject a plea, or *placet*, but if he felt it deserved a hearing

---

11 See Bartlett, *The Fall and Rise of the Irish Nation*, p. 46. 12 *Histoire de Bordeaux*, ed. Charles Higounet (Bordeaux, 1962-74), v, 284. 13 Archives départementales de la Gironde, Bordeaux (hereafter Arch. dép.), MSS C 1594. 14 Arch. dép., MSS C 1077. In Dublin *Pue's Occurrences* (2 March 1756) carried a report from Bordeaux dated 10 February about a meeting of Bordeaux merchants to discuss fitting out the frigates. 15 Arch. dép., MSS C 1077. 16 For Tourny's letter giving the news to his officials see Arch. dép., MSS C 1074, f. 60. I have not been able to locate a copy of Louis XV's order. A news report of the order, dated 3 February from Brussels, is copied from the *London Gazette* in the *Dublin Gazette*, 21 Feb. 1756: 'The French King's Orders were published [at] Dunkirk, for all British Subjects to quit his Dominions before the first of next Month, except such as may obtain his Permission to remain.'

he had to forward the dossier to the secretary for state, Monseigneur le Ministre de St Florentin, who presented it personally to the king. The dossier included the applicant's own reasons for not having to leave France by 15 March, a statement of support from friends or fellow businessmen, and in the case of Catholics evidence from a priest or friend that the applicant was a practising member of the Catholic church. Tourny registered each dossier in an exercise book headed, 'Extraits des placets présentés par les Anglois, Irlandois et Ecossois ...'[17] Each entry gives a summary of the applicant's case, usually half a page or more, with Tourny's comment in the margin. On 24 February he sends Florentin 22 *placet*s, many of them Irish, which he says he has received in two days.[18] The number corresponds with that registered in his note-book between 21 February and early March. On the same day he lists 25 names of those whom he has notified of the king's order.[19] A longer list of 54 names is dated 27 February, giving names, date of the notice to leave France and the name of the person in the house to whom the notice had been handed.[20]

Two difficulties with the evidence should be mentioned at the outset. One is that several of the Intendant's records, usually in Tourny's own hand, are drafts or redrafts of one another, so there are frequent overlaps of names and responses. Secondly, not many of the documents either of the Intendant or the pleaders have precise dates, and in several cases one has to deduce the approximate time of composition from internal evidence.

The overwhelming number of Irish, as distinct from English or Scots, among those pleading to stay is confirmed in Tourny's list drawn up on 5 March, 1756. There are 65 entries of which 55 are Irish: the list gives the family name, dependants, place of origin, religion, number of children, total number of persons, and observations.[21] For example, the entry for the Burk/Burck family reads, 'Burck sa femme, son frère et 4 enfants/ Galoway en Irlande/ Catholiques/ 3 garçons 1 fille/ 7/ La femme est française et les enfants nés à Bordeaux.'

As the number of identifiable Irish in Bordeaux rose so did the number of *placets*. On the following day, 6 March, Tourny has 22 cases ready for Florentin, of which 18 are Irish, 3 Scots and 1 English.[22] These, however, do not go forward because, as Tourny makes clear, he is waiting for details of new procedures from Florentin. Although the king's order applied to 'les sujets du Roy d'Angleterre', Tourny soon distinguishes four categories – old Jacobite families, Irish Catholics, Irish students, and the rest, which incorporate the Scots, the English and Protestant Irish.[23]

---

17 Arch. dép., MSS C 1072, f. 145; this is similar to f. 88 where many of the same names appear. All the submissions were in French. 18 Ibid., 1073, f. 110. 19 Ibid., 1072, f. 96. 20 Ibid., f. 95. Events in Bordeaux were about a week behind what was happening in northern France. A report from Dunkirk dated 21 Feb. states, 'The English settled in this Town are selling off their Effects' (*Dublin Journal*, 13 March 1756). 21 Arch. dép., MSS C 1072, f. 67. 22 Ibid., 1073, f. 100. 23 See ibid., 1072, f. 4 , f. 5, f.89 and f. 143. Three Jacobite names are given: a Scotsman, Charles Alan, and two Irishmen, MacCarthy

Tourny here introduces an ironic refinement to the king's order. The term 'Les Anglois', the English, had the sense in France of those people governed by the king of England; hence the Scots, Welsh and Irish came under the term. Tourny seems to recognise that the Irish Catholics, long colonised by the English, should be handled differently, or at least not be identified as English. The French monarch's presumption was that the coloniser and colonised were as one and to be treated as one. It is an unusual case of the colonised being confused with their colonisers. Tourny's refined categories show an unusual political perception which was confirmed by the responses he got.

Tourny had come to Bordeaux in 1743, a highly competent administrator and a man of vision for the development of the city. One of his objectives was to strengthen ties between the city and its major suburb the Chartrons which spread westwards along the river. It was largely under his direction that Bordeaux became the splendid eighteenth-century city it was. He had certainly added to his work by treating the cases of the Irish with such thoroughness. His reasons were almost certainly to do with their part in Bordeaux's increasing prosperity. One of the earliest complaints about the expulsion order came from the Irish business community who argued that it would seriously damage Bordeaux's trade with the English-speaking world. Seven Irish businessmen who had taken French nationality wrote to Tourny about the importance to business of their Irish and Scots 'commis'.[24] The 'commis' was bookkeeper, clerk, amanuensis, trained on the job and able to run the business in the absence of his master. One of his main tasks was to correspond with clients, who might well be in the Americas, Canada, the West Indies, India, Ireland or England. He had to have a good command of English. One employer makes the point in his *placet*,

> he takes the liberty of pointing out that his correspondence with Great Britain and Ireland being conducted in the English language, it is impossible for him to continue his business without the help of *commis* who have a good knowledge of English and can write the said language.[25]

Each merchant had at least one Irish or Scots commis: 'Sans un Commis un Négotiant est un Ouvrier sans outils,' they wrote. Furthermore, they said, the Irish could be trusted for their loyalty to France. The arguments carried particular weight for Tourny who wanted to continue the work begun by his predecessor Claude Boucher, 'à faire de Bordeaux une ville monumentale.' Tourny had embellished the city with facades, avenues, squares and the 'Jardin Public à la fois

and Denis O'Conor (ibid., f. 89). Students at the Irish College of Bordeaux were exempt from the expulsion as they had automatic French citizenship: T.J. Walsh, *The Irish Continental College Movement*, p. 109 and 'Documents relating to the Irish College in Bordeaux, no. 1', *Irish Ecclesiastical Record*, 47 (1936), p. 101. 24 Arch. dép., MSS C 1073, f. 9. 25 Ibid., 1072, f. 36.

lieu de promenade digne de la haute société bordelaise'.[26] The Irish had in several ways helped him to achieve this.

The placets

It could be argued that the *placets* had a different significance for Tourny from what they had for the individual pleaders. His concern was to maintain the strong business base of the city, theirs was to avoid being sent back to Ireland. On the other hand Tourny was working directly with Florentin, a man with the ear of the king, and there can be little doubt that he carried out the order scrupulously. The Irish Protestants presented few problems and did not plead exemption. The influential John Black for example was sent back to northern Ireland[27] and was asked by Tourny to see that certain of his employees leave France in keeping with the expulsion order. He replied that William Eccles, a Protestant, had already returned to Ireland and that Thomas Barry, also a Protestant, was waiting for a ship to Holland. He asks, however, that his commis Sean Flynn be allowed to stay as he was a Catholic, his wife was pregnant and his affairs in a bad way.[28]

The Irish Catholics took up most of Tourny's attention. What is of interest in terms of postcolonialism is what the Irish thought about the prospect of returning to Ireland and what their image of Ireland was. The fact that the *placets* are highly personal means they provide unique individual histories of exile of a kind seldom found elsewhere in eighteenth-century Irish writing. But their individual stories also become a kind of cumulative record of a community's history, a linking narrative whose several narrators contribute to a common story. These are people who for different reasons were displaced from Ireland. In different ways they found life under the penal laws intolerable and left the country hoping that exile in France would be preferable to English rule in Ireland. As in much subsequent postcolonial literature their aim was to survive in the foreign land of their adoption, but as seldom happens they found in France common cause with an old enemy of their coloniser, England. Their religion turned from being a major hindrance into a passport to common acceptance. Many took French citizenship and all declared their loyalty to the French king.

Individual examples

The case of Irishman Daniel O'Sullivan, commis to James Kearney, a native of Cashel, illustrates the kinds of problem the Irish faced. O'Sullivan had submit-

26 P. Butel and J-P. Poussou, *La Vie Quotidienne à Bordeaux au XVIIIᵉ Siècle*, p. 29.   27 John Black to his brother Robert, 1 Sept. 1758 , Public Record Office of Northern Ireland, D 719, no. 51.   28 Arch. dép. MSS C 1073 f. 62.

ted his *placet* in early March. He explained that because one of his relations was on the run from the English for recruiting soldiers for the king of France, presumably in Ireland, he had sought refuge four years earlier in Bordeaux. He now worked for Kearney and he did not see how he could return to Ireland without incurring very great risks.[29] His fears are corroborated by news in the Irish papers about this time that in Cork Patrick Croneen was sentenced to death 'charged with enlisting Men for the Service of France'.[30] O'Sullivan's application was refused; whereupon Kearney made a personal plea to Tourny. His letter starts with a complaint at the way the French court had treated Irish Catholics, 'ce peuple malheureux. Il est persecuté et méprisé chez lui, il est mal reçu dans tous les états protestants ...' Kearney mentions that there are some 20 Irish commis in Bordeaux's business houses and wonders what they have done to merit being thus chased away.[31] His own commis, Daniel O'Sullivan, 'qui étoit à la tête de mes affaires,' handles all the written side of the business, most of which is in English. By protecting the commis, he argues, one protects business. O'Sullivan was refused again, and the record shows a further representation on 8 April.[32]

Long after the deadline of 15 March Tourny and Florentin were still considering applications for exemptions or postponements, possibly to maintain good relationships with the Irish. For example, as late as 15 April Peter Curtis, a Catholic from Dublin, asked for an extension and got it. He put forward what had become a standard argument – he was from a Catholic family, had been denied a Catholic education in Ireland, so his father had sent him in 1753 to his uncle in Bordeaux, M.Gernon, who had taken French nationality in 1741. Here he had attended the Irish College. A priest in the town, Fr O'Sullivan, vouched for his being a practising Catholic, adding that he knew Curtis' parents in Dublin. In addition, Curtis argued, he was under medical treatment for rheumatism and pleaded to stay until he had recovered. He was granted an extension.[33]

Joseph Rivers

A more comprehensively documented example is that of Joseph Rivers (1722-1805), a native of Dungarvan. There are six documents in his dossier, all in French – his personal plea, together with supporting letters from the Jesuit College he had attended at Poitiers, from previous employers in Bordeaux, from his parish priest in Bordeaux and a reference from his parish priest in Ireland dating back to 1738, the year he left Ireland. He was brought up in Waterford in the care of his uncle, the bishop of Waterford, while his father plied his trade between Ireland and France. His father was arrested and his ships confiscated for transporting recruits from Ireland, but he found his way to France where his son

---

29 Ibid., f. 1.   30 *Dublin Journal*, 6 April and 10 April 1756.   31 Arch. dép., MSS C 1073, f. 3, pp 1-2.   32 Ibid., f. 94.   33 Ibid., 1072, f. 22, 38, 41, 43, 44.

Joseph joined him and went to the Collège Royal in Poitiers run by Irish clergy. This was a small boarding school established by the Jesuits under Louis XIV for the education of Irish boys, and it also served as a refuge and retirement home for Irish Jesuits.[34] A bright student, Rivers won prizes for oratory, poetry and Greek. In the early 1740s, 'il étouffa la passion qu'il avait pour l'étude pour s'employer dans le Commerce,' and he moved to Bordeaux to become a commis.[35] He was apprenticed to various Irish Catholic merchants, to Quin, to the widow of Mitchell, to Galway and Kearney, and finally to Gernon. At least one of these families, the Gernons, had Jacobite sympathies going back to the Williamite war and the treaty of Limerick.[36]

Given this background it is not surprising to hear Rivers argue that he finds himself, 'far from a country [Ireland] so fatal to his family, and where his religion and his education were proscribed.' He adds, 'having regarded France as the haven for the rest of his days and where his father sought refuge and died, [he] has recourse to your Excellency ...' He wants to stay in France, 'so that as a person attached by his family, his religion and his education to the interests of this kingdom he may be able to spend the rest of his days here peacefully and without molestation.'[37]

It might be argued that Rivers, like others in the same predicament, employs a rhetoric of special pleading because he was better off in Bordeaux than he might have been in Ireland. Against this it can be said, as Cullen has argued, that the Catholic interest in Ireland 'actually flourished during the period of the penal laws'.[38] Such arguments however are a distraction from the main issue: they do not negate the historical experience which Rivers here recalls and appeals to. Words like 'fatal', 'proscribed' and 'molestation' convey Rivers' feelings about Ireland as oppressive, even hostile to its Catholics. The language is rooted in a family history of long-standing grievances and harassment, which explains to Tourny and to the king why Rivers is now in France and has no wish to return to his native country.

What is ironic about the choices facing Catholics in Bordeaux is that having enjoyed the liberty and pleasure of integrating with a foreign society and culture, they were driven by the king's order into an essentialist argument about their Irishness. Their future in France depended on their ability to convince Tourny that they were Catholic Irish, victims of an hostility similar to that with which Protestant England viewed Catholic France. Their successful integration into Bordeaux society counted for nothing. What mattered was the evidence they could produce of a history of persecution and colonial abuse.

---

34 Francis Finegan, 'The Irish College of Poitiers: 1674-1762', *Irish Ecclesiastical Record*, 104 (1965), 21, 31-3. 35 Arch. dép., MSS C 1072, f. 105. 36 Richard Hayes, *Biographical Dictionary of Irishmen in France* (Dublin, 1949), p.104. 37 Arch. dép., MSS C 1072, f. 105. 38 L.M. Cullen, 'Catholics under the Penal Laws', *Eighteenth-Century Ireland* 1 (1986), 29.

Ulick Burk

The same rhetorical ploy of explaining the present in terms of a history that is personal but is part of a national narrative, comes through in a plea from an older man Ulick Burk who, like Rivers, lived and worked in the Chartrons. He starts by stressing his historical ties with the Jacobites,

> his ancestor perished in battle with King James I and his grandfather with James II at the battle of Acherim after which his father was obliged to stay in the mountains of Ireland where he died in poverty. The petitioner having been ordered to be detained in the year 1730 for disputes (against a Protestant) very natural for an individual who had lost all his possessions, and his religion being very hampered, was obliged to come to France, where he married a French woman ... he got his two brothers to come, one of whom died at St Domingo, a pilot in the service of the King, the other staying with him in Les Chartrons with the petitioner asks, Monseigneur, for the protection of your Excellency, only able to go into the land of their birth with weapons in their hands ... the petitioner at present has his son a pilot on board a ship at this moment at Rochefort for the service of the King, and transporting troops against the English nation.[39]

More militant than Rivers, Burk's narrative is threaded with conflict between Catholic and Protestant, Irish and English, dispossession and exile. The expulsion order of 1756 would throw him back into that turmoil. He speaks an animosity not often voiced. He and his brothers would have to return to Ireland 'with weapons in their hands'. He knows what proscriptions and persecution to expect. This assessment is put in another way in the already mentioned complaint to the Intendant by Kearney in which he refers to his fellow countrymen as, 'persecuted and despised in their own land'.[40] Burk's narrative is a typical story of conflict with and resistance to the colonial presence, from hiding in the mountains, to disputes, detention and escape. His family dispossessed of their land had taken to recruiting soldiers for England's enemy.

Denis O'Conor

Although scholars have argued that the Irish Administration in Dublin tended to be over suspicious about Jacobite sympathies among Catholics, especially in Munster, in the mid-century the stories of Rivers, Burk and O'Conor indicate that undercover recruitment for the French army from Ireland continued into

39 Arch. dép., MSS C 1074, f. 9. 40 Ibid., 1073, f. 3, p. 1.

the 1750s. O'Conor was from Cork and he makes his part in such an operation the main point of his plea for exemption. He recounts that an Irish gentleman, Herlihy, a lieutenant in Lord Clare's French regiment, had lodged at his inn in Cork while on a recruiting drive. Herlihy was arrested and condemned to death.

> Because the suppliant had accommodated him [Herlihy] as well as the recruits, he was forced to leave his country and his family and put himself under the protection of the king of France so as to avoid the same fate. Having arrived in the present town [Bordeaux] he established himself with his family in the Chartrons, where he has a house and takes in lodgers to make a living.[41]

At the time of O'Conor's pleading the Clare Irish regiment was under the command of Viscount Clare who was the only Irishman to become a marshal of France. The Clare estates in Ireland, 108,000 acres, had been confiscated under King William and given to Keppel, the earl of Albermarle.[42] O'Conor's story links him with a major figure of Irish resistance.

What Rivers, Burk and O'Conor stress in the diverse details of their several cases is a shared sense of injury. They cannot look to Ireland without apprehension. In terms of nationhood Ireland offers them no protection, but in terms of nationality it is their only axis. They despair of Ireland as governed by the English, and yet the expulsion order makes evident the corporate national identity they have from their historical experience of being brought up in Ireland under Protestant nationalism. Their identity as Irishmen is expressed in terms of past suffering and present fears generated by the Protestant administration and, by extension, the English.

Nicolas White

This expression of national identity by reference to a history of persecution is just as evident in the poor and uneducated Irish in Bordeaux as in the narratives of more prosperous individuals like Rivers or Kearney. For example, Nicolas White, who had emigrated to France as a servant to the widow Lee, the proprietor of a firm in Bordeaux, made his plea for exemption in these terms,

> Notwithstanding the lowliness of your petitioner's present circumstances, he is descended from upright people who through their attachment to the

41 Ibid., 1074, f. 64. O'Connor lived with his wife, daughter and his brother. Herlihy was executed in 1752 (L.M. Cullen, 'The Blackwater Catholics and County Cork Society and Politics in the Eighteenth Century', *Cork History and Society*, p. 573).   42 J.G. Simms, 'Protestant Ascendancy, 1691-1714', *New History of Ireland*, iv, 10.

Apostolic Roman Catholic religion (which they always professed, as does the petitioner) lost their property and were subjected to the persecutions which are carried out on Catholics in that country. The petitioner in this sad state of his family having had the misfortune to lose his father and his mother at the age of ten, placed himself in the service of the aforementioned Madame Lee in order to elude the pursuits of the minister of his parish in Ireland who wanted to put him in the capacity of an orphan in the Protestant school and for these same reasons the petitioner determined in the year 1749 to go to France which has always been the haven of his persecuted fellow-countrymen, and where several of his relations have had the honour of serving in the troops of the King and even of losing their lives for the service of his Majesty.[43]

White summarises the two issues which brought the Irish to France and which remain intrinsic to their view of an Ireland that could rightfully call itself a nation – land and religion. England's denial of these rights, together with the heritage of persecution, provides a common cause. If the penal laws were thought to have become less severe in practice than in the letter by the 1750s, Irish exiles believed otherwise. Whether the principle or the threat of the penal laws terrified them, they read those laws as the mark of a country hostile to its native sons.

Matthew O'Connor

Because religion was the most likely reason for exemption it figures prominently in all the *placets*. Suppliants might understandably play rhetorically on the issue to strengthen their case. Matthew O'Connor's argument is unusual in that he rests his case only on religious grounds. He had been in trade in Dublin and argues that,

he found that the laws and regulations of the kingdom of Ireland were not favourable to the Roman Catholic and apostolic religion which he had always professed. As a result he could not remain without exposing himself or at least his family to the notorious harsh measures applied in that country against people of his religion. He decided in the summer of 1754 to leave his country and he arrived here in June of the same year. After a short time he found a place for his only child in a convent in Toulouse run by Maltese nuns and then he returned to Bordeaux to settle.[44]

43 Arch. dép., MSS C 1074, f. 65. The language of the petition suggests it was written for White by a more educated person, perhaps his employer the widow Lee. 44 Ibid., 1072, f. 45.

The simplicity of the argument stands against much of what Molyneux and Swift had written. O'Connor argues that he left because the lot of Catholics was intolerable. Protestant arguments about parliamentary independence or free trade sound almost irrelevant by comparison. Much of Burke's anger about the penal laws in his *Tracts* reflects an implicit sympathy with O'Connor's predicament.

Alexander Brown

Apart from those in trade there were some less conspicuous Irish such as Alexander Brown. His *placet* is supported by Daniel O'Sullivan, a doctor in Bordeaux and by John O'Brien, bishop of Cloyne and Ross. Brown was not a well man and asks for exemption primarily on grounds of health. He suffered from asthma and the Bordeaux climate gave him relief. He begins with a reference to his elder brother who owns family land in Ireland, and goes on to say,

> the suppliant, finding himself suffering from asthma in his country, and besides persecuted on account of his religion and for his attachment to the legitimate prince willingly took the opinion of his doctors three years ago and shipped to France ... He lives a quiet and sober life on his pension waiting until it may please Providence to restore his health and his prince. Even in circumstances where these are restored the suppliant would still fear to return to his unhappy country, apprehensive that he will find his family persecuted or in prison cells. If he is allowed to delay his return he will pray for the success of his Majesty's armies.[45]

Bishop O'Brien mentions in his supporting letter that Brown came from a distinguished family and was a zealous Roman Catholic, 'and as such loyally attached to the interests of the Catholic princes and particularly those of his very Christian majesty'.[46] The bishop attests that Brown's health is his main problem.

Darcy

The thrust of many a *placet* narrative is summed up in one from Darcy, a son of 'established gentry' and brought up in France. He speaks of Ireland in fact and in image, echoing Brown's allusion, as a place of imprisonment. Again an historical consciousness, particularly about land, informs the writing. Because his eldest brother had inherited the family estates in Ireland, 'as the estates of the nobles

45 Ibid., f. 54.   46 Ibid., f. 53.

belong according to the law of England to the eldest alone,' he went to sea as an officer in the French navy. On the death of the brother in Ireland, who had named him executor of his estate, Darcy returned there – probably in the 1740s – to wind up his brother's affairs. He stayed some years in Ireland, experiencing, as he puts it, 'several persecutions in connection with his religion and the laws of the country.' He comes then to the crux of his plea,

> In God's name, Monseigneur, if we Irish Catholics are included [in the expulsion] where can we direct our steps? Prison cells await us in our unfortunate native land where we shall be all the more suspected for having come from France which threatens them with such a well deserved vengeance; if we go to neutral countries at the age of your petitioner, we shall lack acquaintances, knowledge of the language, and even our meagre resources which we shall have to leave behind.[47]

The desperation in this image of the homeless Irish is balanced by the bitter realisation that it is English law which puts Darcy in this predicament. The 1756 expulsion order presents him with two options: either he returns to the contradiction of being a prisoner in his own country, or he pleads to remain free – an Irishman without a country.

As with other applications cited above, Darcy's thought and feelings are shaped by that distressed historical awareness that Ireland is no place for the majority of its people. As the Irish Jacobite Plunkett had written earlier, those who govern there have over the centuries come to 'roul in the same sphear of Inclination and Interest' as the English.[48] For the Irish in Bordeaux the present is the product of a painful past. They see history as having divided Irish people into colonisers and colonised, a history of division determined, not by their own agency, but that of another nation. France provided the opportunity to escape from if not to recover from that history. Joseph Rivers for example wanted to put it behind him. Brown suspects it will continue unabated. The price was estrangement from their native land.

Nationalism and exile

The point acquires fresh pathos and irony when in 1793 during the French Revolution Joseph Rivers has again to plead, this time to the people's representatives, the 'bonnets rouges', on suspicion of being an enemy of the revolution.[49] Rivers' argument is of particular significance. He writes to them, 'I am com-

47 Ibid., 1074, f. 70. 48 Nicholas Plunkett, 'The Improvement of Ireland' (n.d.) Bodleian Library, Oxford, MS Carte 229, f. 1-2. See also Patrick Kelly, 'Nationalism and the contemporary historians of the Jacobite war in Ireland', *Nations and Nationalisms*, pp 89-102. 49 Over 60 Irish were held in prison in Bordeaux in 1793, though Rivers may not have been one of these.

mitted in every way to France, where I took refuge from Ireland nearly 56 years ago, "pour cause de la liberté".[50] His case was accepted. For Rivers, as for the other supplicants, liberty exists only outside Ireland and away from the English.

The voice of the Irish in Bordeaux is markedly different from both the protesting voice of the Molyneux tradition and of the Catholics within Ireland in the 1750s. Lucas, like Swift before him and Grattan later, makes much of the English administration's perfidy, but the rhetoric and abuse of this tradition argues and harries for a future, for a political order that is envisaged as achievable. They speak as if history can be adjusted to some proper agreed vision, and one that would put the Irish Protestant interest on equal terms with that in England. The Bordeaux Irish Catholics had no such hopes. Theirs is a different language, and it differs also from what Dublin Catholics were saying, caught up as they were in a much narrower, even petty argument about the principle of whether to make a declaration of loyalty to the English king. Divisions among them were all too clear in the anti-union riot in Dublin in 1759: while some Catholics protested outside parliament against union with England, the clergy condemned them from the pulpit, and others presented an address of loyalty to the lord lieutenant.[51] Exile and the expulsion order had focused the Bordeaux Catholic Irish on the ambiguity of their predicament. And yet that ambiguity – native Irish excluded from Ireland – was at the core of Catholic protest within Ireland, only they did not enunciate it with the same historical clarity.

The predicament of the Irish in Bordeaux prompted them to look, not towards future change or to constitutional issues, but towards the past, to persecution and land confiscation. They claimed to be escapees from a history of persecution. One after the other the Irish *placets* set the present in terms of the past. The past explains the present. There is no future to speak of. This feature becomes a trait in much twentieth century postcolonial writing.[52] The point may be that writers who are the colonised and who express themselves from within the colonial framework know or subconsciously accept that the institutions of that framework deny them any role in the historical process. They must either conform to colonial history or be excluded, acquiesce in the coloniser's nationalism, which means protesting only in terms of that discourse, or be silent. This is exemplified in Ireland by a document like the address of the Catholics of Waterford to the lord lieutenant during the Seven Years' War. They identified themselves with Britain against France. They subsumed both their religion and their national ties into a statement of loyalty to the king 'at this critical time.'

---

50 Arch. dép., MSS 13, L 29.   51 See Chapter Four above; also Sean Murphy, 'The Dublin Anti-Union Riot of 1759' in *Parliament, Politics and People*, ed. Gerard O'Brien (Dublin, 1989), pp 57-8 and Bartlett, *The Fall and Rise of the Irish Nation*, pp 60-3.   52 See for example in Zimbabwean fiction novels by Stanlake Samkange and Charles Mungoshi.

They speak of 'the full enjoyment of our liberty, trade and properties, which we have been blessed with under his Majesty's most mild and generous government', they express their 'deepest sense of gratitude', they acknowledge 'the wisdom and justice of your Grace's administration.'[53] That way they express their assimilation into their colonisers' ideology. Within the colonial context they thus have no national identity and reflect no historical awareness. The Catholics in Bordeaux on the other hand, speaking from outside the colonial context, refuse the coloniser's ideology and place themselves in an historical narrative which their countrymen in Waterford had also experienced but chose not to speak about.

For the Irish in Bordeaux national identity comes from history, especially a history of exclusion. What stands out in their writing is a history of denials, refusals, hiding, escape. This consciousness has decidedly different emphases and projections to those of Catholics in Ireland and to that of Protestant writers in the wake of Molyneux. For Irish Protestants an appeal to history is an argument to be included, to be accepted within an Anglo-Irish framework. When Lucas says to his Dublin readers, 'I must lay before you a short History of the Foundation, and some Account of the Constitution of the City,' he means to show, as he says later, how 'this Nation was first brought into the Model of the British Government'.[54] Writers like Charles O'Conor did not accept that, nor did they see their way to being as critical as the Catholics in Bordeaux. Their circumstances were quite different. Irish Catholics were in Bordeaux, apart from the prosperity it offered, because they had been ideologically excluded: they had little future in Ireland. Therefore they had physically distanced themselves from the pressures of colonial nationalism, and now defined themselves in terms of its infringements on them as Irish nationals. From the perspective of Bordeaux they could see not just what they lacked in Ireland, but what life offered when not constricted by colonialism.

When Lecky remarked that 'the real history of the Irish Catholics during the first half of the eighteenth century' is to be traced in the countries of Europe, he was marvelling at the 'energy and ability of Ireland', of soldiers, of diplomats, of scholars, put to the service of other nations.[55] This is true of the Irish in Bordeaux, but what is much more significant in the light of this chapter, and which Lecky is silent on, is that they give voice to a particular kind of Irish protest, fuelled not by visions or myths, but grounded in memories of persecution, of being denied one kind of nationalism and history for the sake of another.

Each *placet* cites a personal history. The cumulative effect of these narratives is the story of a group of Irish exiles which is both national and nationalist. If

---

53 *London Chronicle*, 18 December 1759, p. 583.   54 Charles Lucas, *An Apology for the Civil Rights and Liberties of the Commons and the Citizens of Dublin* (Dublin, 1744), pp 9, 11.   55 William H.E. Lecky, *A History of Ireland in the Eighteenth Century*, 5 vols (London, 1892), i, 250, 252.

these exiles had remained in Ireland they would probably have had to suppress these perceptions of their Irish nationality. The crisis of 1756 in Bordeaux brings to light what amounts to a collective statement of national consciousness which had fallen mute within Ireland itself.

CHAPTER SIX

Competing histories:
Charles O'Conor's *Dissertations* (1753)

COMPETING HISTORIOGRAPHIES

Irish writing in English in the eighteenth century differs from much other post-colonial writing around the world in that so much of its energy went into the writing of history. Apart from Swift and Parnell as well as dramatists like Farquhar, Goldsmith and Sheridan, little of the resistance expresses itself in poetry, plays or novels.[1] The writings of Molyneux, Lucas, O'Conor, Grattan, Curran, Burke and several others are sustained by a strong historical conscious-ness. History was the battleground because it was there that Ireland found itself defined. Historical narratives were one of the most influential strategies in the contest for Ireland. English historians like Clarendon and Carte presented a quite different account of the English in Ireland to that found in Lynch, Keating or Mac Cruitín. By the mid eighteenth century the opposing views of the English as either a civilising presence or agents of oppression were clearly drawn. Charles O'Conor's work, particularly his *Dissertations on the Ancient History of Ireland*,[2] approaches these differences in a spirit of scholarship and reconciliation. He attempts to play down nationalist historiography in the belief that traditional hostilities and prejudices are no foundation for the future of a fast changing Ireland.

It is worth recalling the climate of opposing historiographies when O'Conor began to write. The debate prior to the *Dissertations* had dwelt on two issues: first, the antiquity of Irish historical materials, and second, the events of 1641 with some attention to 1689-90. Both had clear ideological significance. As to the first,

---

1 Cf. Carpenter, *Verse in English from Eighteenth-Century Ireland*, p. 25: with the exception of Swift and a few others 'there is a generalised support for England and things English behind much of the verse in this anthology'.

if Irish claims to the antiquity of Irish historical materials were valid then Ireland could argue, as O'Conor did, for a native culture that was equal in dignity to and separate from that of England or any other country in Europe. The nationalist overtones of such an argument challenged England's insistence that Ireland was culturally subservient and raised questions about the cultural and intellectual orientation of eighteenth-century Dublin to London, an orientation reflected in Dublin's architecture, newspapers, theatres and book-trade. Arguments about Ireland's antiquities, while seeming unrelated to political issues such as the Lucas affair, the money bill disputes of the 1750s and 1770s, or Ireland's legislative powers *vis-à-vis* Westminster, went to the heart of the Anglo-Irish relationship by posing questions about Ireland's history, its origins, its self-image, its self-esteem, its cultural identity.

The second topic of heated historical debate concerned the events of 1641 and 1689-90. Protestants like Edward Synge argued, for example, that the so-called rebellion by Irish Catholics in 1641 occurred because 'the Actors ... were Men greatly devoted to the Romish Superstition'.[3] The English were convinced that Irish Catholics had callously murdered Protestants, a view graphically captured in Defoe's *Memoirs of a Cavalier*. When Charles I decided to bring Irish regiments to his assistance in the civil war, the Cavalier reflects,

> This cast, as we thought an *Odium* upon our whole Nation, being some of those very Wretches who had dipt their Hands in the innocent Blood of the Protestants, and with unheard of Butcheries, had massacred so many Thousands of *English* in cold Blood.[4]

Catholic historians said the Irish were provoked by Protestant oppression, and accused English commentators like Sir John Temple of writing as many lies as lines 'in his Romantic Legend of the Irish Rebellion, on purpose to blacken the People'.[5] Temple's *The Irish Rebellion* had convinced generations of Protestants that the events of 1641 were prompted by the ingrained hostility of Catholics towards Protestants, and that Catholics were encouraged in this by Rome.[6] There was a need therefore for government to consolidate a political system in Ireland

---

2 *Dissertations on the Ancient History of Ireland: Wherein an Account is given of the Origine, Government, Letters, Sciences, Religion, Manners and Customs, of the Ancient Inhabitants*, Dublin: James Hoey, for the editor Michael Reilly, 1753. The first edition was published by subscription; there were about 400 subscribers: Charles O'Conor, S.J., *The Early Life of Charles O'Conor (1710-1791) of Belanagare and the Beginning of the Catholic Revival in Ireland in the Eighteenth Century*, 1930, typescript, National Library of Ireland, p. 49. 3 Edward Synge, *A Sermon Preached at Christ-Church, Dublin, on Saturday 23rd October, 1731 Being the Anniversary of the Irish Rebellion* (Dublin, 1731), p. 10. 4 Defoe, *Memoirs of a Cavalier* (1720; Oxford, 1978), p. 192. 5 Hugh O'Reily, *The Impartial History of Ireland* (London, 1749), p. vii; this Jacobite work first appeared under the title, *Ireland's case briefly stated*. 6 Sir John Temple, *The Irish Rebellion* (Dublin, 1646); for the continuing suspicions of Protestants towards Catholics during the eighteenth century in Ireland on this matter see Thomas Bartlett, 'A New History of Ireland', *Past and Present* 116 (August, 1987), 214-15.

which would protect Protestant interests and proscribe Catholics from any position of power or influence. The debate continued into O'Conor's day, notably between his Catholic friend and historian John Curry and the Protestant antiquarian Walter Harris and later Thomas Leland, Professor of History in Trinity College.[7]

These two topics were fundamental to any history of Ireland written in the eighteenth century. Most early English historians had imaged the Irish as barbaric and without any history to speak of. In the early seventeenth century Keating provided the opposing argument in a history of the first inhabitants of Ireland, of their kings, laws and customs.[8] His account concluded with the arrival of Henry II in 1171. Implicitly Ireland's history ends for Keating with the invasion by the English, regarded as a benefit by certain English Protestant writers and a catastrophe by most Irish Catholic writers. Debates about the English invasion and about the 1641 rebellion are part of a much larger controversy about how and why Ireland had lost its ties with its antiquities. The recurring answer in the seventeenth century, found also in O'Conor, is that over the centuries the English had destroyed them by a political and cultural system which was driven by Protestant anxieties about Roman Catholics. The opposing historiographies were built on antagonistic ideologies which by their nature were never objective, always partisan.

O'Conor was singularly equipped to move confidently and critically between the two major cultures of eighteenth-century Ireland. The *Dissertations* was written out of a Catholic Gaelic ethos far removed from Dublin and the intellectual and political currents that shaped Protestant and particularly patriot perceptions of Ireland so influenced by Molyneux and Swift. O'Conor was born in Co. Sligo of Catholic Gaelic aristocratic stock going back to the chiefs of Connaught. After the arrival of the Anglo-Normans 'the O'Conors, with varying success, maintained a semi-regal sway in the western province'.[9] The family had experienced confiscations and subsequent penury. Both his parents' families had Jacobite ties: his grandfather's brother, Owen O'Conor,[10] had been governor of Athlone under James II, and his mother's family, the O'Rourkes, had been honoured in France by James III. O'Conor became fluent in Irish at an early age and

---

7 John Curry (*c.*1702-80), a Dublin physician, had written *A Brief Account from the Most Authentic Protestant Writers ... of the Irish Rebellion 1641*, London, 1747; Walter Harris (1686-1761) replied with *Fiction Unmasked: or, An Answer to a Dialogue Lately Published by a Popish Physician ... wherein the Causes of the Irish Rebellion ... in 1641 are Laid Thick upon the Protestants ...*, Dublin, 1752; Curry continued the debate in *Historical Memoirs of the Irish Rebellion in the Year 1641*, London, 1758. In 1773 Curry published a reply to Leland's version of the 1641 Rebellion in *Remarks on certain passages in Dr Leland's History of Ireland*. 8 Geoffrey Keating, educated in Bordeaux, wrote his history *Foras Feasa ar Éirinn* in about 1633; it circulated in manuscript before being translated from Irish into English early in the eighteenth century: cf. Diarmaid Ó Catháin, 'Dermot O'Connor, Translator of Keating', *Eighteenth-Century Ireland* 2 (1987), 67-87. 9 'Correspondence and MSS of Charles O'Conor', *Historical Manuscripts Commission: Reports*, VIII, i (1881), p. 441. 10 Owen O'Conor (d. 1692); Charles' father was Denis O'Conor (1674-1750).

developed a keen interest in Irish music. When he was fourteen, the family moved to the restored property of Belanagare in Co. Roscommon, where Charles continued his education before going to Dublin in 1727. For his early schooling he sometimes attended local hedge schools and was at times taught privately at home.[11] His interest in Irish literature was first evident in his compilation *Ogygian Tales; Or, A Curious Collection of Irish Fables, Allegories and Histories*, the very title of which points to an indebtedness to the spirit of O'Flaherty's historical work in Irish, *Ogygia, or a Chronological Account of Irish Events* (1684).[12] O'Conor also collected Irish books and manuscripts, and by 1756 he had acquired nine ancient vellum folios, eighteen manuscripts and had transcribed two volumes of extracts from ancient Irish sources.[13] His political concerns are evident in writings like *The Case of the Roman-Catholics of Ireland*, and in his work for the Catholic Committee which he helped found with Curry to campaign for Catholic relief.[14] In the 1750s and 1760s O'Conor and Curry were the two voices to bear the burden of representing the Catholic cause in what Curry called a 'much Slandered, and Injured Country'.[15]

O'Conor's move from the Catholic and Gaelic cultural context of Sligo and Roscommon to Dublin meant that he moved out of the culture for which he speaks and which he mediates to his English readers in the *Dissertations* and into the cultural ambit of the 'other' or contesting culture. He brings to this Anglo-Irish world a knowledge of Irish culture which many in Dublin were either alienated from or simply ignorant of. If the 'Pale' had ceased to exist as a boundary between English power and the native Irish, such a division remained in the socio-cultural mind of Protestant Ireland. O'Conor was one of the first Catholic intellectuals to cross the line and to encourage dialogue.

In O'Conor's case, as in Keating before him, the change of context also helped to clarify points of resistance in his thinking. As will be seen, a major strategy in the *Dissertations* is to resist certain myths about the Irish created by English historians, and implicitly to lay to rest suspicions and prejudices. But O'Conor differs from his precursors, particularly Keating, in that the tactics of his resistance are not simply to restate the essentialist view of Irish culture, but rather to advocate that the essentialist view should accommodate to the processes of history. His goal is the assimilation of ancient Irish virtues into the practices of eighteenth-century Irish institutions and manners. He is the first to advocate hybridity over essentialism, to ask not for the privileging of Irish nationalist perspectives but mutual respect and dialogue.

11 Charles O'Conor, S.J., *The Early Life of Charles O'Conor*, pp 3-9. 12 O'Conor later wrote a defence of O'Flaherty's *Ogygia* in *The Ogygia Vindicated* (Dublin, 1775). 13 'Charles O'Conor', *DNB* (1908), xiv, 856. His uncle, Bishop O'Rourke, had brought back from the continent 'an original autograph volume' of the 'Annals' compiled in the seventeenth century by the 'Four Masters' *(Historical Manuscripts Commission: Reports*, VIII, i, p. 442). 14 *The Case of the Roman-Catholics of Ireland. Wherein the Principles and Conduct of that Party are fully Explained and Vindicated*, Dublin, 1755. 15 Curry to Burke, 8 June 1765, *Correspondence of Burke*, i, 202.

O'Conor's background – Catholic, Jacobite, educated, rural upper class – meant he entered the debates about Ireland's history and the English presence in Ireland from a position quite different from that of Protestant writers. His roots were in the west of Ireland. He was well aware of the implications, particularly the prejudices he would meet. A notice on his death remarked that he was a scholar with 'amiable and engaging qualities' but was debarred from any benefit 'such qualities and circumstances could procure, by being a Roman Catholick'.[16] The point is evidenced by his advice to his eldest son in 1751,

> You live now in a busy, elbowing scene; if you have any sagacity, you will make reflections on every incident and reap instruction and, whatever it be, strive to adapt it to the rank you are to fill hereafter: that of a Roman Catholic in a Protestant country, that of one in a low way, obnoxious to the laws.[17]

This awareness underlies the contentious spirit in much of O'Conor's writing noticeable in early pieces such as *Two Public Letters in Reply to Brooke's Farmer* and *A Counter-Appeal against the Appeal of Sir Richard Cox* (1749). A friend wrote to him from Dublin, 'Your inflammatory *Counter-Appeal* has been roared about the streets.'[18] In 1753, the year of the *Dissertations*, he also produced a new edition of the earl of Castlehaven's *Memoirs*, a work critical of Protestant perceptions of the Catholics in the 1641 rebellion.[19]

The Dissertations

What is soon clear in the *Dissertations* is O'Conor's problem of audience. He was the first Catholic writer of note to address both Catholic and Protestant, Irish and English readers. Accordingly he attempts to rein in his combative and 'inflammatory' urges by a spirit of reconciliation and cautious enquiry. There is an air of hesitancy about the work due in part to his consciousness of the mixed readership and in part to his own doubts about the pertinence of his findings.[20] The structure also reflects a deliberate caution – a set of twelve essays rather than a continuous narrative. The essays range over secular and cultural, not religious issues. The expression shows signs of deliberate care, an acknowledgement of the difficulties of writing in a way that made the same sense to readers of notably diverse cultural ideologies. Not surprisingly some of his most serious statements are open to different readings:

16 *Gentleman's Magazine* 61 (August 1791), 776. 17 *Letters of Charles O'Conor*, 17 November 1751, i, 7. 18 Ibid., 28 October 1749, i, 5, n. 3. 19 *The Earl of Castlehaven's Review; or His Memoirs of His Engagement and Carriage in the Irish Wars* (1680); the book had not been republished since 1684. 20 Advertisement by the editor, Michael Reilly, *Dissertations* [n.p.]; Reilly says O'Conor had put the work into its final form in 1748. For an early attempt to publish the essays one by one, see Charles O'Conor, S.J., *Early Life of Charles O'Conor*, p. 30. A new edition published in 1761 included additional materials.

> The History of the old Inhabitants of this Country is so important, and, at the same Time, so edifying to a free People, that few Subjects merit more their Attention, and hardly any can afford more Political Instruction.[21]

Phrases like 'a free People' and 'Political Instruction' juxtaposed to 'important' and 'edifying' have enigmatic overtones. Catholics could read these as sympathetic to change in Ireland's political institutions, Protestants might wonder why a 'free People', which is how they saw themselves, needed 'Political Instruction'.

The fragmentary structure of the *Dissertations*, perhaps its most surprising feature, is a larger manifestation of the same problems. The essays follow no chronological plan: Section IX for example considers the earliest inhabitants before the arrival of the 'Scots' from Spain, a topic which predates Sections I and II, and then follows it in Section XI with 'An Account of the Monarchy and Royal Line of North Britain' – the ancestors of 'the present Royal Family'[22] – which is a critique of the history of the kings of Scotland from 330BC to the reduction of the Picts in the ninth century. This essay is an attack on 'the voluminous Dreams' of Scottish and English historians of this period.[23] The *Dissertations* concludes with a skimpy account of Irish families who survived the dissolution of the Irish monarchy under Roderic in 1175. If there is an underlying theme to the essays it is not easily discernible.

The absence of narrative continuity presents a problem of how to read the *Dissertations*. One approach would be to read it as a pre-narrative, a body of source material which gives subsequent scholars the basis for a factual and trustworthy narrative. O'Conor stresses the need for scholarship. He gives documentary evidence, he faces up to problems of chronology. This is an unpolemical attempt to scrutinise the evidence of Irish history and thus respond to the repeated charge from England that Ireland had no sources to speak of. But there is no attempt to present the material as a narrative.

Using the term 'Scots' to indicate 'the ancient Inhabitants of Ireland, or the Milesian Race',[24] the twelve essays discuss their Spanish origins, compare accounts of them by Sir Isaac Newton and classical authors with Irish sources, analyse their language, the monarchical system of government and their pre-Christian beliefs and religious practices. After considering their manners, customs and laws prior to the arrival of St Patrick, O'Conor discusses Ireland's transition from a pagan to a Christian society. In each essay there is an air of contention, an awareness that there is a basic problem of facts when writing about Irish history. The essays contribute to an ongoing argument among historians – ancient and modern, Irish and English – about the reliability of Irish sources. O'Conor's approach is to probe, not to win arguments. His scholarship is

21 *Dissertations*, p. v.   22 Ibid., p. 195.   23 Ibid., p. 204.   24 Advertisement by the Editor, ibid., p.[ii].

informed by a wealth of reading, critical of previous scholars, always insisting that those historians who have a command of the Irish language are in a better position to comment than those who do not. Such a stance indicates his seriousness and his desire for authenticity. Yet the nationalist in him is guided by the scholar who keeps demanding that evidence for socio-cultural beliefs and practices be incontrovertible. Ireland's identity lies he argues in its language, art, education, laws and social structures. These rather than chronology or political conflict are the significant features of Irish history.

Of the twelve essays the three longest ones demonstrate O'Conor's priorities. They are Section IV on Ireland's language and letters, Section VIII on manners, customs, commerce and laws, and Section XI on the monarchs of North Britain. The Irish language highlighted in Section IV has a prominent and recurring place of respect throughout the *Dissertations*. It is the primary testament of Irish culture, 'a Monument of Antiquity, many Ages older than the most ancient Inscriptions; and the more valuable, as it is, to this Day, not more beautiful, than intelligible'.[25] Mindful of how concise, expressive and copious the Irish language is O'Conor finds English deficient by comparison.[26] The ancient Irish were great respecters of learning, especially of history and poetry, and the survival of records of these arts through times of wars and invasions, notably by the English, is testimony of the culture's resilience.

Section VIII on manners also highlights poetry among the arts, as well as education. The ancient Irish differed from most European nations in that they did not develop a culture of wealth, of 'sumptuous Equipages and brilliant Outsides'.[27] Their physical isolation from Europe was a protection against frequent invasion, not least by the Romans, 'who first imported Luxury and false Refinements into Europe'.[28] Ireland provided a simplicity of dress and architecture, a 'great Plenty of the Necessaries of Life to its meanest Inhabitants'.[29] The political institutions, the records of civil law and jurisprudence preserved from the fourth century BC, the emphasis on the arts all testify to a learned nation who in the Dark Ages became 'the prime Seat of Learning to all Christendom'.[30] O'Conor checks the urge to write a panegyric on the ancient Irish. He admits that there were times of violence and popular unrest in which they lost sight of the qualities he admires. Those violent times however were not as damaging as the policy of the English who 'took all possible Care to destroy our old Writings' because 'such Works put the Natives too often in Mind of the Laws, Customs and Power of their Ancestors'.[31]

The third essay of note argues that the succession of English monarchs going back from George II to James I, who was also James VI of Scotland, can be traced to the sixth century when Irish monarchical ancestors settled in Scotland.

25 *Dissertations*, p. 38. 26 Ibid., pp 46-7. 27 Ibid., p. 122. 28 Ibid., p. 124. 29 Ibid., p. 140. 30 Ibid., p. 147. 31 Ibid., p. 160.

This contentious argument, which derives from Keating and O'Flaherty, attempts to appropriate the Hanoverians as well as the Stuarts into the Irish monarchical tradition, 'indisputably the most antient in the World'.[32] The point not only gives the Irish reason to be proud of their ancestry but helps conciliate the Hanoverian present with the Celtic past. O'Conor feels so strongly about this that he insists that 'if the Facts in this short Narrative are not indisputably authentic then the whole Irish History is all Romance'.[33] He is reacting against what he calls 'silly and dishonourable Fables' put about by earlier historians.[34]

This final essay on the fate of Milesian families since the English invasion, far from being a conclusion to the rest, is the weakest because by its own admission the evidence is so scarce. The account is punctuated by remarks like, 'I can say but little, for Want of proper Information.'[35] The essay collapses in much the same way as the ancient families had collapsed after the invasion. The final irony is that so little is known of these families 'descended from the most humane and knowing Nation of the old Celts'.[36]

Recovering Ireland

The *Dissertations* is a task of recovery. Over the centuries the English had effectively stifled if not destroyed a large part of Irish culture and then argued that there was no Irish culture to speak of. For instance, Sir William Temple had said that less was known about the ancient history of Ireland than of any country in Europe: 'We know nothing certain of the Affairs or Revolutions of that Island, till the English began their Conquests there.'[37] Dr Johnson, recalling that same observation, encouraged O'Conor to further research;[38] others used it as a justification to berate and denigrate the Irish. The prevailing attitude of colonial historians was, as Dermot O'Connor says, 'that there are no real Antiquities of Ireland, that their Records are not genuine'.[39] Charles O'Conor's reply was that Ireland's culture in all its manifestations gave the Irish substantial cause for pride. He encourages them to take their culture more seriously. To this he adds the

---

32 Ibid., p.183; O'Conor is enlarging the implications of O'Flaherty's remark that Ireland, 'would not submit to be governed by any prince save those decended from the line of her ancient kings' (O'Flaherty, *Ogygia, or a Chronological Account of Irish Events* (1684; trans. James Hely, 2 vols, Dublin, 1793, i, xiv). The argument was dismissed by James Macpherson whom O'Conor replied to in an essay attached to a subsequent edition of the *Dissertations* (1766): cf. Clare O'Halloran, 'Irish Re-creations of the Gaelic Past: the Challenge of Macpherson's Ossian', *Past and Present* 124 (Aug. 1989), 74-8. Later O'Conor noted the objections of Lloyd, Stillingfleet and Mackenzie: *The Ogygia Vindicated*, ed. Charles O'Conor (Dublin, 1775), p. v. 33 *Dissertations*, pp 203-4. 34 Ibid., p. 212. 35 Ibid., p. 230. 36 Ibid., p. v. 37 Wiliam Temple, *An Introduction to the History of England* (London, 1699), p .32. 38 Johnson to O'Conor, Boswell, *Life of Johnson*, pp 227-8. 39 Preface to Keating, *General History of Ireland* (London, 1723), p. iii; although this translation of Keating went through at least five editions by 1738, it was criticised by many, including O'Conor, as frequently inaccurate: cf. Diarmaid Ó Catháin, 'Dermot O'Connor, Translator of Keating', *Eighteenth-Century Ireland* 2 (1987), 67-87; it is presumed that O'Conor read Keating in the original Irish.

innovative point that Ireland's recovered culture provides a considerable poten-
tial to heal Protestant prejudices against the 'mere Irish'. The *Dissertations* were
written out of a need to set the record straight and out of impatience with histories from across the Irish sea. Like many an Irish historian before him he was
weary of abuse. Nearly a hundred years earlier Lynch expressed similar irritation
with Giraldus' slander about the Irish: he is 'that poisoned spring whence all
other writers, who hate Ireland, imbibe their envenomed calumnies'.[40] O'Conor's
pride in his culture thus prompts seemingly contradictory responses – cautious
scrutiny from the scholar in him, anger from the nationalist at foreign abuse, as
well as a conciliatory vision of the future.

As the coloniser had destroyed the culture so the colonised would reappro-
priate it, and O'Conor makes the point that only those familiar with the language are in a position to do this. Recovery was made easier by a new wave of
interest in antiquities in mid eighteenth-century Ireland. As a scholar O'Conor
knew that genuine records were coming to light in his day and were being collected and assessed. His references and notes reflect his scrupulous reading of
printed sources from both sides of the debate in English and Irish as well as
respect for manuscript sources. No matter how sympathetic scholars might be to
Ireland they must be able to read these in the original. In later years he singled
out two historians, an Englishman Ferdinando Warner and the Abbé James
MacGeoghegan in France, as the only two who had recently attempted a general
history of Ireland;[41] but both lacked 'proper materials' and 'skill in our language
for such an undertaking'.[42] O'Conor, wary of 'mythological Stories',[43] is sceptical
of what is unproven and unwilling to comment where he can find no evidence:
'We do not intend in these short Discourses, to make the Panegyric of Ireland at
the Expence of Truth.'[44] The recovery had to be authentic.

O'Conor's cautious scholarship is a riposte to the several dismissive accounts
by Giraldus through to Spenser, Clarendon and Ware. He wants to lift the
debates from politics and national prejudice onto a level of serious and discrim-
inating study. He knew that many of his educated Irish readers were ignorant of

40 John Lynch, *Cambrensis Eversus*, trans. Matthew Kelly, 3 vols (Dublin, 1848-52), i, 97. 41
Ferdinando Warner (1703-68), ordained in the Church of England, wrote on theology and history;
his works included the *Ecclesiastical History of the Eighteenth Century* (vol. i, 1756; vol. ii, 1757), *History
of the Rebellion and Civil War in Ireland (1767)* and *The History of Ireland; from the Earliest Authentic
Accounts to the Year 1771*, 2 vols (Dublin, 1770). In this last he describes the *Dissertations* as the best
work on the early history of Ireland (p. ii) and acknowledges his own debt to O'Conor (pp xx-xxi).
James MacGeoghegan (1702-64), was born in Westmeath and educated and ordained in France; his
Histoire de l'Irlande, ancienne et moderne was published in Paris (vol. i, 1758, vol. ii, 1762 and vol. iii,
1763). O'Conor offered to help MacGeoghegan with his *Histoire de l'Irlande* and made extensive
annotations in his own copy which is in the Library of the Royal Irish Academy, Dublin: Vincent
Geoghegan, 'A Jacobite History: the Abbé MacGeoghegan's *History of Ireland*', *Eighteenth-Century
Ireland* 6 (1991), 41-2. 42 O'Conor, Preface, *Ogygia Vindicated*, p. xxi. MacGeoghegan was able to
consult only one manuscript source, the 'Book of Lecan' which was at the Irish College in Paris
(*DNB* (1908), xii, 531). 43 *Dissertations*, p. 162. 44 Ibid., p. 150.

their own history: it is a shame that those 'who take great Pains to know as much as possible of the History of every other Nation, should be utter Strangers to their own'.[45] Accordingly he writes, he says, like 'a first Discoverer'.[46] The phrase, with its suggestions of Enlightenment scholarship, summarises his objective to be a guide in new intellectual territory, to discover new perspectives. However, many readers were not to know that in spite of O'Conor's more circumspect approach some of the perspectives he offered had already been established by Irish-speaking and Catholic predecessors, especially 'the excellent and learned Mr Roderick O'Flaherty'[47] and the nationalist Keating whose *Foras Feasa ar Éirinn*, known later as Keating's *History of Ireland*, was widely circulated in the seventeenth century.[48] The task of recovery meant not least educating Irish readers as to what their own historians had already written.

O'Conor's nationalist sympathies are rooted in his Gaelic background. Like Keating's translator, Dermot O'Connor, he believed that because Keating's *History* was not 'an infallible Record, perfectly free from Errors and Mistakes' it does not follow 'that the whole of these Accounts is nothing but Fable'.[49] O'Conor does not compromise the nationalist agenda of Keating; he tries to create a firmer platform for it by introducing a more scholarly approach. His circumspection and hesitancy, in a project so important to 'a free People', is a strength not a weakness.[50] Keating had been the major voice in establishing an Irish historiography to counteract the English. He was followed for instance by O'Flaherty, MacCruitín and Reily. Although Keating's *History* was not translated into English until 1713, and then only in a much abbreviated version,[51] it had been known to Irish scholars for many years before that. Keating starts his Preface in combative mood by criticising English historians who 'have industriously sought occasion to lessen the Reputation' of Ireland.[52] He then singles out several English writers who 'have never failed to exert their Malice against the Irish, and represent them as a base and servile People'.[53] O'Conor is less aggressive much of the time but the drive of his scholarship is to build on and refine what Keating had achieved.

Keating's *History* has the strident voice of an historian writing on behalf of his subjected people in their native language. It is combative and polemical. Keating takes a strong nationalist line and includes copious chronologies and genealogies to establish the authenticity of his claims. O'Conor, writing in English over a century later, leaves these out and tones down the rhetoric. Nevertheless the shadow of Keating is discernible throughout. For example, he echoes Keating's account of the first settlers in Ireland,[54] Ireland's support for the

---

45 Introduction, ibid., p. viii. 46 Ibid. 47 Ibid., p. 118. 48 Diarmaid Ó Catháin, 'Dermot O'Connor, Translator of Keating', *Eighteenth-Century Ireland* 2 (1987), 69. 49 Keating, Preface, *History*, p. i. 50 Introduction, *Dissertations*, p. v. 51 *Doctor Keating's History of Ireland*, trans. Dermod O'Connor (Dublin, 1713), 24 pp. 52 Keating, Preface, *History*, p. i. 53 Ibid., p. iii. 54 Keating, *History*, ch. 1; *Dissertations*, ch. 9.

Scots and Picts against the Romans and Britons,[55] the 'Courage and Liberality of the Ancient Irish',[56] their laws and customs,[57] an emphasis throughout on liberty as a fundamental value to the ancient Irish, the importance of the arts, particularly poetry, to Irish culture, and a respect for written records. As to O'Conor's criticism of the English there is little that had not already been said by Keating: he had dubbed them malicious[58] and blamed them for not understanding Irish.[59] Contrary to English 'ignorance and malice' the Irish people 'have signalised themselves in as commendable a Manner to Posterity as any People in Europe'.[60] Keating sums up English historians in an image which encapsulates the anti-English attitude for generations to come. He berates historians from Geraldus Giraldus onwards,

> whom when they write of Ireland, seem to imitate the Beetle, which, when enliv'd by the Influence of the Summer Heats, flies abroad, passes over the delightful Fields, neglectful of the sweet Blossoms, or fragrant Flowers that are in its Way, till at last directed by its sordid Inclination, it settles itself upon some nauseous Excrement.[61]

Keating established a stance and a tone which shadowed Irish historiography through until the *Dissertations*. The battles Keating had fought had continued in various forms well into the eighteenth century, reaching one of their most heated points in the encounter between Sir Richard Cox of Cork, a former chief justice, and the Irish historian Hugh MacCruitín early in the eighteenth century.[62] The *Dissertations* comes some decades after this and needs to be read in the light of it because it makes O'Conor's openness all the more remarkable and his passages of nationalist resistance all the more understandable.

Cox had written his anti-Irish history, *Hibernia Anglicana*, in the late 1680s when Jacobite forces were in control in Dublin.[63] He explains that this history will be 'very useful to the People of England, and the Refugees of Ireland, especially at this Juncture, when that Kingdom is to be reconquered'.[64] The tone is uncompromisingly anti-Irish and anti-Catholic; Protestants have no reason to trust or 'live neighbourly' with the Irish;[65] the bulk of the Irish must be made 'serviceable to the Government', and, alluding to the uprising of 1641, must be 'severely corrected for their past Enormities, and afterwards strictly kept in Obedience'.[66] Turning to Ireland's history Cox sees only barbarism and blood-

55 Keating, *History*, ch.4; *Dissertations*, ch. 11. 56 Keating, *History*, title page; *Dissertations*, pp 68-72, 81. 57 Keating, *History*, ch. 5; *Dissertations*, ch. 8 *et passim*. 58 Keating, Preface, *History*, p. iii. 59 Ibid., p. xi. 60 Ibid., p. xxi; cf. *Dissertations*, p. 4. 61 Keating, Preface, *History*, p. i. 62 Sir Richard Cox (1650-1733), assistant to King William's secretary, drafted the royal Declaration of Finglas after the battle of the Boyne (1690) and became chief justice; Hugh MacCruitín (*c.*1680-1755), from Clare, poet, historian, grammarian and lexicographer. 63 *Hibernia Anglicana; or, the History of Ireland from the Conquest thereof by the English to the Present Time* (pt i, 1689; pt ii, 1690). 64 *Hibernia Anglicana*, p. b. 65 Ibid., p. d. 66 Ibid.

shed. Furthermore the ancient Irish had few riches apart from their cattle, 'and those none of the best'.[67] Their religion was no more than 'Ignorant Superstition' and their customs 'evil'.[68] His conclusion, since echoed by many a British colonial official, was that 'the Irish have as much reason to thank God and the English, for a more Civil and Regular Government exercised over them'.[69] Cox's authoritarian attitude is summed up in his admiration for Elizabeth's declaration on Ireland that 'she will subdue the stubborn by the Sword, but will govern the oppressed by Justice'.[70]

Cox typifies the tradition of colonial discourse towards Ireland which Keating, MacCruitín and O'Conor meant to contest. MacCruitín retaliated in *A Brief Discourse in Vindication of the Antiquity of Ireland* by presenting the ancient Irish as a people of cultural sophistication, orderliness, learning and hospitality.[71] Their art was evident in silver shields and gold helmets presented to their outstanding warriors.[72] He accepts there were periods of violence and barbarism, but the same was true of English history, for example, 'those twenty-eight Saxon Kings of the Heptarchy, part by one another killed, part by their own Subjects murder'd, besides many others depos'd, and forced to fly away for their Lives'.[73] Cruelty and bloody feuds were not peculiar to Irish history. Indeed the suffering of the English after the death of Ethelbert in 616, when they were left prey to the Irish, Scots and Danes, was 'the just Judgment of God'.[74] MacCruitín gives the same reply to Cox's presumption that the Irish were barbarous: 'the Irish Laws and Customs were no way less Civil, nor more Barbarous, through all Ages than those of the other Remote and Neighbouring Countries were.'[75] To insist otherwise is typical of the 'manifest Lies and Fictions' of foreign historians.[76] MacCruitín's advice to 'the indifferent Reader' is 'not to take any Foreign Author to be of any Credit in such Matters of Irish Antiquity, as preceded the English Conquest'.[77] The argument did not end there. MacCruitín's attempt to redress anti-Irish prejudices and to claim the alternative authority of native Irish historians is said to have so angered Cox that he had MacCruitín imprisoned.[78]

O'Conor often picks up the uncompromising nationalist spirit of MacCruitín. For example he too dismisses the 'voluminous Dreams' and 'arbitrary' accounts by foreign historians.[79] His frequent butt is Sir James Ware, a contemporary of Keating and the first major Irish Protestant antiquarian, whose works were being published in Dublin at the time.[80] Whereas MacCruitín is

67 'An Apparatus: or, Introductory Discourse to the History of Ireland', *Hibernia Anglicana*, p. g.   68 Ibid., p. l.   69 Ibid., p. f.   70 *Hibernia Anglicana*, p. 410.   71 *A Brief Discourse in Vindication of the Antiquity of Ireland* (Dublin, 1717), p. 62.   72 Ibid., pp 55, 303.   73 Ibid., p. 148.   74 Ibid., p. 149.   75 Ibid., p. 312.   76 Ibid., p. 309.   77 Ibid., p. 305.   78 Brian Ó Cuív, 'Irish Language and Literature, 1691-1845', *New History of Ireland*, iv, 394.   79 *Dissertations*, pp 204, 208.   80 *The Whole Works of Sir James Ware*, ed. Walter Harris, 3 vols (Dublin, 1739-64). James Ware (1594-1666) was born in Dublin; his father had settled in Ireland as Secretary to the Lord Deputy. He graduated from Trinity College, Dublin in 1610 and was later M.P. for the University and auditor general. Archbishop Ussher encouraged his study of Irish antiquities and in 1654 he produced *De Hibernia et Antiquitatibus eius*

seldom explicit in his attacks on Cox, O'Conor singles out Ware's 'Negligence or negative Credulity'.[81] He mocks him for following Ptolemy's account of Ireland, for giving a whole chapter to 'that Utopian Performance' and foisting it on readers as a genuine account.[82] By 1753 this kind of language was less of a surprise than in MacCruitín's day some decades earlier.

The underlying issue however remained the same – whether the ancient Irish had a history and a culture to be proud of and to retrieve, indeed whether they had a verifiable history at all. The latter question was being answered slowly by Catholic and Protestant, English and Irish collectors alike. O'Conor's efforts were complemented for example by Walter Harris who published *Hibernica, or Some Ancient Pieces relating to Ireland* in two parts in 1748 and 1750.[83] The debate moved onto a more discerning level as more materials became available. Open aggression in O'Conor is accordingly less frequent than in MacCruitín and more pervasively subtle than the occasional outbursts suggest. The tone is more frequently one of infectious pride. He presents the ancient Irish, or Scots as he terms them, as a discrete people, an independent nation, whose 'Politeness, Virtue, and Learning … distinguished the Scottish Nation from all others.'[84] The recurring images indicate a singular maturity, wealth, ease, grandeur:[85] the Irish had 'Advantages, Skill, and Sciences, superior to all other Celtic Nations'.[86] O'Conor insists that the ancient Irish were a nation equal to any other but different, for example in its architecture, its towns, its mode of government. Unlike the English the ancient Irish had regular elections at all levels of government every three or four years. The system was closer to the eighteenth-century German model where several independent principalities operated under one emperor or head, the important difference being that the Irish monarchs were elected and were 'under the Restraint of Popular Councils'.[87] Such differences flowed from the very geographical position of Ireland, its soils, its climate, all of which produced distinctive characteristics and advantages.[88] O'Conor cannot resist a moral eulogy on a society that, contrary to English views, was not built on,

> a vague and inconsistent System, such as Ware and others have represented it: We see the Design, we admire the Wisdom of it: It was calcu-

Disquisitiones. O'Conor's copy of the work, annotated in 1753, is in the National Library of Ireland, Dublin (MS 32494). 81 *Dissertations*, p. 139. 82 Ibid., p. 180; it is interesting to note the comment on Ware in the *DNB*: 'the establishment of Irish history and literature as subjects of study … in modern times is largely due to the lifelong exertions of Ware' (*DNB*, xx. 817). 83 Walter Harris (1686-1761), educated at Kilkenny school and Trinity College, was a lawyer and editor of an English edition of the Latin writings of Sir James Ware; he was granted a government pension in 1748 to enable him to continue his research (*New History of Ireland*, iv, p. lxiv); in 1755 he petitioned the Irish parliament for finance to publish a history of Ireland, but the scheme was not completed (*DNB* , ix, 26); see also for example John Keogh, *A Vindication of the Antiquities of Ireland* (Dublin, 1748). 84 Introduction, *Dissertations*, p. xxxi. 85 E.g. ibid., p. 4. 86 Ibid., p. 31. 87 Ibid., p. 73. 88 E.g. ibid., pp 3-4.

lated for the Promotion of Virtue and Continuance of Liberty, and, in virtuous Times, the People enjoyed all the Advantages of it.[89]

This admiration is the prevailing tone of the *Dissertations*. However, when
O'Conor reflects that this civilisation has left few traces in the texture of life in
eighteenth-century Ireland that tone gives way to much more critical sentiments.
In the vein of many a Gaelic poet before him, he bewails the loss of a glorious
cultural past and blames it on the English. He goes further by using the past to
contrast it with and criticise the present. The contrast is a strategy with strong
nationalist overtones.

The present and the past

He realises that praise for the ancient Irish, an emphasis throughout the
Dissertations, sits uneasily with the fact that in the eighteenth century the descendants of these people have been made subject to England and are expected to
accept her values at the expense of their own proud heritage. An important sub-
text therefore is this implicit commentary on Ireland's present inadequacies. The
spirit of learning, science, liberty, dignity which infused ancient Ireland is offered
as an example of what is missing in the present. By recreating what happened in
the past O'Conor implies and at times draws explicit attention to what is absent
in the present. Instead of benefiting from 'the continued Blessings of Liberty,
which the Inhabitants of this Isle enjoyed beyond all other People in Europe', the
Irish have become a subservient people.[90] This kind of observation prompts him
later to ask, 'Who would think that the Generality of the present Irish are the
remains of a free, learned, and polite Nation?'[91] The question is meant as a rebuke
and is part of a rhetoric of exhortation for the recreation of a national cultural
consciousness. O'Conor tries to be constructive rather than simply angry about
the dismal change, and in this respect he counteracts the pessimism prevalent in
the Gaelic literature he was so familiar with. As one critic puts it, writers in
Gaelic had lost hope in a political future,

> because in rejecting the existing political system the Gaelic poets held out
> no realistic prospect of an improvement upon their position other than a
> vague hope of a fortuitous return to a lost golden age.[92]

O'Conor suggests that the native virtues of that 'golden age' could be retrieved if
the Irish but studied them and tried to assimilate them into present socio-polit-
ical structures: 'The Study and Knowledge of this Ancient People through all the

89 Ibid., p. 81. 90 Ibid., p. 6. 91 Ibid., p.41. 92 Nicholas Canny, 'The Formation of the Irish Mind:
Religion, Politics and Gaelic Irish Literature 1580-1750', *Past and Present* 95 (May 1992), 111.

Stages of their Story, can hardly fail of being edifying to the present Times.'[93] The word 'edifying' is tantalisingly vague about how the transformation might be effected; nevertheless it indicates that O'Conor saw the *Dissertations* as mediating between the past and present – he instructs, offers moral exhortation, encourages his contemporaries, whom he presumes are largely ignorant about Irish antiquities, to think about the past in relation to present day Ireland.

O'Conor's concern is not simply retrieval of the past. He differs from the poets in that his work is not nostalgic or essentialist. He presents the past as different from the present. The past is 'edifying' in a way that the present is not. What has been called in ethnography 'the representation of otherness'[94] has the important function in O'Conor's historiography of describing to the present what it is not; its 'otherness' is its true self. The contrast is a formidable ploy which has often been used in more recent nationalist literatures, for example by Fanon.[95] But that 'otherness' has to be accommodated to the actualities of eighteenth-century Ireland, not least the presence of English institutions and cultural attitudes.

O'Conor's anti-colonialism

The implication that eighteenth-century Irish readers should resuscitate their cultural identity becomes clear if we focus on those moments when O'Conor abandons his mild and cautious tone to admit quite different feelings of resentment and bitterness against the English. It has been argued that O'Conor's conciliatory manner was part of a burgeoning interest in Gaelic culture in the mid eighteenth century, also evident in Scotland and Wales. This was thought to have 'the capacity to serve as an integrating factor for the different "British Dominions"'.[96] O'Conor and Curry 'sought to revise the Protestant view of the Irish past and not merely confront it with one in which Protestants were cast, as they were by MacGeoghegan, as alien tyrants'.[97] Parts of the *Dissertations* support such views, but the very opposite impression seems true if one looks at his outbursts against the English.

He accepts that Ireland's demise as a nation is in some measure the fault of the Irish themselves, but such lapses are insignificant in comparison with what the English have done.[98] His rhetorical outbursts against the invading English provide a strong anti-colonial undercurrent to the text. The first comes in a pas-

93 Introduction, *Dissertations*, p. xxxviii. 94 James Clifford, *The Predicament of Culture: Twentieth-Century Ethnography, Literature and Art* (London, 1988), p. 24. 95 Frantz Fanon comments that the search by African intellectuals to recover their past is directed 'by the secret hope of discovering beyond the misery of today ... some very beautiful and splendid era whose existence rehabilitates us both in regard to ourselves and in regard to others' (*The Wretched of the Earth*, p. 170). 96 Jacqueline Hill citing William Nicolson in 'Popery and Protestantism, Civil and Religious Liberty: The Disputed Lessons of Irish History, 1690-1812', *Past and Present* 118 (1988), 104. 97 Leighton, *Catholicism in a Protestant Kingdom*, p. 125. 98 *Dissertations*, p. 141; see also p. 83; for Ireland's reputation as a dull nation see Pope, *Dunciad Variorum*, I, ll. 23 and note.

sage which develops remarks from the Introduction about Henry II's invasion which 'in a few Months dissolved a Monarchy which stood out against all Shocks for more than two thousand Years'.[99] This brief outburst finds fuller expression in the long chapter on the language, letters and sciences of the ancient Irish: these survived the worst of times, in particular the presence of the English:

> That Nation attacked Ireland with the fairest Prospect that ever People had of subjecting a Neighbour Country; unfortunately for them and our Nation they neglected it: Content barely with giving our Government and Constitution the last Stroke, they cruelly gave us no other in their Place, for four hundred Years; but left the Land for a Field of Anarchy and Slaughter to the unfortunate Natives, who during that Time, made it their chief Study to torment and menace one another; as the Great Sir John Davis honestly and justly laments in his Relation of those fatal Days. Notwithstanding, I say, that the People of England have laid our Government, in this Manner, fairly prostrate, and all true Liberty in its Grave; yet they have been Eye-Witnesses that our Poetry and other Arts survived both.[100]

Careful reading shows that this is not simply an angry account of past history, of the confrontation between 'them and our Nation' in 'those fatal Days'. The narrative slips subtly from historic to primary tenses carrying the hurt of the past into the present. A remark like, 'the People of England have laid our Government ... fairly prostrate' implies that the situation continues in the present. If the English had provided 'equitable Government' instead of giving 'the last Stroke' and burning 'all the Books and Laws which this Kingdom ever produced' both they and the Irish would now be enjoying a different history.[101]

O'Conor's second outburst follows shortly afterwards where he praises the role of the bards in Ireland's resistance to the English: 'those bitter writers' exhorted their patrons to rebellion – except they called it by another name, 'nothing less than the Spirit of Liberty, and the Assertion of the Rights of their Fathers'.[102] Citing his own translation of a bardic poem, the longest quotation in the book, O'Conor gives his eighteenth-century audience a feel for the kind of protesting sentiments he admires. The bard cries out in resentment at the English:

> What! are we not the Prisoners of the Saxon Nation ... Power exchanged for Servitude, Beauty for Deformity, the Exultations of Liberty for the

---

99 Introduction, *Dissertations*, p. xxxviii. 100 Ibid., p. 59. 101 Ibid., p.161; Leighton argues, on the basis of such comments, that O'Conor thought the arrival of the English could have been a blessing to Ireland (*Catholicism in a Protestant Kingdom*, p. 123). 102 *Dissertations*, p. 63.

Pangs of Slavery, a great and brave People for a servile, desponding Race! ... In most Parts of the Kingdom, how hath every Kind of illegal and extrajudicial Proceeding taken the Pay of Law and Equity? And what must that Situation be, where only our Security ... must depend upon an intolerable Subservience to this very lawless Law? ... this late free Ireland has become metamorphosed into a second Saxony![103]

This contrast between past liberty and present servitude is picked up by O'Conor later and applied explicitly to the eighteenth century. The ancient Irish mode of government operated in a spirit of persuasion and good example, a spirit strengthened by the advent of Christianity in the fifth century,

It were to be wished that this was still the Case, without temporal Rewards to allure, Incapacities to corrupt, and Inquisitions to torture Men into the true Religion; and until this is the Case, until Government desists from the Encouragement of Apostacy, and consequently of every Kind of hypocritic Immorality, it will be Burlesque to talk of Liberty in the Sense that the wise Ancients understood it: On any other Terms, sacred Freedom is, in fact, but a mere Monopoly, and the Property only of those, who are compelled to come in.

Happy the Government now in Europe which cannot be charged with such Absurdities in Religion, or these Ecclesiastic Alternatives of Liberty and Slavery within the same Country! The Civil and Religious Constitution of Ireland was the Reverse of all this; and such a Constitution alone should bring its History (in our own unhappy Times) into Repute![104]

What the bard inveighed against remains true in 'our own unhappy Times'. The penal laws manifest the 'servitude' and 'deformity' the bard spoke of. Burke said of such 'lawless Law' that it was 'rather of the nature of a grievance than a Law'.[105] The supposed liberty of the English constitution is its very opposite in Ireland, 'a mere Monopoly': Irish history can only be brought back into repute by her own ancient constitution. There is no need for the institutional glosses of the coloniser because Ireland has its own native resources for equity and liberty.

Conflicting images

The problem was how to achieve this. O'Conor offers implicit guidelines in the contrast he draws between Henry II and St Patrick.[106] These two figures typify

103 Ibid., pp 61-2. 104 Ibid., p. 86. 105 Burke, 'Tracts relating to Popery Laws', *Writings and Speeches of Edmund Burke*, ix, 462. 106 St Patrick 'was one of the few historical figures to command the

contrasting behaviour towards Ireland. Henry is synonymous with deceit and deliberate destruction, Patrick with consideration. Henry and Pope Adrian IV, 'under the Pretext of Religion, and Reformation of Manners did not scruple to associate for the Subversion of both, in this divided Kingdom'.[107] Henry's deceit was to pretend justice while fomenting divisions.[108] The politics of Ireland were but a game to him, until he decided to invade: then 'he pulled off the mask'.[109] Patrick by contrast exemplifies how an outsider should behave. Patrick came not as a coloniser but as a missionary, 'a Briton, but a Roman by Education'.[110]

> He did not think it consistent with his Duty as a Missionary, to give his Advice, and even his Assistance, in the Reformation of our political Government: He assisted to the furthest Limit that the Genius of the Nation would permit: He went no farther ... Ireland, on his Entrance knew nothing of Servitude, or arbitrary Domination. His Business as a Politician consisted in correcting the Intemperance of Liberty ... Religion and Government must flourish under such a Guide.[111]

Patrick's contribution to politics and culture, particularly the spirit of respect and the constructive criticism he brought to Ireland, stands as an example of how to resolve the divisions emanating from Henry's invasion and more recently from the penal laws. Whereas Henry set the trend of conquest with no deference to native traditions, Patrick fostered 'the Genius of the Nation'. As a result of Patrick's influence, 'Ireland became the prime Seat of Learning to all Christendom';[112] in the wake of Henry the English suppressed the Irish, they burnt their books and rejected their laws. Patrick, far from rescuing the Irish from supposed barbarism, encouraged their best qualities; Henry and the English settlers by contrast promoted barbarism and, after four hundred years, consolidated the 'deformity' of their rule so lamented by the bards.

The implication of the contrast is that Ireland would recover something of its self-respect if the English and the Irish themselves would turn from the spirit of Henry to that of Patrick. That transformation is the key to recovering a national cultural identity, but as the *Dissertations* so often suggests, that would require a critical knowledge of Irish history: not the history written by English sympathisers, but the history of pre-invasion Ireland written by Irish historians versed in the Irish language. O'Conor is asking for a socio-cultural history, not a political history. Political structures flow from the customs, social values, artistic achievements of the society. Much of the *Dissertations* therefore is given, not to

respect of both the Catholic and Protestant religions' in the second half of the eighteenth century in Ireland (Clare O'Halloran, '"The Island of Saints and Scholars": Views of the Early Church and Sectarian Politics in Late-Eighteenth-Century Ireland', *Eighteenth-Century Ireland* v (1990), 7). 107 *Dissertations*, p. 219. 108 Ibid., p. 221. 109 Ibid., p. 223. 110 Introduction, ibid., p. xxiv. 111 Ibid., pp xxiv–xxv. 112 Ibid., p. 147.

causes and consequences of public events, not to the rule of kings or chronology, but to explaining how the society worked, its government, the virtues of its rulers, its customs, language, music, poetry, religion, its values, its commerce. This was the Ireland that had been lost, and by contrast the alternative to eighteenth-century Ireland under English rule. O'Conor argues that by insinuating the spirit of Ireland's precolonial culture into contemporary Ireland both the past and the present would be well served.

However, the argument conceals a conflict between the currents of nationalist and resistance history and O'Conor's conciliatory purposes. The tension points to a fundamental paradox in O'Conor's task. Certain aspects of the *Dissertations* are testimony to his desire to reconcile Catholic resistance historiography and the tradition of Protestant colonial historiography. But what O'Conor seems not to realise is that parts of the text work strongly against reconciliation. On the one hand he argues that a knowledge of history would bring about the wished for accommodation between Catholics and Protestants, a kind of hybridity of the two cultures. On the other hand the essays are a search for a discrete cultural identity which by its nature allows no accommodation. To present his Protestant and Catholic readers with an image of the Irish as a people with a cultural heritage to be proud of is to insist on their 'otherness'. The native Irish, as the final essay shows, have a privileged place in that image. The English on the other hand are presented as responsible for the destruction of that identity and for continuing the spirit of oppression which informed that destruction.

O'Conor's cautious scholarship, far from ameliorating this perception, reminds readers, implicitly the Protestants among them, that the voice of history will vindicate him. Writing of good government in ancient Ireland and of the ability of the ancient kings Moran and Feredach 'to bring Harmony out of Misrule', he writes,

> What an Incentive to honest and worthy Conduct! What a Lesson to hesitating Principle! What a Spur to drowzy Authority … Such Characters often extend their Government beyond the Grave: They sow their Seeds of laudable Emulation in Minds yet unborn … These Examples must remind great Men of what they ought to expect, and of what they must justly dread from true History; true History, I say, whose Voice will be heard, when the Power, which may bribe or silence it, loseth all Operation.[113]

Tuathal Teachtmar, who began 'the great Work of rescuing his native Country from Thraldom', gave the example of how to rekindle the spirit of correcting gov-

113 Introduction, ibid., pp xv-xvi.

ernment's hesitancy, its 'drowzy Authority'.[114] The 'dread' of history is the moral demand it makes on succeeding generations to match its achievements and hence gives the 'spur' to act in the positive spirit of Patrick to reclaim for Ireland what the spirit of Henry continued to deny. The underlying warning seems to be that if readers turn a deaf ear to the voice of conciliation, they will eventually have to listen to the voice of history.

Contesting liberty

Further evidence of O'Conor's nationalist orientation is his argument on liberty. The concept was already well worn in debates about Ireland which is hardly surprising in an age excited by Locke and Montesquieu. However, O'Conor's treatment of liberty differs markedly from anyone else's. Liberty had become the Protean catch-word on all sides – of the 'patriots' in the Irish parliament, of Whigs at Westminster, of Irish émigrés on the continent. 'The Irish,' wrote the Abbé MacGeoghegan in France, 'are deprived of that liberty which, according even to their oppressors, should be the portion of all mankind.'[115] On the other hand liberty was the saving grace of Protestants in their arguments against the slavish religion of Rome: 'We will to the Death, preserve that Liberty, which alone can make Life valuable, and the Purity of that Religion, which will best qualify us for Immortality.'[116] Liberty was the key concept in English Whig constitutional thought as reflected for example in the law lectures of Blackstone. Locke had argued that man enters into a social contract 'the better to preserve himself, his liberty and property'.[117] Thomson wrote his poem 'Liberty' (1735) 'to trace Liberty from the first ages down to her excellent establishment in Great Britain'.[118] The goddess Liberty proclaims,

> By those three virtues be the frame sustained
> Of British freedom – independent life;
> Integrity in office; and o'er all
> Supreme, a passion for the commonweal.[119]

In Sterne's *Tristram Shandy* Uncle Toby says the preservation of liberty is England's reason for going to war:

> For what is war? what is it, Yorrick, when fought as ours has been, upon principles of *liberty*, and upon principles of *honour* – what is it, but the

114 Ibid., p. xvii. 115 MacGeoghegan, *Histoire de l'Irlande*, iii. 798, cited by Vincent Geoghegan, 'A Jacobite History: the Abbé MacGeoghegan's *History of Ireland*', *Eighteenth-Century Ireland* 6 (1991), 41. 116 Henry Brooke, Letter I, *The Farmer's Six Letters to the Protestants of Ireland* (Dublin, 1745; London, 1746), p. 5. 117 Locke, 'Of Civil Government', sect. 131, *Works of Locke*, iv, 414. 118 Thomson, 'Dedication to His Royal Highness Frederick Prince of Wales', *James Thomson Poetical Works*, ed. J. Logie Robertson (London, 1965), p. 310. 119 'Liberty', V. ll. 120-3.

getting together of quiet and harmless people, with their swords in their hands, to keep the ambitious and the turbulent within bounds?[120]

Hume described freedom of speech as the hallmark of English life:

> There is nothing more apt to surprise a Foreigner, than the extreme Liberty we enjoy in this Country, of communicating whatever we please to the Publick, and of openly censuring every Measure which is entered into by the King or his Minister.[121]

What is unusual about O'Conor's references to liberty is that, far from repeating the phraseology of British nationalist rhetoric, as Lucas had done, O'Conor subverts it by asserting that the Irish had their own tradition of liberty and had 'held their Liberties longer than any other People in Europe'.[122] But that record had been changed by the English. He remarks, rather sarcastically, 'that even the most violent Assertors of Liberty mean it only for themselves'.[123] The consequence has been endless conflict:

> The Contest between Liberty and Faction can be found in no History better illustrated than in that of Ireland. Let us take it in Review. A careful Attention on so variegated a Prospect may teach some of us a great deal of that Wisdom whose Place is taken up by more local Judgments, and political Anomalies; Sores, productive of national Phrenzies whenever they rankle in the Breasts of Governors and Legislators.[124]

The conflict leads to the absurd consequence, 'Liberty and Slavery within the same Country!'[125]

The image of rankling sores, an allusion to long-standing prejudices, is a quite different impediment to liberty from those invoked by English writers. For them liberty is a constitutional and moral issue going back to Magna Carta. It had constantly to be defended, not against prejudice, but arbitrary power and money. Bolingbroke's *Craftsman* repeatedly warned against avarice, corrupt ministers and the dangers 'which constantly attend all advances to *arbitrary Power*'.[126] Gay satirised the corrupting power of money in *The Beggar's Opera*. Pope envisaged Britain 'sunk in lucre's sordid charms';[127] Thomson's goddess of Liberty warns against 'corruption's soul-dejecting arts', in particular a 'thirst for gold'.[128] O'Conor points to none of these but to English and Protestant prejudices, to

---

120 Sterne, *The Life and Opinions of Tristram Shandy* (London, 1906), p. 445. 121 Hume, 'Of the Liberty of the Press', *Essays, Moral and Political* (Edinburgh, 1742), p. 9. 122 *Dissertations*, p. 88. 123 Ibid., p. 168. 124 Introduction, ibid., pp xxxviii–xxxix. 125 Ibid., p. 86. 126 *The Craftsman* no. 430 (28 September 1734) in *Lord Bolingbroke: Contributions to the 'Craftsman'*, ed. Simon Varey (Oxford, 1982), p. 177. 127 'Epistle to Bathurst', l. 145. 128 'Liberty', V, ll. 307, 335.

their 'Encouragement of Apostasy.' That has made liberty the prerogative of the Protestants.[129]

O'Conor argues that liberty has different traditions among different peoples and is not a benefit to be distributed at the behest of the English. Liberty had its own history and tradition in Ireland which had escaped the dangers bemoaned by Thomson because of Ireland's physical remoteness from Europe. O'Conor attributes the corruption of liberty in Europe and England to the Romans who,

> first imported Luxury and false Refinements into Europe; who spoiled the Morals, as they destroyed the Liberties, of many great Nations, whom without Distinction, they very civilly styled Barbarians.[130]

Ireland by contrast had developed the arts and cultural characteristics of its supposed Spanish roots and thus established its self-sufficiency and happiness on a different tradition. The result was that 'the ancient Iberians of Ireland had Advantages, Skill, and Sciences, superior to all other Celtic Nations'.[131] The Irish tradition of liberty had been corrupted not from within by luxury and avarice, but by England's deliberate political and religious policy of subjection.

The failed dream

The same tensions in O'Conor between nationalist sympathies and a conciliatory thrust to bring together government and people as a single cultural and political entity emerge again some years after the *Dissertations* when O'Conor and others encouraged Thomas Leland (1722-85) to write his *History of Ireland* (1773). Leland, Professor of History at Trinity College, Dublin, author of *The History of the Life and Reign of Philip, King of Macedon* (1758), was the person O'Conor thought had the abilities to write a history of Ireland that would transcend religious and political differences. Such a history would continue the spirit of the *Dissertations* and do justice to Ireland's diverse cultural traditions:

> It is a pity that a man who distinguished himself thro' Europe by writing the life of a monarch of a remote country and age, should not bestow part of his abilities to adorn (and what is better) instruct and reform his own country.[132]

129 *Dissertations*, p. 86.   130 Ibid., p. 124.   131 Ibid., p. 31.   132 Charles O'Conor to Chevalier O'Gorman, 1 September 1767 (H.M.C., report 8, vol. i (1881), p. 486), cited by Joseph Liechty, 'Testing the Depth of Catholic/Protestant Conflict: The Case of Thomas Leland's 'History of Ireland', 1773', *Archivum Hibernicum* 42 (1987), 16. On O'Conor's encouragement of Leland see Walter D.Love, 'Charles O'Conor of Belanagare and Thomas Leland's "philosophical" history of Ireland', *IHS* 13 (March 1962), 2-5.

The reform would come from a new perception of Ireland, a fusion of the Catholic Irish historiography of Keating and the Protestant traditions. The two major cultures would fuse in a new narrative of Ireland. Leland told O'Conor that his guiding principle would be 'a liberal indifference to all parties English & Irish, civil and religious',[133] in other words the kind of history for which the *Dissertations* had prepared the way. The aim has the air of attempting to reconcile the irreconcilable and it is not surprising that O'Conor's hopes were disappointed. In spite of the disclaimer Leland's 'indifference' was not as comprehensive as he promised. Nevertheless O'Conor's hopes, supported by Burke, were that Irish history would now be written in a way that served neither colonial nor nationalist interests.

The two formidable obstructions in the way of any Irish historian, Catholic or Protestant, were the prejudices of English historiography and the hagiography of Gaelic historians, both of which emanated from opposing political ideologies. Although Leland fell victim to them he started out from a clear awareness of their dangers. O'Conor had handed on to Leland Keating's perception of this root conflict between English prejudices and Ireland's self-respect. Keating had written,

> I have observed that every modern Historian, who has undertaken to write of Ireland, commends the Country, but despises the People ... It grieved me to see a Nation hunted down by Ignorance and Malice, and recorded as the Scum and Refuse of Mankind, when upon a strict Inquiry they have made as good a Figure, and have signalised themselves in as commendable a Manner to Posterity as any People in Europe.[134]

Leland, though less personal in his observations, makes a similar observation about the Irish:

> Depressed for many ages, and reduced to a mortifying state of inferiority, stung with the reproaches, with the contempt, and sometimes with the injurious slander of their neighbours, they passionately recurred to the monuments of their ancient glory, and spoke of the noble actions of their ancestors in the glowing style of indignation.[135]

Leland is sympathetic to the tradition out of which O'Conor was writing and the difficulties it faced: histories of Ireland were 'for many years dictated by pride, by resentment, by the virulence of faction',[136] and native Irish historians had to con-

---

133 Leland to O'Conor, 5 January 1769, cited by Liechty, 'Testing the Depth of Catholic/Protestant Conflict', *Archivum Hibernicum* 42 (1987), 16. 134 Keating, Preface, *History*, pp xx-xxi. 135 Leland, *History of Ireland*, i, vi. 136 Ibid., iii.

tend with the contempt and sometimes the slander of their English neighbours. Their reaction was understandable if not always admirable: they wrote with indignation and with overweening pride in their ancient history;[137] they 'were naturally tempted to exaggerate'.[138] Like O'Conor, Leland also respected the testimony of the bards. He describes the ancient Irish as 'the greatest lovers of justice', and adds, in a phrase reminiscent of John Davies and O'Conor, 'with shame we must confess that they were not taught the love of justice by the first English settlers'.[139] Leland shares O'Conor's view that Ireland's internal disorders were to blame at times for the successes of their invaders, the Danes and the English.

What is noticeably absent from Leland, perhaps deliberately so and a consequence of 'liberal indifference', is a sense of Irish grievance or outrage. The hurt of those who had been colonised does not come through. His account includes ridicule of the English, pathos and a strong sense of the inevitability of English domination, but little sense of injury at what the English had done in Ireland. Although Leland's comments on the invasion mock the initial bravado of the English and explain why the Irish were no match for the English, there is nothing of the nationalist tradition out of which O'Conor was writing, nothing of the anger that 'the People of England have laid … all true Liberty in the Grave'.[140] Leland writes of the invasion,

> Had those first adventurers conceived that they had nothing more to do but to march through the land, and terrify a whole nation of timid savages by the glitter of their armour, they must have speedily experienced the effects of such romantic madness. But their valour was happily directed by prudence and circumspection, and hence they gradually prevailed over their enemies, no less brave, but inexperienced, improvident, and disunited.[141]

The word 'happily' in this context would have been impossible to Keating or O'Conor, likewise words like 'valour', 'prudence' and 'circumspection' giving the English invaders the edge over the disorganised Irish. The phrase 'prevailed over' nicely avoids issues of injustice or suffering. Leland is frequently more concerned to assess the English than to consider the offence felt by the Irish. Ireland's suffering is often rather an instance of English wrong-headedness than of injustice. Leland writes of the parliament at Kilkenny in the reign of Edward III,

> Pride and self-interest concurred in regarding and representing the Irish as a race utterly irreclaimable. The desperate resistance of the oppressed,

137 Ibid., vi. 138 Ibid., xlviii. 139 Ibid., xxxvi-xxxvii; cf. *Dissertations*, p. 161: had the Irish 'received from England the Benefit of equitable Government, it would go infinitely further towards securing their Obedience, than the Burning of all the Books and Laws which this Kingdom has produced.' 140 *Dissertations*, p. 59. 141 Leland, *History of Ireland*, i, 39.

or the violence of national vanity, were readily mistaken for the outrages of a natural cruelty and barbarism.[142]

Leland's sympathy for the Irish, 'desperate' and 'oppressed', leads less to an analysis of the damage done to Ireland, as in Keating and O'Conor, than to blame of the English. Leland is the first major Anglo-Irish historian, writing from a Protestant Irish perspective, who presents Irish history as the product of English prejudices. But this does not develop into anything like O'Conor's commitment to a national history rooted in an independent cultural tradition, an absence compounded by Leland's own admission that he was 'totally unacquainted with the Irish language'.[143] The reason was that Leland was unsympathetic, let alone indifferent to the Catholic dimension of that tradition. For instance writing about the Catholics and the requirement under James I that anyone for public office had to swear the Oath of Supremacy, he says,

> That indolence and acquiescence to which the errours of popery reduce the mind, added to the shame of deserting their communion, seem to have kept back these men from any advances towards conformity.[144]

Such sentiments confirm the charge that Leland's 'treatment of Catholicism was harsh and conventionally Protestant'.[145] O'Conor accused him of abandoning impartiality for money or promotion in the church.[146] Clearly Leland would not be able to synthesise his own perceptions of Irish history with O'Conor's. Protestant historiography in the example of Leland was no more willing to negotiate between its essentials and the movements of history than Keating had done.

No subsequent Irish historian in the eighteenth century took up Leland's failure or O'Conor's conciliatory aims. This can be explained in part by the fact that O'Conor had occupied an unusual place in Dublin's intellectual life. Other Catholic historians did not have O'Conor's contacts with Protestant intellectuals like Leland nor ready access to resources available to Protestant historians. O'Conor was unusual in that he obtained the singular permission of Leland to use the Trinity College library and, equally unusual, he was invited as a Catholic to work on a committee of the Dublin Society to promote the study of Irish antiquities.[147] His close Catholic friend John Curry was notably sceptical whether these contacts would benefit Irish historiography;[148] neither Curry nor O'Halloran made a significant advance on O'Conor.[149] O'Conor's argument that Ireland's Celtic past provided guidelines, however romantic, for reforming the present was also neglected.

---

142 Ibid., 322.   143 Ibid., iv.   144 Ibid., ii. 440.   145 Liechty, 'Testing the Depth of Catholic/ Protestant Conflict', *Archivum Hibernicum*, 42 (1987), 20.   146 Walter D. Love, 'Charles O'Conor of Belanagare', *IHS* 12 (March 1962), 15.   147 Ibid., 16.   148 Ibid., 10-15.   149 Sylvester O'Halloran, *An*

So what, we might ask, happened to O'Conor's spirit of reconciliation between Catholic and Protestant historiography, of trying to remove the colonial impress on histories of Ireland, of trying to improve the image of the Catholics in Protestant eyes, and vice versa, of giving the Irish a sense of pride in their ancient history and thus stimulating them to recover their cultural identity? That spirit resurfaces briefly in O'Halloran who, writing against Leland, argued that 'the Irish nation was constituted by both Protestants and Catholics, who were "assuredly one nation".'[150] But by the early nineteenth century the Keating-O'Conor push to promote scholarly respect for Ireland's ancient culture had faded or been appropriated to more obvious political purposes. For some it passed into a 'romantic nostalgia' which was part of a new wave of nationalist sentiment.[151] For others, like Maria Edgeworth and her father, it held no attraction.[152] By the 1790s Ireland had become a great deal more polarised than O'Conor had known in the 1760s. The conflicting interests he wrestled with in his *Dissertations* found stark expression first in the rising of 1798 and then in the Union of 1800. General Hutchinson, son of the provost of Trinity College, looked on these events as indicative of Ireland's ingrained divisions. He supported Catholic aspirations but thought the country too deeply immersed in political corruption and religious prejudices to make reconciliation even a remote possibility:

> If ever there was a country unfit to govern itself, it is Ireland; a corrupt aristocracy, a ferocious commonality, a distracted government, a divided people. I solemnly believe that the great mass of every religious persuasion in this country have no wish so near their hearts as to enjoy the power of persecuting each other. The Catholic would murder the Protestant in the name of God; the Protestant would murder the Catholic in the name of law. Both sects seem to consider their common country only as an extended field of battle, where each are at full liberty to display their sanguinary dexterity.[153]

Ireland's efforts first to rewrite itself and then to assert its own identity had both failed.

Introduction to the Study of the History and Antiquities of Ireland (London, 1772). 150 Leighton, *Catholicism in a Protestant Kingdom*, p. 111. 151 Donald MacCartney, 'The Writing of History in Ireland, 1800-1830', *IHS* 10 (September 1957), 361 *et passim*. 152 After a short-lived interest in Irish antiquities 'they thought that extensive education among all classes was the best remedy for tradition': Marilyn Butler, *Maria Edgeworth: A Literary Biography* (London, 1972), p. 364. 153 Cited by Frank MacDermot, *Theobald Wolfe Tone and His Times*, p. 278.

CHAPTER SEVEN

Edmund Burke:
the divided Irishman

BURKE AND EMPIRE

Edmund Burke was one of the most eloquent advocates of empire in the eighteenth century. It is not difficult to cite passages to demonstrate that he thought Ireland but a part, and a subservient part, of the British empire, that he regarded Westminster as the centre of that empire and the arbiter of Ireland's best interests. Writing from Westminster in 1773 to Sir Charles Bingham in Dublin about a proposal from the Irish parliament for a tax on absentees, he sums up his understanding of the bonds of empire. He sees nothing 'invidious' about the central authority of Great Britain:

> But if it be true, that the several bodies which make up this complicated mass, are to be preserved as one Empire, an authority sufficient to preserve that unity, and by its equal weight and pressure to consolidatethe various parts that compose it, must reside somewhere: that somewhere can only be in England. Possibly any one member, distinctly taken, might decide in favour of that residence within itself; but certainly no Member would give its voice for any other except this. So that I look upon the residence of the supreme power to be settled here; not by force, or tyranny, or even by mere long usage, but by the very nature of things, and the joint consent of the whole body.[1]

Here are the well-known markers of Burke's organic theory of empire, complex yet unified, held together by common consent and natural law. Theory flowers into metaphor in a speech of 1785:

1 'Letter to Sir Charles Bingham', 30 October 1773, *Writings and Speeches of Edmund Burke*, ix, 488.

pre-eminence and dignity were due to England; it was she alone that must bear the weight and burden of empire; she alone must pour out the ocean of wealth necessary for the defence of it. Ireland and other parts might empty their little urns to swell the tide; they might wield their puny tridents; but the great trident that was to move the world, must be grasped by England alone.[2]

Few Englishmen, let alone Irishmen, have expressed the global vision of the British empire more imaginatively. The image of 'the great trident' bespeaks the realpolitik of colonial discourse from the eighteenth to the twentieth centuries echoing Thomson's lines, 'O blest Britannia! in thy presence blest,/ Thou guardian of mankind! whence spring alone/ All human grandeur, happiness, and fame.'[3] Burke had no difficulty subsuming Ireland into this vision and he saw no contradiction between it and his life-long campaign for equity and justice in Ireland. When the Catholic Committee in Dublin sent him three hundred guineas in recognition of his work for them, he refused the gift on the ground that his contribution to the relief of the Catholics was reward enough. He goes on,

> My Principles make it my first, indeed almost my only earnest wish, to see every part of this Empire, and every denomination of men in it happy and contented, and united on one common bottom of equality and justice. If that Settlement were once made, I assure you, I should feel very indifferent about my particular position, or my particular situation, in so well constituted a Community.[4]

Ireland and conquest

But if these sentiments are weighed against Burke's reading of Irish history earlier in his life a much more complex and ambiguous attitude to empire and to England emerges. To the younger Burke the English presence in Ireland was not a result of 'the joint consent of the whole body' but of conquest, and Henry II 'well knew, from the internal weakness and advantageous situation of this noble island, the easiness and importance of such a conquest'.[5] Burke's account of how the English settled themselves against the wishes of the Irish is unequivocal in its anti-colonial language. The English policy was to keep 'a vanquished people in obedience to the conquerors', they 'put themselves at the head of the tribes whose chiefs they had slain', and 'partly by force, partly by policy, the first English families took a firm root in Ireland'.[6] The language recalls Gulliver's description

2 *Parl. Hist.* xxv, 649 (19 May 1785). 3 Thomson, *Liberty*, V. ll. 2–4. This was a recurring trope during the century; see for example David Mallet, *Britannia: A Masque* (1755). 4 17 August [1779], *Correspondence of Burke*, iv, 121. 5 'Abridgment of English History', *Writings and Speeches of Edmund Burke*, i, 509. 6 Ibid., 514.

of the despised coloniser and stands in stark contrast to Burke's later thoughts addressed to Bingham.

A comparison of Burke's account of Henry's invasion of Ireland with Molyneux's indicates the divergence between the two and is a pointer to Burke's ambivalence towards England. The many debates about Ireland's relation with England during the century kept coming back to this question whether Ireland was originally conquered by England. Burke said yes, Molyneux said no. Molyneux's *Case of Ireland* argues that no force was used. The Irish voluntarily accepted Henry:

> Here we have an Intire and Voluntary Submission of all the Ecclesiastical and Civil State of Ireland, to King Henry II without the least Hostile Stroke on any side; We hear not in any of the Chronicles of any Violence on either Part, all was Transacted with the greatest Quiet, Tranquility, and Freedom imaginable.[7]

The Molyneux tradition understood Henry as one 'whom the Irish had voluntarily accepted as their lord, who had come to protect them from the violence of the Anglo-Norman adventurers, to reform their Church, and bring order into their country'.[8]

Burke rejected this central tenet of Anglo-Irish thought and stands much closer to a Catholic even nationalist position in his historical understanding of how Ireland was drawn into subjection by England. It is ironic that he was challenged to own up to such views by one of his more radical opponents in Dublin in 1780. A correspondent calling himself Nathan asked him,

> Permit me to put the following Queries for your consideration. Was Henry 2nd justifiable by the law of Nations, or rather did he not violate the natural Rights of another nation, in his Invasion of Ireland.
>
> Were the People of Ireland bound thenceforth by the success of that Invasion to unconditional submission to the Legislature of England.[9]

Burke's reply is not recorded, but the questions came at a turbulent time for him and touched a sensitive nerve.

His lukewarm response at Westminster to Lord North's measures for relief in Ireland had sparked widespread abuse of him in Ireland where the mood was increasingly reformist. The Irish received Lord North's proposals with gratitude and were looking for further concessions both on Poynings' Law and on the penal laws. Burke's constituents in Bristol on the other hand were angry that he

---

7 *The Case of Ireland*, pp 30-1. 8 Goddard Henry Orpen, *Ireland under the Normans, 1169-1216*, 2 vols (Oxford, 1968), i, 265. 9 27 Jan. 1780; cited by Thomas H.D. Mahoney, *Edmund Burke and Ireland* (London, 1960), p. 91.

showed any sympathy for North's moderate trade concessions for Ireland. In addition opposition in England to Catholic relief was mounting, spearheaded by Lord George Gordon's Protestant Association which was bent on the repeal of the Catholic relief Act of 1778. These were the early signs of an anti-Catholic fanaticism which boiled over in the Gordon riots in June 1780. Ironically just at this time the Irish Catholic peer Lord Kenmare writes to Burke praising him for his long-standing commitment to Ireland's interests and his work on their behalf at Westminster. Kenmare speaks of 'the vast Obligations Humanity lies under to you and your Connexions, who took the lead in setting our Parliament the Precedent in England', and assures him that apart from being misunderstood 'by some hasty Spirits here' he has the support of 'the most Sensible and respectable part of your Countrymen'.[10]

Whatever Burke said it seems he made enemies on both sides of the Irish sea. In both quarters critics blamed him for not being committed to their particular concerns. Bristol merchants expected him to favour their trading interests against Ireland's and the Irish looked to him as their man in Westminster who would push for religious, commercial and constitutional reforms in Ireland. Burke straddled the divide.

Lord Kenmare, just after reading that early and unpublished 'Elegant Abstract of our Penal Statutes', presumably the *Tracts relating to Popery Laws*, applauds Burke's comprehension of and rootedness in Ireland's history.[11] The work is in many respects an unqualified attack on England's subjugation of Ireland, of her Catholic religion, property laws, education, family traditions, in fact every aspect of Irish life that constitutes cultural identity. The hostile rhetoric of that work may well have been the reason why Burke never published it. At the time of writing in the early 1760s he was looking for a place in the English political system.[12]

The 1641 rebellion: colonial and resistance readings

An issue in the *Tracts* which demonstrates this attachment to his Irish roots and reflects an important aspect of his Irish identity is his reading of the 1641 rebellion. Burke had been aware since his student days that most published histories of Ireland were a construct of English prejudice. They presented the rebellion as an unprovoked and violent attack on the innocent English settlers. Hume's account of what happened in Ulster reflects the emphasis and tone of earlier English historians like Clarendon and Temple:

> The stately buildings and commodious habitations of the planters, as if
> upbraiding the sloth and ignorance of the natives, were consumed with

10 18 February 1780, *Correspondence of Burke*, iv, 204.   11 Ibid., 203.   12 Walter D. Love, 'Burke's Transition from a Literary to a Political Career', *Burke Newsletter* 6, no. 2 (1964-5), 376-90.

fire, or laid level with the ground. And where the miserable owners, shut up in their houses, and preparing for defence, perished in the flames, together with their wives and children, a double triumph was afforded to their insulting foes.

If anywhere a number assembled together, and assuming courage from despair, were resolved to sweeten death by revenge on their assassins, they were disarmed by capitulations and promises of safety, confirmed by the most solemn oaths. But no sooner had they surrendered, than the rebels, with perfidy equal to their cruelty, made them share the fate of their unhappy countrymen.[13]

English readers could not but join in astonishment that their defenceless and peaceful countrymen had been so mercilessly murdered in this barbaric way. The passage carries all the expected markers of colonial discourse which Burke so objected to – the compassionate virtuous English struck down by perfidious and cruel Irish, courage met by cold-blooded murder; the more innocent the English the more evil the Irish. The cardinal sin of the Irish was that the massacre was unprovoked and therefore irrational. Such an event was the worst dream of Swift's Houyhnhnms.

Burke is said to have tried to persuade Hume that received accounts of the rebellion were exaggerated if not untrue.[14] In the *Tracts* he resists this kind of colonial discourse by setting it side by side with his own postcolonial version. On the one hand he re-enacts the colonisers' view of fickle and unreliable Catholics. The penal laws, they think, are necessary to protect the State against the danger of rebellion. Their argument runs that while the Catholics,

> were possessed of landed property, and of the influence consequent to such property, their allegiance to the Crown of Great Britain was ever insecure; the publick peace was ever liable to be broken; and Protestants never could be a moment secure either of their properties or of their lives. Indulgence only made them arrogant, and power daring; confidence only excited and enabled them to exert their inherent treachery; and the times, which they generally selected for their most wicked and desperate rebellions, were those in which they enjoyed the greatest ease and the most perfect tranquility.[15]

The language catches the key anxiety in the settlers' mind that the master cannot trust his servant who simply takes advantage of any kindness or indulgence as an incitement to rebellion.

13 David Hume, *History of England*, 6 vols (London, 1848), iv, 62-3. 14 See Michel Fuchs, 'On a loss of philosophical temper and stylistic composure: Ireland and its effects on Hume's discourse', unpublished paper, 1996, and Robert Bisset, *The Life of Edmund Burke*, 2 vols (London, 1800), ii, 426; Bisset defends Hume. 15 'Tracts relating to Popery Laws', *Writings and Speeches of Edmund Burke*, ix, 478.

To counteract this Burke enjoins Irish readers to reject such inscription of themselves and turn to their own history of the event based on Irish sources:

> there is an interior History of Ireland, the genuine voice of its records and monuments, which speaks a very different language from these histories, from Temple and from Clarendon, these restore Nature to its just rights, and policy to its proper order.[16]

An example of what Burke may have had in mind is a document from the Catholics after the rebellion as to why they took up arms. They thought the English were determined to wipe out the Catholic religion. In addition they argued,

> All Natives here were deprived of the Benefitt of the Auncient fundamental Lawes liberties and Priviledges due by all Lawes and Justice to a Free people and Nacion and were particularly due by the Municipall Lawes of Ireland.[17]

They follow this striking sense of separate nationhood by claiming their right to ancient possessions, complaining, 'that the Subjects of Ireland especially the Irish are thrust out forceably from their Ancient possessions against and without Coulor of Right and could not have propertie …'[18]

Burke is more attentive to such voices than to English historians behind whose accounts he sees something quite different. He introduces the 'very different language' based on his reading of the Irish sources which show,

> that these rebellions were not produced by toleration, but by persecution; that they arose not from just and mild government, but from the most unparalleled oppression. These records will be far from giving the least countenance to a doctrine so repugnant to humanity and good sense, as that the security of any Establishment, civil or religious, can ever depend upon the misery of those who live under it.[19]

The polarisation of words like 'toleration' and 'persecution', 'security' and 'misery' indicates the vehemence of Burke's re-writing of the colonial account. This new vocabulary, so much more direct than Molyneux's or Swift's, antithetical rather than ironic, berates the English for a policy that insults while it fails its own purposes. The reasons that provoked the rebellion continue in legislation like the

16 Ibid., 479. 17 'Papists' Reasons for taking up Arms' [?1641], *The Manuscripts of the House of Lords*, Addenda, 1514-1714, xi, ed. Maurice F. Bond (London, 1962), 304. 18 Ibid. 19 'Tracts relating to Popery Laws', *Writings and Speeches of Edmund Burke*, ix, 479. He expresses similar sentiments in a letter to Dr William Markham, *Correspondence of Burke*, ii, 285.

penal laws which 'will rather be disadvantageous to the publick peace than any kind of security to it'.[20] Yet, as with Molyneux and Swift, Burke is not arguing for independence but for security and peace within the empire.

The underlying anger of Burke's attack on the penal laws, like that in his account of the 1641 rebellion and in his later criticism of the Ascendancy in the 1790s, stems from a perception summed up in a letter to a friend in the Irish parliament, Sir Hercules Langrishe:

> For a much longer period than that which had sufficed to blend the Romans with the nation to which of all others they were the most adverse, the Protestants settled in Ireland, consider themselves in no other light than that of a sort of colonial garrison, to keep the natives in subjection to the other state of Great Britain. The whole spirit of the revolution in Ireland was that of not the mildest conqueror.[21]

This spirit of oppression was nothing new. It did not spring from Protestant anxiety or animosity towards Catholics in the seventeenth century because it existed 'in that harassed country before the words Protestant and Papist were heard of in the world'.[22] It came to a head in the seventeenth century under Lord Stafford and provoked the rebellion of 1641. The penal laws were a later manifestation of that same sense of hatred for a conquered people which could be traced back into pre-Reformation times.

Burke's account of the 1641 rebellion together with its broad historical contextualisation is both unusual and yet fundamental to an understanding of his feelings about Ireland and his hostility to English historiography. That commitment surfaces in unpublished form before he enters parliament in the 1760s, and again in the closing and despairing years of his political career in the 1790s. Yet none of his speeches contain the slightest suggestion that England kept 'a sort of colonial garrison' in Ireland. To better understand the strength and passion of this suppressed area of his thought one needs to look at his earliest writings.

Burke's early cultural nationalism

The Reformer (1748), a weekly paper Burke edited in his last months as an undergraduate at Trinity College, set out to criticise Dubliners for their unashamed indulgence of English culture at the expense of their own. His particular target was the manager of the Theatre Royal in Smock-Alley, Thomas Sheridan, as well

20 'Tracts relating to Popery Laws', *Writings and Speeches of Edmund Burke*, ix, 479. 21 'Letter to Sir Hercules Langrishe' (1792), *Writings and Speeches of Edmund Burke*, ix, 615. 22 Ibid. This is not to deny the importance of religion in Ireland's history; Burke wrote in the 'Tracts': 'No country, I believe, since the world began, has suffered so much on account of Religion; or has been so variously harassed both for popery and for Protestantism' (*Writings and Speeches of Edmund Burke*, ix, 471).

as patrons of the theatre, who typified the uncritical acceptance of 'English prejudice': 'so greedily do we swallow that Tide of fulsom *Plays*, *Novels*, and *Poems* which they [the English] pour on us'.[23] *The Reformer* rallies its readers to throw off the English slur that the Irish are a nation of dullards and to engage seriously with the cultural problems and capabilities of Ireland, to promote Irish writers, to support the Arts and Sciences and to be much more critical of Sheridan's anglophobic theatre. He touches on a problem that has been noted of so many of Ireland's artists from Charles Macklin to Joyce, and was later to include Burke himself:

> It is not more our Intention to expose Dulness, than to relieve from the vitiated Relish of pert and ignorant Coxcombs, such Productions of our own as promise Genius. Merit in Perfection may be easily seen, but it will require a Taste and Penetration extraordinary to discover it in the Bud – and how worthy a Labour this is, may appear by the Number of excellent Men this Nation has from time to time produced, and who the Moment their Parts begin to ripen, were forced to leave it for more indulgent Regions; depriving us at once of the Benefit and ornament we should have from their residing amongst us.[24]

The repeated sense of 'us' and 'this Nation' in the first number of the paper makes clear Burke's commitment to the fostering of a national cultural identity. But frustration soon sets in because he recognises early in his life that the Irish are uninterested in his vision. He comes to admit in a later number, 'no civilized People in Europe are less concerned for the Welfare of their Country than we are'.[25] The very title of the paper underscores Burke's intention to reform Ireland's slovenly self-esteem. It demonstrates that before he had ever been to England his mind and heart were publicly involved in Ireland's cultural predicament as a country given over to foreign influences. These were the intellectual convictions and sympathies he took with him to England and which he then had to reconcile with the complex demands that a seat in Westminster was to make on him.

More than a decade later he was writing his *Tracts relating to Popery Laws* where his criticism moved from cultural to legal issues. The commitment and frustration are just as evident. Much of that work was probably written during Burke's employment in the early 1760s in Dublin as private secretary to William 'Single-Speech' Hamilton, secretary to the lord lieutenant Halifax. Working so close to the lord lieutenant Burke gained first-hand experience of how the English administration perceived and discussed Ireland. It seems likely that as secretary to Hamilton he drafted speeches for him,[26] which would mean that in

23 *The Reformer*, 1, *Writings and Speeches of Edmund Burke*, i, 67. 24 Ibid., 68. 25 *The Reformer*, 9, ibid., 106. 26 See Joel J. Gold, 'In Defence of Single-Speech Hamilton', *Studies in Burke and His*

his official capacity he wrote for the administration while in his private hours he would be criticising that same administration in his *Tracts*. His career pulled him in one direction, the Castle and colonial discourse, while Ireland and resistance pulled him in the other. The experience shows in the *Tracts* where he impersonates the thought of English lawmakers with caustic irony,

> We found the people hereticks and idolaters; we have, by way of improving their condition, rendered them slaves and beggars; they remain in all the misfortune of their old errors, and all the superadded misery of their recent punishment.[27]

The brutality of this voice serves as a platform for the main purpose of the *Tracts* which is to reproach the English for their arrogance, deviousness and infringement of rights, particularly after the Treaty of Limerick. The penal laws, he argues, go against what was agreed for Catholics at Limerick and countermand the promise in the Treaty of greater tolerance for Catholics:

> Judge whether the Roman Catholicks have been preserved ... from any disturbance upon account of their Religion; or rather, whether on that account there is a single right of Nature, or benefit of society, which has not been either totally taken away or considerably impaired.[28]

In the light of such criticism it seems paradoxical that Burke supported the patriots' agenda for 'colonial nationalism', that is 'the demand for domestic self-government within an imperial framework'.[29] Yet he believed that outside that framework, that is outside the security and commercial ties with England, 'Ireland would be the most compleatly undone Country in the world'.[30] If there was a contradiction it lay not in the concept of colonial nationalism but in England's abuse of the concept, its repeated resort to repressive legislation, its determination to keep Ireland subservient. Even that argument is curious coming from Burke since he had long argued that Ireland had been conquered by the English and that the relation between the two countries started out as coloniser to colonised. Modern readers looking back with the advantage of hindsight might well ask why Burke should be surprised at England's conduct. It was foolhardy to expect anything else.

The anger of those subjected to colonial rule seldom blames the coloniser for not keeping his part of the bargain, not least because colonialism does not operate by bargains. Burke however implies that many centuries of colonisation do lay a moral onus on the coloniser. After ruling Ireland for five hundred years and

Time 10, 2 (Winter 1968-9), 1140. 27 'Tracts relating to Popery Laws', *Writings and Speeches of Edmund Burke*, ix, 468. 28 Ibid., 472. 29 J.G. Simms, *Colonial Nationalism*, p. 9. 30 'Letter on the Affairs of Ireland' (1797), *Writings and Speeches of Edmund Burke*, ix, 676.

more, he argues, the English should respect the moral demands of equity and justice. There would be no peace in Ireland unless such a moral bargain applied. Stability only comes with justice. As he said of the British imperial presence in India, the first step is revolution to give it power; 'the next is good laws, good order, to give it stability'.[31] Stability in Ireland depends on the same 'good laws'. Burke wrote to John Curry of the Dublin Catholic Committee who had thanked him for his assistance to the Catholics,

> My endeavours in the Irish Business, in which I was indeed very active and very earnest, both in public and in private, were wholly guided by an uniform principle, which is interwoven in my nature, and which has hitherto regulated, and I hope will continue to regulate my conduct, I mean an utter abhorrence of all kinds of public injustice and oppression, the worst species of which are those which being converted into maxims of state, and blending themselves with law and jurisprudence corrupt the very fountains of all equity, and subvert all the purposes of Government. From these principles I have ever had a particular detestation to the penal system of Ireland.[32]

His mission was to fight against that 'public injustice and oppression' which the English administration practised in Ireland. Because English interests prospered 'in the distress and destruction of everything else', Ireland remained troubled by agrarian discontent as seen in the Whiteboy disturbances of the 1760s and trade disputes in the 1770s.[33] Burke's dilemma, as he discovered in his years as member of parliament for Bristol, was how to promote his English constituents' interests while securing justice for Ireland, how to be a covert Irish nationalist and yet keep his seat in the English parliament. His sympathies rested with Ireland in this lopsided relationship, but power he knew lay with the English.

A conflict of interests: the rhetoric of conciliation

Burke's paradoxical stance towards Ireland is best understood not as an inherent inconsistency in his thought but a product of the rhetorically awkward if not ambivalent space he occupied as an Irishman in the House of Commons. Burke the politician at Westminster was the Protestant son of Catholic parents from Munster who had circumvented the penal laws. By conforming to the church of Ireland and revoking their allegiance to the Catholic church Burke's parents had given the family a new start. Burke's father had cleared the way for himself to practise as an attorney.[34] Their sons could enjoy educational and professional

31 'Speech on Opening of Impeachment' [Fourth Day, 16 Feb. 1788], ibid., vi, 317. 32 14 August 1779, *Correspondence of Burke*, iv, 118. 33 Ibid., 15. 34 Conor Cruise O'Brien, *The Great Melody: A Thematic*

prospects denied to their many Catholic relations. Burke went to the Protestant university, Trinity College, and to the Middle Temple in London with a view to practising law in Dublin. Throughout his formative years Burke visited and kept in regular touch with his mother's side of the family, the Nagles in Munster. They provided a personal and affectionate link with 'the Irish Gaelic world'.[35] He assisted them with books and from his relatively powerful position across the religious divide he advised them on education and agriculture. His encouragement sprang from strong sympathy: 'I am really sollicitous for the welfare of all the people about the Blackwater, and most grateful for their friendship ... for I consider you all as one.'[36] In spite of Burke's rise to parliamentary prominence he never neglected these Catholic Munster connections. The lifestyle that went with office at Westminster meant he acquired a country estate at Beaconsfield, which he actively farmed, and a house in London both of which were always open to family and friends from Ireland.

However, he had also to consider the demands of the Rockingham Whigs and of his patron Lord Rockingham who was an absentee landlord with estates in Ireland. Although Burke served both these interests – the informal, historical and family ties with Ireland and the parliamentary career he was making for himself in England, critics have yet to agree on whether or how Burke reconciled these opposing concerns in his writings. R.B. McDowell argues that they caused no internal tensions in Burke because he looked rather to 'the common literary and political heritage, the way of life, and the friendships shared by men of education, property and enterprise in both countries'.[37] This assertion, however, takes no account of Burke's strong historical sense of Ireland's ill-treatment as described in his pre-parliamentary writings. He was too intelligent a reader of history to put that hurt behind him once he acquired a seat in parliament. Conor Cruise O'Brien speaks of 'the friction between outer Whig and inner "Jacobite"' which he says 'was productive of that oblique aggressiveness which is the driving force of irony'.[38] Kiberd gives pertinent examples of how this 'friction' informs much of what Burke wrote on India and the French Revolution: 'Ireland provided him ... with a metaphor for the world beyond Dover, affording points of comparison which helped to explain events in places as far-flung as India or the Americas.'[39] The point is that the Burke at Westminster who applauds the inheritance of 'so happy a Constitution and so flourishing an empire' is the same Burke who drew up 'The Address and Petition of the Irish Catholics'. In that document he highlights the servile position of Catholics under that same constitution,

Biography and Commented Anthology of Edmund Burke (London, 1992), p. 10. Burke's mother and sister probably continued to practise as Catholics. 35 R.B. McDowell, Introduction to Part II, *Writings and Speeches of Edmund Burke*, ix, 391. 36 Burke to Garrett Nagle, *Correspondence of Burke*, i, 289. 37 McDowell, *Writings and Speeches of Edmund Burke*, ix, 394. 38 Introduction, *Edmund Burke: Reflections on the Revolution in France*, ed. Conor Cruise O'Brien (London, 1969), p. 43. 39 Kiberd,

a servitude the more intolerable as it is suffered amidst that liberty, that peace, and that security, which, under your majesty's benign influence, is spread all around us, and which we alone, of all your majesty's subjects, are rendered incapable of partaking.[40]

Like much that Burke wrote and did for Ireland this piece did not bear his name. The question arises as to how this dualism – feelings of sympathy for and outrage over Ireland and loyalty to the English Whigs – affects his parliamentary writings and speeches. Where and when do his rhetorical energies seem curbed or restrained, and on what occasions does he expatiate, exhibiting that 'stream of mind' which Johnson said was 'perpetual'?[41]

Burke's speeches and letters about Ireland point to an inner struggle between his public and his private self. His writings on Anglo-Irish trade relations in the late 1770s illustrate how he was caught between English and Irish loyalties. The revolt by the American colonies and the increasing unrest in Ireland made the 1770s particularly trying years for the English parliament as it faced the first serious threat to its colonial authority and the unity of its empire. As Burke remarked, the sheer distance between England and America made it difficult to enforce the will of Westminster on the American colonists. Ireland, being so much nearer, presented no such problem. But England needed the support of Ireland in its dispute with the American colonists. The late 1770s and early 1780s are marked by Ireland's attempts to make the most of this situation by drawing concessions for itself, culminating in legislative independence in 1782. A key area of debate was England's trade restrictions on Ireland. England's tactic at the start of the American war was to ensure first call on provisions from Ireland to supply Britain's army and navy. By 1778 the war was having an adverse effect on the Irish economy.[42] In April 1778 the Irish peer Lord Nugent introduced at Westminster a set of resolutions proposing that Ireland be granted unrestricted trade with the British colonies. Wool and woollen goods were excepted. Only tobacco and indigo were barred from direct import and there would be no duty on the import of sailcloth, cordage and cotton yarns from England. Many members were sympathetic arguing that Ireland could better help England in the war with the American colonists if trade restrictions were eased. Speaker after speaker agreed that Ireland had been the victim of what Nugent and Byng called England's 'narrow policy'.[43] Lord Beauchamp added cynically that 'Ireland must continue for ever to smart under the prevailing hand of Great Britain'.[44] Opposing voices argued that Britain should protect, not liberalise her trade.

Inventing Ireland, pp 17-20. 40 'Address and Petition of the Irish Catholics' (1764), *Writings and Speeches of Edmund Burke*, ix, 432. Catholics had Burke's permission to present the Address to the lord lieutenant in 1777. 41 Boswell, *Life of Johnson*, p. 696. 42 Dickson, *New Foundations*, p. 147. 43 *Parl. Hist.* xix, 1105, 1109. 44 Ibid., 1126.

'The present measure,' said Pelham, 'would be highly detrimental to the manufactures of this country.'[45]

Burke spoke several times in the debate well aware that the issue presented him with a conflict of interest. He represented Bristol which was a major trading city and his support for the proposals would anger his constituents. Before Burke's final contribution to the debate members of parliament had circulated copies of the new trade proposals to their constituencies. The response, especially from trading cities like Manchester, Liverpool, Preston and Glasgow was prompt and hostile claiming that more liberal trade laws for Ireland would damage England. Burke's speech on 6 May 1778 attempts to allay such fears. He disagrees that Ireland would pay less tax and dismisses the argument that the proposals would lead to commercial equality: 'The great disproportion of capital effectually destroys the possibility of equality.'[46] English merchants would keep the advantage in terms of both prices and exports: their anxieties had no foundation in practice. The Irish respected parliament. A delay or refusal would not bring rebellion. He adds caustically, 'They were patient and loyal, and therefore, he supposed, they were crushed.'[47]

The opening paragraph of this speech illustrates much about Burke as mediator between England and Ireland. It also provides examples of the antithetical manner of his thought. Mediation implies strategies to reconcile opposites and Burke's voice in the opening passage offers an image of Ireland, reminiscent of Swift's injured lady impoverished by an oppressive England. The relationship, he says, has been counterproductive. He accuses England of 'a kind of left-handed policy' that keeps Ireland 'under the most cruel, oppressive, and unnatural restriction':

> Deprived of every incentive to industry, and shut out from every passage to wealth, she had inwardly lamented, but she had never complained of her condition. She had gone the most forward lengths in serving the interest, and defending the rights of Great Britain. She had assisted in conquests from which she was to gain no advantage, and emptied her treasury, and desolated her land to prove her attachment and loyalty to the government of this country.[48]

Such self-inflicted damage, and all because of loyalty to England, serves to praise the Irish while castigating the English. Ireland's loyalty provides the base for Burke's appeal for justice – Ireland wants justice not pity, wisdom not generosity – and for his assurance that the Irish unlike the Americans will not rebel: 'their loyalty and zeal was superior to complaint; they might despair, but they would not resist.'[49] The proposals were but the first step towards a better deal for

45 Ibid., IIII.   46 'Speech on Irish Trade', *Writings and Speeches of Edmund Burke*, ix, 521.   47 Ibid.   48 Ibid., 520.   49 Ibid., 521.

Ireland. He tells the speaker of the Irish House, Sir Edmund Perry, 'It is a great deal to have broken up the frozen Ground, though things are not at this instant quite ready for the last and most perfect Culture.'[50]

While Burke argues that England will lose nothing by granting the proposals and Ireland will be stronger, there lurks a sub-text that nothing stands between Ireland and rebellion – except her loyalty. The only security against that is just and wise government, an argument that dates back to Burke's pre-parliamentary writings. That same aggressive anti-colonial language – phrases like 'inwardly lamented', 'no advantage', 'emptied', 'desolated' – infuses many of the sentences. The emphasis on loyalty is a noticeable difference from earlier writings, prompted possibly by the fact that now he stands at the centre not on the margins of power. But this talk of rebellion is no more than a rhetorical threat. If it were realised, it would cut the tight-rope Burke treads so adroitly between Ireland's discontent and England's war needs. It was not long before Burke lost the support of his Bristol electors and he failed to keep his seat at the next election.

What is absent from such rhetoric is the sustained derision of England found in Burke's earlier writings and which would be a feature of Grattan's and Curran's speeches in the Irish Commons during the next few years. Although Burke's criticism has an unmistakable moral directness, it moves towards reconciliation, not confrontation. The rhetoric moves through oppositions in order to show that conciliation is a moral necessity and an honourable possibility.

By the time Nugent's resolutions were adopted in a modified form in May 1778 the climate for the rhetorical strategies Burke practised in this debate was changing dramatically. Soon the English initiatives were seen in Ireland as inadequate. France had joined the war on the side of the American colonists. England needed more recruits for the army and Ireland was the obvious source. As England's needs became clear, Ireland became bolder in her stance. In a move to encourage Catholic enlistment to the army concessions were made in the penal laws, for example, allowing Catholics to take leases not for 31 but 999 years. But the Irish parliament was unwilling to release money to pay for the new militia. Anxieties about the French spreading the war in America to Ireland saw the establishment of a new kind of militia, the Volunteers, who were independent of government. Ireland was in the first phase of a 'semi-revolutionary crisis' which was to lead to Grattan's push for legislative independence.[51] A feature of this new era in Irish politics was a shift in the rhetorical climate. Ireland's heightened sense of confidence and the growing anxiety in England meant a more brazen and sometimes bitter language in Ireland about the English and this prompted Burke to change his conciliatory strategies to a more partizan rhetoric.

50 19 May 1778, *Correspondence of Burke*, iii, 448.   51 H. Butterfield, *George III, Lord North, and the People, 1779-80* (London, 1949), p. v.

He has no problem expressing strong pro-Irish sentiments in his private letters, but as always is much more circumspect in public. He wrote to Perry in August 1778 about the changes he saw in Ireland. He is pleased, he says, to hear politicians speaking up for liberty and justice.

> You are now beginning to have a Country; and I trust you will complete the Design … I am persuaded that when that thing called a Country is once formed in Ireland, quite other things will be done, than were done whilst the Zeal of men was turned to the support of a party and whilst they thought its Interests only provided for in the distress and destruction of every thing else. Your people will begin to lift up their heads and to act and think like men; and the Effects will be answerable.[52]

If read out of context, this could be taken for a radical voice of nationalist pride. He never expressed such sentiments in parliament.

Burke and Fox: varieties of anti-colonial protest

At times Burke's attempt to hold in balance the interests of his native country with those of England can be obtrusively awkward as we see if we compare him with Charles James Fox in debates on Ireland late in 1779. Of the many critics of England's treatment of Ireland in the shadow of the American war Fox comes closest to and yet is significantly different from Burke in his criticism. Together with Burke he was a frequent speaker on Ireland in the late 1770s, putting the Whig view on liberalising trade, critical of the ministry for dragging its feet on Irish affairs, supportive of Grattan, and as convinced as Burke that if the ministry treated Ireland as they had done the American colonists they would court equally disastrous results. Burke told his Bristol constituents, 'To read what was approaching in Ireland, in the black and bloody characters of the American war, was a painful, but it was a necessary part of my public duty.'[53]

Although Fox shares the general thrust of Burke's views on America and India, it is on Ireland that his language and emphases are notably different. Fox keeps a straight line of attack; Burke's stance is less stable, shifting between sympathy for Ireland and loyalty to Westminster as the heart of the empire. The following extract is from Fox's contribution to the debate on the Address of Thanks to the king in November 1779. Because Fox's roots are unequivocally English and his national loyalties undivided the speech is more direct, less shaped by antitheses. His attack on Lord North makes no comparisons between say Irish loyalty and English oppression. Ireland, he says, 'afforded one of the most critical situa-

---

52 12 August 1778, *Correspondence of Burke*, iv, 15.   53 'Speech at the Guildhall in Bristol', 1780, *Writings and Speeches of Edmund Burke*, iii (eds Warren M. Elofson with John A. Woods, 1996), 633.

tions in which the two kingdoms ever stood with respect to each other'.54 He does not ironically imply what should be done. He mocks without suggesting remedies. The language is free of a moral vocabulary. The energy of the writing dwells instead on the muddled evasiveness of North's ministry, particularly the claim in the king's speech that the present plight of Ireland was unrelated to England's conduct of the American war. The report of his speech comes to a climax with a string of rhetorical questions:

> The noble lord at the head of the Treasury could not surely be in earnest when he declared that the American war had nothing to do with the affairs of Ireland. Did not that ill-fated project appear most conspicuous in every circumstance of the present condition of that kingdom? What stripped Ireland of her troops? Was it not the American war? What brought on the hostilities of France and put Ireland in fear of an invasion? Was it not the American war? What gave Ireland the opportunity of establishing a powerful and illegal army? Certainly the American war! When he called the associated forces an illegal army, he did not mean to cast any odium upon the associations. He was equally ready to acknowledge the necessity and the merit of the plan: but it was the accursed American war that made that measure necessary, and rendered it illegally meritorious.55

He goes on with equal force to expose England's negligence towards Ireland, his aim to ridicule, not to point the way forward. The rhetorical question is Fox's key figure. He uses it less for its ironic barbs than to highlight the ministry's inconsistency and incompetence. The presumed answers drive home his disagreement with ministry. The ministry is the issue on Fox's mind rather than a solution to the Irish problem. This is anti-government, not anti-colonial, rhetoric. The ministry is again the issue a few weeks later in Fox's speech on the earl of Upper Ossory's motion of censure on the ministry over its conduct towards Ireland. Fox attributes Ireland's new confidence to the ministry's weakness: 'It was the calamities of the empire which had made Ireland poor; but it was the incapacity and negligence of government that had rendered her bold and daring.'56

Burke too criticises government. In the debate shortly afterwards on a motion censuring the ministry for neglecting Ireland Burke challenged the ministry to treat Ireland with the same 'obstinate perseverance' as it treated America. As they were sure to lose America, so they would lose Ireland. His sarcastic string of rhetorical questions has an ironic grotesqueness which carries the argument well beyond Fox's anti-ministerial attack. Burke sees incidents in America mirrored in Ireland, in Dublin as in Boston:

54 *Parl. Hist.* xx, 1126. 55 Ibid., 1127. 56 Ibid., 1197-1242 (6 Dec. 1779).

A mob had rose in Dublin, and non-importation agreements had taken place; why not, like ill-fated Boston, shut up the port of Dublin, burn Corke, reduce Waterford to ashes? Why not prohibit all popular meetings in that kingdom, and destroy all popular elections? Why not alter the usual mode of striking juries, as was done by the Massachusetts Bay charter bill? Why not bring the Dublin rioters over to this country to be tried by an English jury?[57]

Burke mockingly dares the ministry to treat one colony like another knowing that they dare not. And yet whereas America, 'in her revolt, has had a choice of favours held out to her', Ireland who remained loyal is left 'unattended to, and unpitied'.[58] The argument, as in much resistance writing, stresses the injustice and the hurt to Ireland.

This is compounded when he turns to 'the example held out to Ireland, by our conduct towards America.' The administration turns a deaf ear to loyal Ireland, driven 'to the last stage of human misery and distress' while rebellious America has won 'a free trade with all the world.'

Burke then undercuts his indignation at the contradiction – a note seldom found in Fox on Ireland – with a fawning disclaimer about himself as an Irishman in Westminster. He ends by expressing 'his warmest gratitude to this country, which had raised him from an humble situation', his criticism was but the result of 'the best of his judgement'; whatever would benefit Ireland he was sure would benefit England,

> but if ever any concesssions on the part of his native country should be insisted upon, derogatory to the interest and prosperity of this country, he would be one of the first men in that House, in the character of a British senator, to rise and oppose [in] the most peremptory and decisive manner, any proposition tending directly or indirectly to any such point.[59]

The tone of obsequiousness in these closing remarks leaves the reader wondering why Burke needs to shift his ground, what these self-conscious remarks have to do with his case for Ireland. The transformation from confident, ironic, critical spokesman for the aggrieved Irish to loyal British senator looks gratuitous, and yet it is a fair reflection of the division within him between a deep-seated concern for Ireland and a reverence for the empire of which Westminster was the final arbiter. As he said on America, 'Let the Colonies always keep the idea of their civil rights associated with your Government.'[60] He knew at times like this that Ireland and Westminster were divided and he did not know how to hold them together.

---

57 6 Dec. 1779, 'Speech on Trade Concessions to Ireland', *Writings and Speeches of Edmund Burke*, ix, 538. 58 Ibid., 539. 59 Ibid., 541-2. 60 'On Conciliation with the Colonies' (1775), *Writings and*

Burke on India

He has no such difficulty with India on which he wrote a great deal more than on Ireland, and a brief analysis of the opening of one of his speeches on India illustrates the greater ease and application with which he addresses colonial exploitation there. The point is not strange in that in speaking of India or America Burke was free of those family, historical and cultural ties which affect his writing about Ireland. Also, India's relation with England was different to Ireland's: India was administered under charter by the East India Company, a distant and strange country to many, whereas Ireland was so close at hand, with its complex political, religious and economic forces intertwined with England's. And yet these differences do not entirely explain why Burke was so expansive on India and, by comparison, so reticent on Ireland.

In terms of postcolonial writing there are obvious similarities between Ireland and India: both were part of the empire and therefore Burke's notion of universal human rights would apply equally to both countries. Yet India rather than Ireland prompted Burke to those eloquent moments where he so clearly enunciated that view:

> We are all born in subjection, all born equally, high and low, governors and governed, in subjection to one great, immutable, pre-existent law, prior to all our devices, and prior to all our contrivances ... by which we are knit and connected in the eternal frame of the universe, out of which we cannot stir.[61]

Conquest makes no difference to this. What he says of India – 'No conquest give[s] such a right by which it may rule others at its pleasure' – applies to Ireland.[62]

The sheer volume of Burke's writings on India indicates a much greater readiness to speak like this about that far distant colony than on Ireland. There is a sense of enquiry, exploration about his approach, followed by the notorious exhaustiveness which he applies to the injustices of the East India Company under Warren Hastings. Of all his writings those on India, he said, 'showed the most industry, and the least success'.[63] He brought to the thankless task an astonishing knowledge of that country's history, culture, economics, geography and current administration to support his analysis of how the people of India were being abused in the name of empire. The same principles had matured earlier in his thinking about Ireland. He told Sir Hercules Langrishe that he had started work on India at about the time he wrote his letter to Lord Kenmare about

Speeches of Edmund Burke, iii, 164.   61 'Speech on Opening of Impeachment', Writings and Speeches of Edmund Burke, vi (ed. P.J. Marshall, 1991), 350.   62 Ibid., 462.   63 'Letter to a Noble Lord', Writings and Speeches of Edmund Burke, ix, 159.

Catholic relief in Ireland in 1782. India provided 'another distressed people, injured by those who have vanquished them, or stolen a dominion over them'.[64] The charter company's lack of respect for religion, culture and resources differed in degree but not in kind to what had happened in Ireland. India was Ireland writ large. Accused in 1785 of saying the affairs of Ireland were trivial in comparison Burke replied that in principle they were not, 'but they must be ignorant or inhuman, who said, that Ireland in her present circumstances so feelingly called on Britain as the undone millions of India'.[65] Burke chose not to speak of Ireland with the same energy or copious imagination as he did of India which suggests that India became for Burke a kind of surrogate Ireland.

The opening of his celebrated speech on Fox's East India bill (1783) illustrates his profusion of ideas and principles of empire in several ways. Fox had introduced his bill to redress the maladministration by the East India Company, what he called 'a government of anarchy and confusion'.[66] Burke starts by highlighting the gravity of the task. He asks sarcastically 'whether our knowledge of the grievances has abated our zeal for the correction of them'; a remedy, he says, 'is demanded from us by humanity, by justice, and by every principle of true policy'.[67] As of Ireland, so here he remarks on the silence of the ministry on 'the interest and well-being of the people of India'. What he likes about Fox's bill is the demand 'that a *whole* system ought to be produced ... a legislative provision, vigorous, substantial, and effective'.[68] That was more than he asked for Ireland. As with England's treatment of Ireland over trade in the 1770s so now in India he warns that bad government could lead to rebellion:

> I must beg leave to observe, that if we are not able to contrive some method of governing India *well*, which will not of necessity become the means of governing Great Britain *ill*, a ground is laid for their eternal separation.[69]

The task of parliament therefore is 'to preserve the British constitution from its worst corruption', and the best way to achieve that is to write into the instruments of government 'the rights of men, that is to say the natural rights of mankind'.[70] Burke is quickly into a favourite theme, the constitutional liberties of all citizens as enshrined in Magna Carta. These underwrite his concept of empire. Without them empire, and indeed colonialism, have no justification. For that reason they need to be formally recognised:

> Indeed this formal recognition, by the sovereign power, of an original right in the subject, can never be subverted, but by rooting up the holding radical principles of government, and even of society itself.[71]

---

64 'Letter to Sir Hercules Langrishe' (1792), ibid., ix, 635. 65 'Speech on Debate on Address', 25 Jan. 1785, ibid., ix, 585. 66 Cited by Loren Reid, *Charles James Fox: A Man for the People* (London, 1969), p. 181. 67 *Writings and Speeches of Edmund Burke*, v (ed. P.J. Marshall, 1981), 381. 68 Ibid., 382. 69 Ibid., 383. 70 Ibid. 71 Ibid., 384.

Subjection of a nation by a stronger nation is no licence to ignore these rights for, as he might have argued about Ireland, 'political power and commercial monopoly are *not* the rights of men; and the rights to them derived from charters, it is fallacious and sophistical to call "the chartered rights of men".'[72]

Before Burke launches his attack on particular abuses he establishes that the East India Company charter is not a licence but a trust, and the underlying principle of that trust, as in all parts of the empire, is the benefit of the people governed. Precisely the same argument, taken from Locke and Molyneux, informs his unpublished *Tracts relating to Popery Laws* where he states that laws take their validity from the consent of the people, a consent 'to whatever the Legislature ordains for their benefit' – and 'no one is so gross and stupid as not to distinguish between a benefit and an injury'.[73] The East India Company is accountable to parliament that the people of India benefit from and are not exploited by these charters. If parliament passively acquiesces in the Company's conduct it becomes 'an active accomplice in the abuse'.[74]

From this theoretical base he moves into his analysis of the Company and of India, 'infinitely diversified by manners, by religion, by hereditary employment'.[75] The analysis is not just sympathetic to the oppressed millions of India, it mediates India from the perspective of those who are exploited.[76] Of all India's invaders over the centuries – Arabs, Tartars, Persians and now the English, all prone to rapacity and tyranny – none matches the English for oppression and abuse: 'The Tartar invasion was mischievous; but it is our protection that destroys India. It was their enmity, but it is our friendship.' The English, like Swift's prototype colonists, 'a crew of pirates', are rapacious looters. Burke rises to one of his most vicious anti-colonial passages:

> Animated with all the avarice of age, and all the impetuosity of youth, they roll in one after another; wave after wave; and there is nothing before the eyes of the natives but an endless, hopeless prospect of new flights of birds of prey and passage, with appetites continually renewing for a food that is continually wasting.[77]

This flow of scorn has an imaginative energy which contrasts with the pent-up anger of his much briefer account of the English conquering Ireland in the *Abridgment*. The rapacity of the English in India made them the worst of colonists. They had not touched India in any meaningful way:

> With us no pride erects stately monuments which repair the mischiefs which pride had produced, and which adorn a country, out of its own

72 Ibid. 73 'Tracts relating to Popery Laws', *Writings and Speeches of Edmund Burke*, ix, 454-5. 74 Ibid., v, 385. 75 Ibid., 390. 76 Cf. Bhabha on 'cultural difference' of which the aim is 'to rearticulate the sum of knowledge from the perspective of the signifying position of the minority that resists totalisation' (*The Location of Culture*, p. 162). 77 *Writings and Speeches of Edmund Burke*, v, 402.

spoils. England has erected no churches, no hospitals, no palaces, no schools; England has built no bridges, made no high roads, cut no navigations, dug out no reservoirs. Every other conqueror of every other description has left some monument, either of state or beneficence, behind him. Were we to be driven out of India this day, nothing would remain, to tell that it had been possessed, during the inglorious period of our dominion, by any thing better than the ouran-outang or the tiger.[78]

The desolate landscape is made hideous by the animated images of English administrators turned into birds of prey with insatiable appetites.

Burke is not done yet. He turns from India back to England where the young officials who have drunk 'the intoxicating draught of authority and dominion' are welcomed home while the complaints of India are lost over 'a remote and unhearing ocean.' The benefits of their Indian fortunes contrast starkly with the suffering they have left behind:

Here the manufacturer and husbandman will bless the just and punctual hand, that in India has torn the cloth from the loom, or wrested the scanty portion of rice and salt from the peasant of Bengal, or wrung from him the very opium in which he forgot his oppressions and his oppressor.[79]

The 'worst corruption' of the empire filters back into England in a cycle of oppression and self-aggrandisement. That is the dynamic of colonialism described by Swift and repeated by postcolonial critics into the twentieth century. Burke's fellow Irishman Sheridan, persuaded by Burke to speak on the impeachment of Hastings, resorted to similarly harrowing and grotesque images. He likened the so-called 'protection' of Hastings' administrators to a vulture,

Like a vulture with her harpy talons grappled in the vitals of the land, they flap away the lesser kites and then they call it protection. It is the protection of the vulture to the lamb.[80]

Burke's metaphoric flights are even more ghoulish. If the proximity of Ireland both physically and emotionally restrained him, India released him. Burke's place as an Irishman in Westminster with his strong brogue, essentially an outsider, made it virtually impossible for him to speak about Ireland in the House of Commons in this expansive, authoritative, uninhibited way. Burke never gives Ireland full rein in public, only in his closet.

---

78 Ibid. 79 Ibid., 403. 80 Sheridan's speech, 13 June 1788, cited by Madeleine Bingham, *Sheridan, the Track of a Comet* (London, 1972), p. 246.

The colonial discourse of the centre

India isn't all Burke is speaking against here. A more fundamental target is the dominating discourse from the centre at Westminster. The argument as in his writings on Ireland and America is that England has repeatedly placed her own political and economic interests ahead of the empire. Burke keeps coming back to principles of justice and equity enunciated in that favourite reference point of his, Magna Carta. The pertinence of Magna Carta is that it had, in Burke's view, salvaged England from its own abuses of power. The plot of the *Abridgment of English History* makes this clear. England was a country colonised severally by the Romans, the Danes and the Normans. For several centuries there was 'no respected order in the state' only anarchy and misery for the majority of the people.[81] The succession of monarchs was uncertain – some were unscrupulous exploiters, a few wise and innovative. The shifting and uncertain fortunes of the people and the endless struggle for power are finally brought to stability and security in 1215 by Magna Carta with the separation of the judiciary from the executive. Magna Carta establishes justice and equity before the law. That, argues Burke, is the fundamental benefit of empire.

However, Burke knew from his upbringing in Ireland the many contradictions between such a theory and practice. Although an eloquent supporter of empire and therefore in theory not anti-colonial, he repeatedly contested the discourse emanating from succeeding ministries in England which ignored the argument from Magna Carta. To better understand what he was writing against, it is important to identify some features of that colonial discourse as it pertained to Ireland.

Throughout the eighteenth century that same overbearing attitude evident in Poynings' Law and the Declaratory Act recurs in parliamentary debates. For example it stands out clearly in the 1770s in the speeches of the leader of the Commons, Lord North. Not unsympathetic to Ireland, North shared his ministry's belief that Ireland's dependence on England exemplified the kind of relationship that should exist between the mother country and its colonies. Clearly it is different from Burke's. The colonies, and North uses the word much more frequently than Burke, were created primarily for England's benefit. North remarked in a debate on Ireland in 1779,

> By every principle of justice, of the law of nations and the custom of the other powers of Europe who had settlements and distant dependencies, the mother country had an exclusive right to trade with and to forbid all others from having any intercourse with them. Such an exclusive right was of the very essence of colonisation, for what nation under the sun

---

81 'Abridgment of English History', *Writings and Speeches of Edmund Burke*, i, 384.

would spend their blood and treasure in establishing a colony and protecting and defending it in its infant state, if other nations were to reap
advantages desirable from their labour, hazard and expense?[82]

The mother country has primacy in whatever sphere she sees fit.

Irish writers contested this argument throughout the century. As Wolfe Tone
put it in 1790: 'It is convenient, doubtless, for England, and for her instruments
in this country, to cry up the "good of the empire" because it lays the power of
Ireland at her disposal.'[83] North trades on none of the more common myths
about Ireland – Catholic sympathy for France, Irish resentment about lands confiscated in the seventeenth century, hostility to Protestants. In fact he has little to
say about the Irish. His argument is about Westminster's power. Constitutional
and economic power emanate from the centre. This argument had been gathering momentum since 1770 when the ministry looked to Townshend as the first
resident viceroy in Dublin 'to recover direct power for the King's government'.[84]
The issue had been severely tested by the American war. North regarded parliament as the supreme authority of the empire and it had to be defended from
'threats on all sides, from Crown, people and colonies'.[85] In the debates on
America he talked about 'the just dependence of the colonies on the Crown of
Great Britain':[86] North's response to the American colonists was, 'We must
punish, control, or yield to them.'[87] In the early 1770s North saw no threat from
Ireland and his confidence is evident in the debate that followed Townshend's
prorogation of the Irish parliament over a money bill in December 1769. At
Westminster an opposition member, Boyd Walsingham, argued that
Townshend's action had been unconstitutional. 'What is this, Sir,' he asked
North, ' but adding insult to oppression, but laughing at the idea of all order, and
smiling while they stab the essence of all liberty to the heart.'[88] The juxtaposition
of 'smiling' and 'stabbing' insinuates a duplicity that makes Townshend's action
all the more damnable. Grenville spoke next, echoing Gulliver on colonialism in
the remark: 'the dignity of this nation has been sacrificed to plunder the inhabitants of Ireland'.[89]

Lord North by contrast employs the myth of colonial prosperity.
Walsingham's images of Ireland, he says, are a fabrication, 'pathetic pictures of
national calamities', his 'melancholy colours ... the child of the imagination'.[90]
With greater daring than Bishop Berkeley twenty years earlier North claims that
Ireland is a land of plenty – trade is on the increase, property values are rising,

---

82 Debate on Lord North's Propositions for the Relief of the Trade of Ireland, 13 Dec. 1779, *Parl. Hist.*, xx, 1279. 83 *Spanish War! An Inquiry how far Ireland is Bound, of Right, to Embark in the Impending Contest on the Side of Great Britain* in *Life of Theobald Wolfe Tone*, ed. William Theobald Wolfe Tone, 2 vols (Washington, 1826), i, 334. 84 Peter D.G. Thomas, *Lord North* (London, 1976), p. 59. 85 Thomas, *Lord North*, p. 54. 86 *Parl. Hist.*, xvii, 1163. 87 Ibid., 1167. 88 Ibid., xvi, 947. 89 Ibid., xvi, 949. 90 Ibid., 950.

and with the exception of parts of the west of Ireland where peasant laziness is attended by wretchedness, 'all is a continual scene of abundance and festivity'.[91] In North's view the myth of a prosperous and happy colony has materialised in Ireland and Gulliver's ironic puff about wise and virtuous British governors has been vindicated.

North's images of 'abundance and festivity' are not without ambiguity in that they exonerate Westminster's control while pointing up a ready source of supply should England need it. But North's determination to project Ireland as a contented and prosperous dependency became increasingly hollow as the 1770s unfolded. In 1770 Ireland witnessed the highest imports for more than a decade, there was a serious shortage of wheat, a failing corn harvest and in the months that followed a financial crisis which brought bankruptcy to many merchants.[92] The rising costs for the army and for patronage contributed to a growing budget deficit. Trade in Ulster began to decline because of a fall in demand for linen and in cattle prices. The changing economic situation prompted some 40,000 to emigrate from Ulster to America between 1769 and 1774.[93] North had to change his rhetorical tactics, even more so as Ireland became a more crucial factor in the war against America and with the threat from France. In the Irish trade debates of 1778-9 North accepted that Ireland had been a victim of prejudicial policy. In 1779 he was pushed to acknowledge of Ireland what had long been thought in America that in all matters pertaining to the colonies England put her own interests first: 'No one had a greater desire to serve Ireland than he had: but the commercial situation of this country was by no means to be thought able to give way in favour of the trade of that country.'[94]

The report of Burke's scathing response to this speech reiterates the self-destructive tendency of North's policy towards both Ireland and America.

> He said, that every measure for some years past, particularly such as had led us into the American war, were avowedly adopted under the idea of *rendering government* powerful and paramount over the several dependencies of the British empire; yet what was the consequence? We had lost already *one third* of the empire past redemption; Ireland was ruined and bankrupt; the reins of government were become so loose, that tumults and insurrections were daily feared; on the other hand if any measure should be adopted to quiet the minds of the people there, Great Britain itself being on the eve of ruin and bankruptcy, it was objected to upon the ground of danger, lest it should cause tumults and insurrections at home.[95]

91 Ibid., 951; the increase in Ireland's trade was mainly with Britain and the trans-Atlantic countries (L.M. Cullen, *An Economic History of Ireland since 1660* (London, 1987), p. 54). 92 Ibid., pp 68-74. 93 Dickson, *New Foundations*, pp 140-3. 94 *Parl. Hist.*, xx. 137 (15 February 1779). 95 'Speech on Irish

Burke depicts England 'powerful and paramount' over the empire, while threatened on her doorstep by 'tumults and insurrections'. What he advocates is more liberal trade policies which would secure rather than threaten the bonds of empire. The issue is not to insist on the power of the centre but to encourage the prosperity of the margins. 'What was given to Ireland, he contended, was not *taken away* from this country, but *secured* to it.'[96] As he said of America, there would be no discontent in Ireland if Britain would only be generous,

> nor do I apprehend the destruction of this empire, from giving, by an act of free grace and indulgence, to two millions of my fellow citizens, some share of those rights, upon which I have always been taught to value myself.[97]

By the end of 1779 North's colonial discourse had moved to a more conciliatory stance. He still insisted that colonialism gave certain exclusive rights to the mother country, but he faced ever increasing sympathy for Ireland in the House and events in Ireland took a more threatening turn – a boycott of British goods, a reduced supply bill from the Irish parliament and the formation of the Irish Volunteers. These last were a militia formed in 1778 for the defence of Ireland against France and drawn chiefly from the Protestant middle-class. Supported by the Catholics they brought a new dimension to Irish politics, not least because 'they were a force outside the control of the administration but at the same time they were a necessity for national defence'.[98] In this changed political climate North became more conciliatory arguing now that Ireland had been rather harshly and unpolitically treated, past laws may have resulted from 'narrow prejudices' or 'a blind policy'; he noticed 'a more liberal spirit' on both sides of the water.[99] Critical of ministry's past prejudice and self-interest towards 'our sister kingdom', he proposed 'to open new sources of commerce to her and such as it would be impossible for Ireland to obtain without the liberality and indulgence of this country'.[100] Reminders about England's primacy gave way to the language of partnership: the two countries were 'but one people' and Ireland was the only part of the empire 'to which we could look for assistance in the moment of peril'.[101]

Burke's persistent attack on England's narrow policies during these debates is tempered by his ambivalence towards Westminster. He tries to negotiate between

---

Trade', 15 February 1779, *Writings and Speeches of Edmund Burke*, ix, 527-8. 96 Ibid., 528. 97 'On Conciliation with the Colonies', *Writings and Speeches of Edmund Burke*, iii, 158. 98 Edith Mary Johnston, *Ireland in the Eighteenth Century* (Dublin, 1974), pp 150-1. There were 50,000 Volunteers by December 1779 (Dickson, *New Foundations*, p. 149). Burke says of the Volunteers, 'this army did not so much contradict the spirit of the law, as supersede it': letter to Thomas Burgh, 1 January 1780, *Writings and Speeches of Edmund Burke*, ix, 557. 99 *Parl. Hist.*, xx, 1272-7 (13 December 1779). 100 Ibid., 1280-1. 101 Ibid., 1282.

a beleaguered Ireland and a self-serving England, imaging England now as mother, now as plunderer, encouraging the Irish to become 'a country' against North's idea of a dependency. Yet all the time the object of his attack was shifting its ground to the point where North accepted Ireland on all but equal terms. Events had run with Burke and the Whig sympathisers and against North and the ministry. This forced the old colonial discourse on Ireland of well over a century into a new phase of self-criticism and revaluation. Ironically events in Ireland were moving faster than North dared countenance. While he was framing his conciliatory approach to Ireland's trade, the more fundamental issue of legislative independence was already the talk of political circles in Ireland. Drennan addressed a pamphlet to Burke in 1780 in which he wrote,

> a free trade implies a free constitution ... and our trade can with as little reason be called free, as a prisoner would be set at liberty by drawing the bolts that fasten him to the ground, while he is still secured within the four walls of his dungeon.[102]

North brushed aside rumours of this mood as 'merely speculative'.[103] By 1782 Grattan had made it a reality and North had been ousted from office.

Burke's reaction to Ireland's legislative independence was characteristically ambiguous. Although long-standing injuries were at last redressed, such as sections of Poynings' law and the Mutiny Act, and positive benefits secured like the independence of the Irish judges, he was nevertheless apprehensive:

> A new order of things is commencing. The old link is snapped asunder. What Ireland will substitute in the place of it in order to keep us together, I know not – I say, what *Ireland* will substitute; because the whole is now in her hands.[104]

Yet within a few sentences he remarks, 'If things are prudently managed, Ireland will become a great country.'[105] The same mixture of hesitancy and pride is evident a few weeks later when he tells Lord Charlemont in Dublin that any loosening of ties between England and Ireland would be 'a blessing of a very equivocal kind'.[106] In the wake of the French Revolution he feared that the rebellious spirit in Ireland made it all the more imperative that her bonds with England be strengthened.[107] His political sense of Ireland's place in the empire,

---

102 Drennan, *A Letter to Edmund Burke*, p. 21. The letter asked Burke to put aside 'party' interest and 'make himself instrumental in the attainment of this great national object [political independence]' (p. 37). 103 *Parl. Hist.*, xx, 1284. 104 To the Duke of Portland, 25 May 1782, *Correspondence of Burke*, iv, 455. 105 Ibid. 106 Ibid., 12 June 1782, 460. 107 Burke spells out his opposition to total independence for Ireland in 1795 when the Catholics joined with the United Irishmen in their anti-English protests: 'The Language of the day went plainly to a separation of the two Kingdoms. God forbid,

especially with regard to defence, cannot however suppress the emotional and cultural pull of his native land. Stressing that he was born in Ireland and benefited from his upbringing there, reassuring Charlemont that 'a natural, faithful, and cheerful alliance, will be a far securer link of connexion than any principle of subordination', he encourages Charlemont as if speaking to all Ireland, 'Go on and prosper, and improve the Liberty you have obtained by your Virtue, as a means of national prosperity and internal as well as external union!'[108]

Burke's letters show that his heart was in Ireland, wrestling with it, loving it, frustrated by it. Only occasionally do his parliamentary speeches reflect the same range and depth of emotion. More often they indicate his loyalty to the counterclaim of wider and more complex concerns among the Rockingham Whigs at Westminster. In pleasing the latter he often came under fire from Ireland. His opposition to the French Revolution meant that by the end of his career he had become a person to ridicule and an enemy to the cause of radical elements in Ireland, as seen in these verses,

> I said to old Burke, for d'ye see he could cry,
> When France had resolved to be free,
> What argufies grunting like hogs in a stye?
> Why, what a blind fool you must be!
> Don't you see the world's wise, and that freedom's the work
> Engaged in, by sea and on shore:
> And if to the lantern you go, my friend Burke,
> We ne'er shall be plagued with you more.[109]

In one of the few speeches he made in the debates leading up to the grant of legislative independence for Ireland in 1782, his sense of being pulled in opposite directions is poignantly clear. His remarks are a curious blend of impassioned commitment and failure. Saying that he had always tried 'to relieve Ireland from the tyranny and oppression' of England, he comments,

> It had been his misfortune to have been misrepresented, and to be held forth as an enemy to that country ... It was a little hard for him, of all men, to have experienced this fate, because, in the days of the subordination of Ireland, when she lay at the foot of England, depressed, humiliated, and a sufferer, he had ever pleaded her cause with zeal, with sincerity, and all the arts of persuasion that he possessed; but as in those

that anything like it should ever happen. They would both be ruined by it' (Burke to Thomas Hussey, 18 May 1795, *Correspondence of Burke*, viii, 246-7). 108 Ibid., 12 June 1782, iv, 460. 109 'Freedom's the Work' in James Porter, *Billy Bluff and Squire Firebrand, with a Selection of Songs from 'Paddy's Resource'*, 13th edn (1794; Belfast, 1840), p. 83. During the French Revolution people were hanged from the lamp-posts.

days Ministers were not to be moved by prayer, and by intreaty, all he could say, had but little effect. Having done his utmost, however, to serve his native country, when oppressed and miserable, now she was to be placed on a footing of equality with Great Britain, it only remained for him to congratulate her on her having recovered from her debasement, and give his vote in contributing to exalt her to that degree of elevation and liberty, that was her undoubted and just right.[110]

110 'Speech on Affairs of Ireland', 17 May 1782, *Writings and Speeches of Edmund Burke*, ix, 582.

CHAPTER EIGHT

Maria Edgeworth:
Castle Rackrent[1]

To move from Burke and the political debates at Westminster to the remote rural Ireland of Maria Edgeworth's novel *Castle Rackrent* (1801) seems a substantial shift from the centre to the margin, from arguments of great moment about empire, nations and justice to an anecdotal fictional account of life on a distant Irish estate. The worlds are so far apart that they appear to have nothing in common. But this is to miss the point that the landed estate was at the heart of Burke's notions of empire as well as of Molyneux's *Case*. As seen earlier it was the focal point of dispute between settlers and the dispossessed, a sign of contradiction, dispute and shifting identities.

In many ways *Castle Rackrent* marks a major moment in Ireland's attempt to deal with just these issues. It is the first novel out of Ireland to reflect if not analyse a landed Protestant family whose roots go back into Ireland's complicated history and, even more radical, to give the guiding voice, not to a landlord, but to an illiterate serving man. It places at the centre of the narrative a character who in previous fiction, drama and in much political writing had been peripheral, if noticed at all. The horizons of the countryside which the narrator inhabits are the boundaries of his mind. He probably has not heard of Molyneux or O'Conor; Swift and Burke may be but names to him. To give such a person control of the story left readers confused between horror and amusement.

Castle Rackrent is recognised as having brought a new dimension to fiction in English – the local as national – much as Burns and Crabbe were doing in poetry: the fact that this happens in Ireland in the 1790s can be seen as a not unexpected consequence of the long debates mentioned earlier. Edgeworth

---

1 The edition used is in *Maria Edgeworth's 'Castle Rackrent' and 'Ennui'*, ed. Marilyn Butler, London, 1992 (hereafter *Castle Rackrent*).

lodges those debates in the particulars of local people. Thady becomes the epit-
ome of his nation's characteristics. The novel brings to attention that mundane
dimension of Irish rural life which many in Ireland regarded as too familiar to be
worth recording, and yet such estates and their management had long been a key
issue in the political argument between Ireland and England.

The Edgeworths and Ireland

Maria Edgeworth was more obviously settler stock than Molyneux or Swift.
Born and educated in England, she was the eldest daughter of the family who
moved to their Irish estate at Edgeworthstown in the summer of 1782. Maria was
fourteen. Her father, Richard Lovell Edgeworth, a forceful man of wide-ranging
interests in science, literature, education and politics, had brought up his daughter to read voraciously in English and French and to assist him with the business
of the estate, prompting her remark that his many acts of 'liberality ... were
remembered by the warm-hearted people among whom he lived'.[2] Edgeworth
was an improving landlord whose intellectual curiosity and orientation were not
westwards into Ireland but towards parliament and the bookshops of Dublin,
and across the Irish sea to England and France.

Yet the very success of the Edgeworth estate raised ghosts of this settler
family's chequered past in Ireland. The lands had been granted to Francis
Edgeworth, a lawyer and clerk of the crown in Ireland, in 1619. The family's
presence thus dated back to James I's policy of settling Protestants on lands confiscated from Catholics.[3] Succeeding generations of Edgeworths, often spendthrift and eccentric, were glad of the revenue from their estate but more
concerned with their standing at court. In the late seventeenth century Francis'
son, John, knighted by Charles II, raised a regiment to fight for King William
against James II. When Sir John's son Frank died, Maria's grandfather succeeded
to the estate, which had been reduced by family litigation. He married Jane
Lovell, daughter of a Welsh judge and had eight children of whom Maria's
father was the second son. He came into the estate when his elder brother
Thomas died. He had attended school in Edgeworthstown, where he was
taught by Patrick Hughes, the same master who had taught Oliver Goldsmith,[4]
and later moved to school in England and then Trinity College in Dublin. His
time in England, where Maria was born and educated, was a relatively brief gap

2 Cited by Anne Thackeray Ritchie, Introduction, '*Castle Rackrent' and 'The Absentee'* (London, 1895),
p. xx. 3 Marilyn Butler, *Maria Edgeworth*, p. 13. Maria's father referred to the estate as 'landed property by the right of Conquest' (Edgeworth to Mrs Clifton, 13 Dec. 1792, cited by Butler, *Maria
Edgeworth*, p. 112). 4 Vivienne Abbott, *An Irishman's Revolution. The Abbé Edgeworth and Louis XVI*
(Newbridge, 1989), pp 2-3; one of Richard's cousins in Edgeworthstown, Henry Essex Edgeworth,
later became the Abbé Edgeworth who was chaplain to Louis XVI at his execution. Edgeworth's uncle
Robert had turned Catholic and emigrated to France (*An Irishman's Revolution*, pp 5-8).

in the family's history in Longford. This family estate, so steeped in settler history, was where Maria Edgeworth wrote *Castle Rackrent* and was to be her home until her death in 1849.

Maria, like her father and grandfather, had a strong if ambiguous feel for this family's history. Not only had it been preserved by her grandfather in family annals, known as the Black Book, by her grandfather, but her father too wrote an autobiography of his times there which Maria finished after his death.[5] These several narratives, together with *Castle Rackrent*, tell the Edgeworth story over and over again as if trying to renegotiate its relation with its own history in Ireland. *Castle Rackrent,* drawing on family records for many of its characters and situations, metamorphoses history into a fictional saga stretching over four generations of Rackrents. The date which Maria Edgeworth puts into the sub-title of the novel, 'before the year 1782',[6] deliberately distances the action from the late 1790s when she was writing because both she and her father saw a decided contrast between that reckless and dissolute lifestyle of their forbears and the present exemplary and innovative management of the estate. The point is made explicit in the Preface written by her father: 'the manners depicted in the following pages are not those of the present age'; people move forward from their 'follies and absurdities' stimulated by 'new habits and a new consciousness'.[7] National identities change, he argues, 'and the present generation is amused rather than offended by the ridicule that is thrown upon its ancestors'.[8] The amusement suggests the novel is offered as a backward look from a fresh perspective.

The confidence of the Preface does not conceal an obvious difficulty. In a complex and divided Ireland one wonders who precisely Edgeworth means by 'the present generation' of readers: Irish readers, including Catholic gentry, or just Protestants? The phrase certainly includes readers in England. The immediate implication is enlightened Protestant gentry like himself and his daughter who are mature enough to put behind them the scandalous conduct of many of their ancestors who so exploited their tenants and neglected their own family estates. But not all Edgeworth's neighbours shared his views: some were divided on whether the novel was a satire or simply absurd; others were 'enraged'.[9] The claim that landlords' habits had changed was denied many years later by Maria's half-sister Harriet who wrote in 1849,

> even yet, we fear that the working of the encumbered estates Commission
> will show that the Sir Kits and Sir Condys are not extinct & that their
> propensities, if not so very glaring & obtrusive as those of their progeni-

5 *The Black Book of Edgeworthstown and Other Edgeworth Memories*, eds H.J. and H.E. Butler, London, 1927 and *Memoirs of Richard Lovell Edgeworth*, 2 vols, London, 1820 . 6 'An Hibernian Tale taken from facts and from the manners of the Irish squires before the year 1782.' 7 *Castle Rackrent*, p. 63. 8 Ibid. 9 Mrs S.C. Hale, 'Edgeworthstown, Memories of Maria Edgeworth', *Art Journal*, Nov. 1866, p. 228.

tors have in fact been attended with consequences not a jot less disastrous to others & to themselves.[10]

In the light of these diverse reactions the bold assertiveness of the Preface reads like the self-justification of an improving landlord who wanted to redeem his family's record, and by extension the settler presence. Even though the novel depicts the likes of his ancestors wasting their opportunity for constructive and humane developments in Ireland he had learned to make good their errors.

The ambiguous narrator

If the title *Castle Rackrent* conjures up expectations of heartless exploitation of Irish tenants, the character of the narrator quickly disarms such expectations. This is not a protest novel against domineering landlords, a horror story of deprivation, at least not on the surface. The narrator, Thady Quirk, is incapable of such direct engagement: he is 'an illiterate old steward',[11] Catholic Irish, loyal to the Rackrent family, 'one of the most ancient in the kingdom'.[12] What Thady calls the 'Memoirs of the Rackrent Family' are thus mediated by a narrator who seems a toady, 'without enlargement of mind to draw any conclusions from the facts',[13] whose loyalty leaves us wondering whether he is not blind to much of what is happening around him, if not to the damage done to Ireland by the likes of the Rackrents. He is a servant telling the tale of his masters. The amusement stems largely from his apparent innocence. Yet his blinkered naïveté and garrulous anecdotes are part of a more puzzling character whom we have reason to suspect sees more than he tells. Old Thady's very language with its rural Irish syntax, grammar and expression roots him in a culture and class which, as Maria Edgeworth demonstrates in other novels, was renowned for its cunning manipulation of settler landlords. What she may not have been so aware of is that her choice of Thady as the narrator allowed a kind of mediation between master and servant, Protestant and Catholic, which could be highly subversive.

Thady is based on the old steward at Edgeworthstown, John Langan, who had long fascinated Maria:

> I heard him when I first came to Ireland, and his dialect struck me, and his character; and I became so acquainted with it, that I could think and speak in it without effort: so that when for mere amusement, without any idea of publishing, I began to write a family history as Thady would tell it, he seemed to stand beside me and dictate.[14]

10 Article about Maria in Harriet's hand for the *Commercial Journal and Family Herald*, Nov. 1849 (Bodleian Library, Oxford, Edgeworth Adds. Box 2, f.4). 11 Preface, *Castle Rackrent*, p. 62. 12 *Castle Rackrent*, p. 66. 13 Preface, ibid., p. 62. 14 Maria Edgeworth to Mrs Stark, 6 Sept. 1834 in *A Memoir*

This 'mere amusement' became a desire to write Thady into print, hence 'this illiterate old steward' tells his tale 'in his vernacular idiom' to her as his 'editor'.[15] The freedom she gives him is as much a token of her innocence as of what she supposes is his. As the Preface puts it, 'those who were acquainted with the manners of a certain class of the gentry of Ireland some years ago will want no evidence of the truth of honest Thady's narrative'.[16] He is simply telling the truth about the decline of the family. The relationship is typical of what postcolonial critics have observed about the way the settler writer approaches the indigene. Her fascination comes from a curiosity with his difference, in particular the way he speaks. The Edgeworths had thought at first, 'to translate the language of Thady into plain English', but soon found that 'Thady's idiom is incapable of translation'.[17] That difference is alluring yet dangerous because its amusing surface conceals a cultural way of thought she is ignorant of. Her desire to describe or record is driven by a presupposition about his naïveté and ignorance. His supposed backwardness is a given of her cultural norms and therefore a subject for amusement as being deviant and at the same time harmless. He poses no threat and her writing is an attempt to capture him in words for her unsuspecting English readers. Her fascination thus leaves the story in the hands of a narrator she thinks she can trust. But there is much in the novel to suggest that his story is layered with meanings much more complex if not subversive than she or her father would want to admit.

Maria Edgeworth's choice of Thady achieved one important objective. She allays English prejudices. The novel was written with English readers in mind, as she makes clear in the glossary and notes; her father reinforces the point in the Preface. Thady looks like an Irish stereotype of the English imagination, a rural Irish character of little education, whose life has been spent in service to one family, who has never been to Dublin, knows little about the world, who speaks an awkward and sometimes incomprehensible English, but who seems commendably faithful and completely without malice. He seems no threat to anyone, amusing to listen to and therefore easy to accept. Edgeworth's achievement here is that she creates a narrator who by his very idiosyncrasies allays whatever hostile prejudices English readers may have against the Irish in the wake of the 1798 rebellion.

By thus disarming her readers and cajoling them into listening to Thady, Edgeworth lays the ground for what becomes her main focus, the fortunes of the Rackrent family. Thady tells the story not just of the decline of a big Irish estate, but of an estate inherited by a family that was once Catholic, then conformed to

of Maria Edgeworth with a Selection from Her Letters, ed. Frances Edgeworth, 3 vols (1867), iii, 152. Maria's father introduced John Langan to Marc-Auguste Pictet, a visitor to Edgeworthstown, as 'l'original de ce bon Thady' (the original of good Thady): Marc-Auguste Pictet, *Voyage de trois mois en Angleterre, en Ecosse, et en Irlande* (Geneva, 1802), p. 186. 15 Preface, *Castle Rackrent*, pp 62-3. 16 Ibid. 17 Ibid., p. 63.

the church of Ireland, and which over four generations ruined the estate by aping the life-styles sometimes of their ancestors and sometimes of the Anglo-Irish gentry. But Thady tells the story in such an amusing way that the reader can be excused for not pondering on its darker ironies. The Edgeworths assured readers this was an Ireland long gone.

What we shall see in this chapter is that Thady's narrative, despite his loyalty to the Rackrent family, is infused with a critical irony that operates on two levels. It can be read as a rambling maudlin account of colonial-style living, or as a narrative which through irony becomes an anti-colonial critique of the way the English have subverted Ireland's Catholic gentry. Thady is the typical mimic man of postcolonial literature, 'a contradictory figure who simultaneously reinforces colonial authority and disturbs it'.[18] His story tells of loyalty and of ruin. The fact that the Rackrents hastened their own collapse makes no substantial difference to the ambiguities in Thady's account. His apparent innocence is the most troubling feature of his character.

The Rackrents

To appreciate Thady's ironic role it is important to clarify the world he inhabits and the family he serves. Castle Rackrent is situated in rural Ireland, well away from Dublin. Thady seems never to have been to Dublin, let alone England, yet those centres of influence keep intruding on Castle Rackrent. The Rackrents, their friends and neighbours, the O'Neils of Ballynagrotty, the Moneygawls of Mount Juliet's Town, the O'Shannons of New Town Tullyhog, whether they acquired their titles by conformity or not, shared the privileges enjoyed and sanctioned by the Protestant government in Dublin. The last of the line Sir Condy wins a seat in the Irish parliament and spends his winters in Dublin. The lifestyle of such gentry illustrates the colonial ethos of Thady's world. The family to which he is so faithful, old Catholic stock, the O'Shaughlins, had sold out to settler politics and culture. Sir Patrick O'Shaughlin inherited the estate on condition that 'he should by act of parliament take and bear the surname and arms of Rackrent'.[19] The reference may be to the Act of 1704 which allowed a Catholic to inherit 'the whole real estate' only if he conformed to the church of Ireland within a year of the owner's death,[20] or to the earlier Act of Resumption of 1700 which cancelled Catholic legislation on Irish estates passed under James II and gave Protestant trustees powers that 'all and every the honours, baronies, manors, castles ... may be disposed of in the most beneficial manner to the public'.[21] Either way the old Catholic O'Shaughlins could inherit the estate only if they had

18 Jenny Sharpe, 'Figures of Colonial Resistance', *The Post-Colonial Studies Reader*, p. 99.   19 *Castle Rackrent*, p. 66.   20 'An Act to Prevent the Growth of Popery', 1704, *Irish Historical Documents, 1172–1922*, p. 191.   21 *English Historical Documents, 1660–1714*, ed. Andrew Browning (London, 1953), pp 720–1.

renounced their faith and accepted a name which labels them as exploiters of their own people. Whether they remained crypto-Catholics or not, the change of name formalised their standing in the eyes of the government.[22] The word 'castle' in the title reinforces the point because it was the English who introduced castles to Ireland in Anglo-Norman times. Castles were initially synonymous with conquest and colonial rule. The O'Shaughlins had succumbed to the colonisers.

Old Thady claims to be too intent on affirming his loyalty to the family to dwell on these awkward historical issues or indeed on the family's spendthrift habits. Even so, the story he tells makes clear that the Rackrents abused the estate and its tenants in various ways: some were so riotous and careless that they totally neglected the estate, others so mean that they destroyed its spirit. Sir Patrick who, like Sir Condy later, died from drink, lived so carelessly and hos-pitably that his body was seized for debt at his funeral. His hospitality is a reminder of his old Irish ties, in this case the custom known as coshering by which the lord would keep open house to his supporters.[23]

His son Sir Murtagh was the opposite. Educated in the law, he thought only of money. He married a widow, heiress to the Skinflints, who ran the estate with frightening efficiency and financial benefit to herself while he gave his energies to lawsuits, driving his tenants, extorting payment from them in coin and kind at every turn. Thady thanked his stars, 'I was not born a gentleman to so much toil and trouble.'[24] This selfish generation bleeds the energies and resources of their tenants as the worst of the 'new' English might have done.

Sir Murtagh is succeeded by his younger brother Sir Kit. The family has now been so assimilated into English ways that he has left for England where he serves as 'a young dashing officer' in the army.[25] His initial urge is to join the ranks of Irish absentee landlords who take full advantage of the benefits of colo-nialism by living in England off the income of their Irish estates; as a critic of the time puts it, to 'riot and blaze abroad, while some thousands of their fellow Citizens are starving for want of their Help at home, and their country is reduc'd to Beggary, and a deadly Consumption.'[26] Such criticism abounded through the eighteenth century in Ireland. Absentees usually left their estates, as Sir Kit does, in the hands of agents or middlemen, often Catholics, 'who grind the face of the poor'.[27] But when the money runs out Sir Kit marries a Jewish heiress he meets

---

22 Kevin Whelan argues that there were many more Catholic and crypto-Catholic landlords than has previously been acknowledged: 'An Underground Gentry? Catholic Middlemen in Eighteenth-Century Ireland', *Eighteenth-Century Ireland* 10 (1995), 10-11. 23 Coshering, according to Burke, was the Irish version of the older English custom by which subordinate barons 'should receive their lord and all his followers' ('Abridgment of English History', *Writings and Speeches of Edmund Burke*, i, 489). 24 *Castle Rackrent*, p. 70. 25 Ibid., p. 72. 26 Samuel Madden, *Reflections and Resolutions proper for the Gentlemen of Ireland, as to their Conduct for the Service of their Country* (Dublin, 1738), p. 7. In 1783 there were 394 absentee landlords who spent an income of £188,980 abroad (*Walker's Hibernian Magazine*, (1783), pp 174-6); for an analysis of absentees see L.M. Cullen, 'Economic Development, 1750-1800', *New History of Ireland*, iv, 172-3. 27 *Castle Rackrent*, p. 73.

at Bath, 'with I don't know how many tens of thousand pounds to her fortune', and returns to the estate.[28] The brief account of his life ends with him being shot in a duel, leaving his creditors to bemoan his demise.

The last of the Rackrents, Sir Condy, has all the marks of a Protestant gentleman. He is educated to the law at Trinity College and in London, knows that he is to inherit the estate so does not apply himself to his studies and returns to Castle Rackrent. Popular with the tenants but careless of his accounts, he soon finds all the income of the first year committed and interest rising. Edgeworth here suggests the final twitch of the old Irish spirit – generous to a fault, Sir Condy falls prey to his agents. His kindness and carelessness go hand in hand to ruin him. Jason, the upstart son of Thady, a Catholic who has conformed and trained in the law, gives the final blow to the family. He so insinuates himself into the management of Sir Condy's debts that he gradually assumes financial control of the estate and in a famous closing scene brings Sir Condy to sign away the Rackrent lands and the castle to himself, or a higher bidder. In the end the Rackrents are rackrented by Jason, one of their own kind.

Thady's closing remark to his story is as enigmatic as his own part in the tale of woe,

> As for all I have set down from memory and hearsay of the family, there's nothing but truth in it from beginning to end: that you may depend upon; for where's the use of telling lies about the things which every body knows as well as I do?[29]

What he tells may well be the truth. What we don't know is whether it is the whole truth.

Irish self-destruction

The plot of *Castle Rackrent* endorses the irony of conforming servant rackrenting conforming master, which in turn suggests a thread of self-destruction. The plot moves from the O'Shaughlins' initial compromise, to capitulation or at least assimilation into the ways of absentees, to the final forfeiture of the estate. If this Catholic family had not bargained with the English lawmakers in the first place, the estate would have been forfeited by Sir Patrick, probably to a settler or some other conforming family. But by trading off his cultural and religious birthright he sets the family on a course that leads to forfeiture of another kind – to the grasping son of the family's serving-man. The old Irish O'Shaughlins, descended from the kings of Ireland, fall prey to upstart Irish who are much cleverer at playing the colonial system to their own advantage. The settler laws have so trapped

28 Ibid., p. 75. 29 Ibid., p. 121.

the old family as to make them seem victims of their own good intentions. It could be argued, particularly by the English, that the Rackrents have only themselves to blame.

Thady's narrative has a beguiling ambiguity. He tells the story of the Rackrents ruining themselves, yet his loyalty prevents him from explicitly acknowledging the failings all around him. The characteristics that bring about this ruin are a curious combination of Irish and English flamboyance, traditional Irish generosity and a taste for English amusements. The consequences are careless management and the horror that the estate will have to meet the costs. Even if these traits were 'a colonial variation upon the concurrent extravagances of the homeland', Ireland will pay.[30] The epitaph on Sir Patrick's tombstone is an ironic tribute to his folly: 'Sir Patrick Rackrent lived and died a monument of old Irish hospitality.'[31] Although Maria Edgeworth means to inform her English readers about the complex forces at work in Ireland – the customs and culture, the exploitation of tenants by middlemen, absentees, religion – Thady's narrative confirms rather than corrects that image of the uncaring and hard-drinking Irish found in contemporary novels and plays. Maria Edgeworth admits as much in the closing paragraphs:

> All the features in the foregoing sketch were taken from the life, and they are characteristic of that mixture of quickness, simplicity, cunning carelessness, dissipation, disinterestedness, shrewdness and blunder, which, in different forms, and with various success, has been brought upon the stage, or delineated in novels.[32]

Whether she is thinking of stage Irishmen like Sheridan's Sir Lucius O'Trigger or Charles Macklin's Sir Callaghan O'Brallaghan, she continues in characters like Sir Condy and Thady an image of the Irish as amusingly generous, impetuous, devious and incompetent.[33] Sir Patrick's carefree hospitality, Jason's cunning, their belief in the fairies and Sir Condy's mock wake are variations on that disparaging view of the Irish first put about by Giraldus and continued by Spenser and Davies, both of whom were respected by the Edgeworths. *Castle Rackrent,* despite the Edgeworths' claim that the novel was designed to counteract stereo-

30 Oliver MacDonagh, 'The Nineteenth Century Novel and Irish Social History: Some Aspects', 14th O'Donnell Lecture (Cork, 1970), p. 5. 31 *Castle Rackrent*, p. 84. Whelan cites the example of George Ryan of Tipperary in the 1780s: he found the demands of his neighbours to be hospitable too much and left for Toulouse where he could live 'without the ruinous expenses of ostentatious entertaining expected of him' ('An Underground Gentry?', *Eighteenth-Century Ireland* 10 (1995), 29). Cf. Tom Dunne, 'Maria Edgeworth and the Colonial Mind', 26th O'Donnell Lecture (Cork, 1984), p. 14: 'Edgeworth's fascination with the native Irish world was traditionally colonial in that she portrayed it as both barbarous and seductive.' 32 *Castle Rackrent*, p. 121. 33 Sir Lucius O'Trigger appears in Sheridan's *The Rivals* (1775) and Sir Callaghan O'Brallaghan in Charles Macklin's *Love à la Mode* (1759).

types of the Irish, offers a settler view of them. The compassionate humour, far from mitigating the image, gives a paternalistic colour to the writing. Yeats said of Thady that 'he stands in the charming twilight of illusion and half-knowledge'; Roger McHugh noted that from the mid nineteenth century Maria Edgeworth was regarded as an Ascendancy writer 'who got little nearer to the Irish peasantry than the threshold of the Big House at Edgeworthstown from where she observed them'.[34]

The glossary and notes also have a paternalist flavour in that they provide English sense to Irish sayings and customs. They not only mediate Thady to the English reader but do so with the learning and authority of an interpreter, of the settler to the uninitiated. One critic calls this commentary 'the secondary text' and adds that it is 'obviously the more reliable and authoritative one, and in it, the voice at least of the colonist class, or rather, of its liberal minority, *is* present'.[35]

The Rackrents as victims

But we should be wary of dismissing the novel as a settler's amusing view of the Irish. Its ironies and humour prevent a single reading. In another and important sense the Rackrents are victims of the colonial system. Their engaging qualities of generosity and national pride make them vulnerable to that system. None of them lives by half-measures. Sir Patrick is notoriously hospitable; Thady is decidedly indolent, more interested in the past and gossip than work, while his masters veer between riotous and extortionate living. Sir Condy was 'a fool all his days'.[36] Georgian England presumed and respected a more even temper in its gentlemen landlords than that displayed by the Rackrents. This is summed up as 'politeness' – 'its civilised if secular outlook, its faith in a measured code of manners, its attachment to elegance and stateliness, its oligarchical politics and aristocratic fashions'.[37] In this age of commerce when English gentry were 'thriving in their own private fortunes, and at the same time promoting the public stock', Addison could exclaim, 'If we consider our own country in its natural Prospect, without any of the Benefits and Advantages of Commerce, what a barren and uncomfortable Spot of Earth falls to our Share!'[38] Some English landed gentry in both fiction and fact preferred hunting and drinking, but many who started out the century as small landowners, like the Whitbreads, became considerable figures by combining their land and business interests.[39] By contrast none of the

---

34 W.B. Yeats, Introduction, *Irish Tales by Maria Edgeworth and John and Michael Banim* (London, [1891]), p. 7; Roger McHugh, 'Maria Edgeworth's Irish Novels' *Studies*, 27 (1938), 556.   35 Tom Dunne, 'Maria Edgeworth and the Colonial Mind', p. 8.   36 *Castle Rackrent*, p. 121.   37 Paul Langford, *A Polite and Commercial People: England 1727–1783* (Oxford, 1992), p. 1.   38 *Spectator*, no. 69 (19 May, 1711), *The Spectator*, i, 295.   39 See Roy Porter, *English Society in the Eighteenth Century* (London, 1982), pp 81–2. Many farmers were prospering as Arthur Young noticed when he toured Ireland in the 1770s, and Ireland's trade and industry figures showed a marked improvement in the latter half of the century (see Cullen, *Economic History of Ireland*, pp 95–8).

Rackrents understands either politeness or money. They either lack the business acumen or apply it ruthlessly. From Sir Patrick who 'had his house, from one year's end to another, as full of company as ever it could hold',[40] to Sir Condy 'who hated trouble, and could never be brought to hear talk of business',[41] they give no thought to improving the estate. This fictional world of *Castle Rackrent*, set before 1782, stands in marked contrast with the actualities of Edgeworthstown which by 1800 had become a model of an improved estate under the management of Maria Edgeworth's father.[42]

For all their faults the Rackrents are victims of alienating forces beyond Thady's or their own comprehension. No reference to the English in the novel suggests other than a force that dissipates Irish values, culture and heritage. The protest against the effects of English laws is implicit from the day Sir Patrick agrees to change his religion and his name. Castle Rackrent is a microcosm of Ireland as a product of England. Lured from their Catholic Irish heritage into the English dispensation, the O'Shaughlins slide into an alien way of life. By changing their name to Rackrent they exchange their Irish identity, which is culturally cohesive, for a name signifying exploitation, and a much less certain identity. For all their generosity they lose whatever links they have had with Gaelic culture for an identity determined by the English. Thady's oft repeated loyalty to the family is a loyalty to a chimera, to something that no longer exists. Without any deliberate objectives, the newly named Rackrents flounder in a cultural no-man's land somewhere between their Irish heritage and English expectations. Sir Patrick O'Shaughlin, given the option of keeping the estate in the family, conforms, 'seeing how large a stake depended upon it';[43] Sir Murtagh, empowered by the English laws, brings a mind obsessed with legal exactions and a Skinflint wife who terrifies the tenants. Between them they alienate themselves from their tenants: 'They knew her way, and what with fear of driving for rent and Sir Murtagh's lawsuits, they were kept in such good order, they never thought of coming near Castle Rackrent without a present of something or other.'[44] If Sir Murtagh lacks his father's Irish trait of generosity his younger brother Sir Kit has removed himself both spiritually and physically to England. Forced by overspending to find a rich wife he returns to the estate with a Jewish heiress who understands nothing of Ireland. Thady soon realises she is 'a stranger in a foreign country',[45] but in fact both are strangers because both look to England, and particularly Bath, for their cultural norms. The last of the line, Sir Condy, although raised on the estate, has spent his formative years in the Protestant English milieu of Trinity College and London. His wife, Isabella, daughter of Captain Moneygawl, reminds us of her English cultural ties by acting Juliet and by her frequent allusions to Shakespeare, which Thady does not understand.[46] Isabella

40 *Castle Rackrent*, p. 66. 41 Ibid., p. 93. 42 See Butler, *Maria Edgeworth*, pp 85-7. 43 *Castle Rackrent*, p. 66. 44 Ibid., p. 69. 45 Ibid., p. 76. 46 Ibid., pp 88, 90.

eventually leaves Sir Condy, thus mirroring the difficulties between old and new, Catholic and Protestant traditions. The same was hinted at in the other Rackrent marriages starting with Sir Murtagh and his wife who 'had a great deal of sparring and jarring between them'.[47] In the end Sir Condy has to leave the castle for the lodge, a move that symbolises his final displacement from the ties and traditions of the O'Shaughlins.

The new generation transgresses the old

Implicit in much of the above is the relentlessly divisive and destructive power of the English presence in Ireland. Allusions to England or its laws are made without exception to the detriment of the Rackrents and by implication of Ireland. Allusions to absenteeism, to Bath, to parliamentary elections, to expensive winters in Dublin during the parliamentary session all suggest that Castle Rackrent looks for its vitality to a social, economic and political ethos it does not understand. Displaced from their own culture the O'Shaughlin descendants live on the margins of this foreign world.

Yet the power behind the settler ideology insinuates itself into the Rackrents' fortunes most damagingly in the person of a local, Thady's son, Jason. He becomes agent to Castle Rackrent, a position that enables him ironically to manage not the welfare of the estate but the bankruptcy of its master. We are introduced to him at the start as 'attorney Quirk': 'he is a high gentleman, and never minds what poor Thady says, and having better than fifteen hundred a year, landed estate, looks down upon honest Thady'.[48] If the Rackrents' response to the English presence is a careless enjoyment of its benefits, young Jason takes a more cunning approach. He acquires the power of the law before moving in on the spoils that await him. The latter part of the novel, 'History of Sir Condy Rackrent', concludes with the confrontation between the two, Jason and Sir Condy, between Thady's son and Thady's master, between the new and the old Irish. From childhood the two of them seemed destined for traditional and complimentary roles, landlord and tenant, but by the end of the novel these roles are so disrupted as to be reversed. Sir Condy and Jason had their early schooling in the village together; both then took different routes to a legal education: Sir Condy takes the conventional route followed by middle-class and landed gentry, from Trinity College to one of the Inns of Court in London, while Jason, 'a good scholar from his birth and a very 'cute lad',[49] becomes an attorney by serving an

47 Ibid., p. 71. 48 Ibid., p. 66. 49 Ibid., p. 74. To qualify as an attorney Jason would have had to conform to the church of Ireland and spend a five year apprenticeship with a practising lawyer. He could have served the apprenticeship in say Dublin, Cork or Limerick while continuing to manage the affairs of the estate. Many agents resided in Dublin in order to be close to banks and visited their estates and tenants from time to time: Arthur Young, *A Tour in Ireland with General Observations on the Present State of that Kingdom made in the Years 1776, 1777, and 1778 and brought down to the end of*

apprenticeship. Thady thought first to send him to be a priest, 'but he did better for himself'.[50] He starts as a clerk to Sir Kit's agent, then begins leasing land and is given control of Sir Kit's accounts. By the time Sir Condy returns to inherit the estate Jason has been appointed agent. The impending conflict between them is between two kinds of historical forces in late eighteenth-century Ireland – respect for tradition, an ancient family's inheritance and the much more flexible pragmatism of money backed up by the law. Sir Condy's training in the law had been something of a formality. As a Protestant gentleman inheriting an estate he did not need to take it seriously enough to have to depend on it for his security or his income. A contrasting figure in Edgeworth's fiction is Lord Glenthorn in *Ennui*, who loses his title and then trains as an attorney. His diligence and per-severance bring him success at the Dublin bar and a happy marriage. Sir Condy makes no attempt to use his legal training to help himself out of his financial dif-ficulties; quite the opposite. He starts to appease Jason with leases and rents. Thady tells us,

> my son requiring to be paid for his trouble, and many years' service in the family gratis, and Sir Condy not willing to take his affairs into his own hands, or to look them even in the face, he gave my son a bargain of some acres, which fell out of lease, at a reasonable rent.[51]

Jason by contrast is determined to extract his financial dues and since 'he had been studying the law, and had made himself attorney Quirk', he cleverly posi-tions himself to take advantage of Sir Condy's financial problems.[52] As Sir Condy's creditors close in, Jason contrives with them to take custody of his assets in order, he tells Thady, 'to make things easier than if all the land was under the power of a total stranger'.[53] That seeming goodwill turns to the hard reality that Jason has bought up Sir Condy's debts and is able to say of Castle Rackrent, 'it's all … lawfully mine, was I to push for it'.[54] Jason brings the spirit of rackrenting to bear on Sir Condy by issuing a final demand on the monies owed to him. He drives Sir Condy to sell him Castle Rackrent to pay off the debts. Old traditional Ireland has been outwitted by the cunning acquisitiveness of their own progeny schooled in the art of rackrenting.[55] The old order has become indebted to the new in a way that spells its own ruin. Not satisfied with the Rackrent estate, Jason then has Sir Condy sign away 'all right and title to those lands that you know of'.[56]

1779, 2 vols (Dublin, 1780), ii, Pt. II, 18. 50 *Castle Rackrent*, p. 74. 51 Ibid., p. 87. 52 Ibid., p. 106. 53 Ibid., p. 100. 54 Ibid., p. 109. Dunne raises the possibility that Jason, together with his father, 'achieved the common peasant dream, noted in many contemporary accounts, of repossessing the land which they believed historically and rightfully theirs' ('Maria Edgeworth and the Colonial Mind', p. 10). 55 Cf. Butler, *Maria Edgeworth*, p. 357: Jason 'was the parasite of the old system, not the herald of a new'. 56 *Castle Rackrent*, p. 117.

Thady's ambivalent response

As a father 'Old Thady' is both proud of and outraged by his son. In keeping with his role as servant he expresses moral indignation at his son's final demand on Sir Condy: 'Is it you, Jason, that can stand in his presence, and recollect all he has been to us, and all we have been to him, and yet use him so at the last?'[57] But the tone here, as of much of Thady's narrative, is difficult to pin down because we are not sure whether he is posturing, or is sincere. He is so ambiguous a figure that some have argued he is secretly supportive of Jason's manoeuvres, others that he is a 'duplicitous Caliban'.[58] He strikes a pose from the start which smacks of a cunning awareness that obsequiousness is the surest way to insinuate himself into the favour of his masters: 'My real name is Thady Quirk, though in the family I have always been known by no other than "honest Thady"'.[59] He also comes to be known affectionately as 'Old Thady.' The point gained is that a servant nick-named 'honest' and 'old' has the trust and favour of his master while the rest live under the presumption of being dishonest. His obsequiousness gains him the additional benefit outside his work to wield power among the locals: for example, Thady is able to ensure that Jason's offer to purchase a lease from Sir Kit will not be contested: 'I spoke a good word for my son, and gave out in the country that nobody need bid against us.'[60] That power is the reward of his much vaunted 'loyalty' to the family. But loyalty in turn has to be set beside his insatiable curiosity to eavesdrop on conversations between Sir Kit and his wife and Sir Condy and Isabella. His responses to Jason's machinations are equally ambiguous. In private he expresses a kind of piqued indifference: 'I wash my hands of his doings,' he says at the start, and at the end seems not to care whether Jason wins his lawsuit or not.[61] Yet in public he remonstrates and weeps at what Jason is doing to Sir Condy. Bemused at the legal knowledge of his attorney son he seems caught between secret pride and public horror.

Thady can be read as the prototype servant, the colonised native who understands that because his security depends upon compliance with the system he needs to display total loyalty. That is the way to whatever benefits are available to him. As one of the dispossessed, he lives off the bounty of his masters, and that requires a show of behaviour in keeping with their expectations. But we have little idea how deep his subservience, loyalty, trustworthiness go. A loyal servant must be seen to accept no other point of reference than his master's, least of all his own cultural roots. This manifests itself when, given the moral choice of

57 Ibid., p. 109. 58 E.g. Sandra M.Gilbert and Susan Gubar, *The Madwoman in the Attic* (London, 1979), pp 150-1: 'this steward who appears to serve his lords with such docility actually benefits from their decline, sets in motion the machinery that finishes them off, and even contributes to the demise of their last representative.' See also Mitzi Myers, ' "Like the Pictures in a Magic Lantern": Gender, History, and Edgeworth's Rebellion Narratives', *Nineteenth-Century Contexts* 19, no. 4 (1996), 381. 59 Ibid., p. 65. 60 Ibid., p. 74. 61 Ibid., pp 66, 121.

siding with Sir Condy or Jason, Thady supports Sir Condy; to do otherwise would be to betray his basic ploy. The colonised cannot openly side with one another against their master without suggesting rebellion. In Thady's case his moral protest always comes at moments when the contest is already decided in Jason's favour, giving the impression that while the servant in him has one role to play the father has another.

Jason dispossesses the Rackrents and by implication the ancient family, the O'Shaughlins. Such dispossession would have been unthinkable in the old Gaelic order. But Jason is fulfilling the designs of the penal laws which encouraged Catholics to conform to the church of Ireland so that they could inherit and purchase land, enjoy life-long leases, be educated, practise a profession, exercise the law to their advantage, live like a settler. As Burke realised, the penal laws set Catholic Ireland against itself.[62] In *Castle Rackrent* there is the added indignity of one conforming Catholic exploiting another. The novel ends with further legal wrangles between Jason and Sir Condy's widow. Division and destruction pervade the novel.

Narrative strategies of failure

This sombre undercurrent in what is often a humorous tale raises difficult questions about the emplotment of the novel. The ending is neither generically comic, wanting the final prospect of a revitalised world, nor is it tragic. The opening voice of the Preface is that of an enlightened Protestant Irish landlord who invites readers to look back to less enlightened times, suggesting satire. The plot of Thady's story indicates time and again that circumstances are more powerful than dreams and that the characters' hopes and desires are constantly undercut by the exigencies of mundane living. The absence of a resolution to the Rackrents' problems confirms Edgeworth's departure from fictional modes which English readers might readily recognise from Defoe or Fielding or Fanny Burney. The guiding narrative voice of an ill-educated local Irish serving-man immediately unsettles the reader's expectations of either a generic telos or a reliable authorial centre. The fact that the narrator is rural Catholic Irish, and not English or an omniscient voice, is a major factor in what looks like a highly subversive strategy to decentre authority, or at least wrest it from an English to an Irish perspective.

But what her narrative strategy also achieves is something more than she may have intended. The novel can be read as a story about what happens in Ireland when the native Irish assume control, when they take over estates and try to live like English landlords. The Rackrents are all patently unable to command respect or engender confidence. When they author themselves, they can hardly be taken seriously.

62 'Address and Petition of the Irish Catholics' (1764), *Writings and Speeches of Edmund Burke*, ix, 431.

The telos of the plot raises questions also about the scheming Jason and his equivocal father. Unlike other novels such as *Moll Flanders* which also have ill-educated but crafty narrators, *Castle Rackrent* ends not with repentance or a moral vision or a marriage to indicate that characters have learned the errors of their ways. Marriage as a closing trope of a happy resolution is deliberately dismissed both with the collapse of Sir Condy's marriage and the failure to marry Jason to Judy, daughter to Thady's sister's son: 'Jason did not marry, nor think of marrying Judy, as I prophesied and I am not sorry for it.'[63] Instead, the story closes in a tangle of unresolved bad feelings. This ending contributes to an elusive sense that Thady is an incompetent story teller. He fails to tie up the ends of his own story.

The Rackrents' failure can be read as Ireland's failure, an inability to handle responsibility, to exercise authority when wrested from England. This also shows in other ways. The title *Castle Rackrent* hints obliquely at the convention found, for example, in Fielding and Richardson, and continued by Jane Austen, of alluding to some big house or landlord as a point of reference for stability and moral values. The title plays with just such English expectations of a large country house, possibly on the site of an old castle, the focus of the surrounding countryside, where the family's influence has been felt for hundreds of years. Castle Rackrent is a quite different place. For example, the house is not large enough to accommodate all Sir Patrick's guests, some of whom choose to lodge in the chicken-house. There are some predictable features – a cellar, an avenue and a lodge – yet the building is so close to other houses that Thady can walk out and talk to children playing in the street. O'Shaughlin's town takes its name from the house, suggesting that it too exhibits not elegant spaciousness or extension, but tightness, a lack of respectful distance. Thady remembers Sir Condy as a child playing barefoot in the streets with Jason and other children. At the close of the novel the townspeople crowd to the windows of the house and Sir Condy has to speak to them through a window. The want of physical space reflects perhaps a want of imaginative space.

The castle: site of contest and displacement

The term 'Castle' raises further ironies not least because of the English origins of the term. The first castles in Ireland were built by the Anglo-Norman invaders to protect settler families against what Spenser called 'that savage nation'.[64] These castles were alien. The title word 'Castle' therefore may hint that this is an estate at the heart of Ireland's history of confiscations: the English confiscated it and fortified it with a castle; it was repossessed by the Irish, confiscated again and later put in the hands of Sir Patrick on condition that he conform. Coming at

63 *Castle Rackrent*, p. 121.   64 Spenser, *A View of the Present State of Ireland* , p. 1.

the end of this torrid history, the Rackrents fail dismally whether seen in the mould of their ancestors or as imitators of settler families bent on improving Ireland in English ways.[65] Colonialism has let them loose in a cultural no-man's land. They tried to take control of the adversarial space and failed. Part of the reason was their life-style reflected the weaknesses rather than the strengths of the two contesting cultures.

Castle Rackrent falls short of the pretensions of its name. It boasts no improving landlord to match Richard Lovell Edgeworth, or Fielding's Squire Western or Austen's Darcy. This is not Castletown House nor Carton Court. Castle Rackrent and its family typify the opposite. In both condition and size the castle stands in contrast to other big houses in eighteenth-century Ireland renowned for their improvements and the prosperous management of their Anglo-Irish landlords. The fiction has the O'Shaughlin family, 'one of the most ancient in the kingdom', reduce themselves physically and economically from a glorious memory to the penury of the last of their line. Sir Condy starts to sell off land and finally has to move out of the castle 'for good and all'.[66]

The literal as well as figurative displacement of Sir Condy in the closing pages brings to mind the ending of *Gulliver's Travels* in that, like Gulliver, the Rackrents are worse off at the end than they were at the start. But unlike Gulliver they have learned nothing. The last of the Rackrents, Sir Condy, dies after a drinking bout, just as the first, Sir Patrick, had done suggesting a point-less circularity in the family annals.[67] The absence of any meaningful cultural or economic direction makes them prey to their own whims and the machinations of Jason. The Celtic heritage of the O'Shaughlins is superseded by forces as ahis-torical and impersonal as Jason's money and settler laws. This is one face of colonised Ireland. Money and greed are the only traces of authority at the end of the novel. Read in this light the novel is an indictment, however amusing, of the old Irish stock who conformed and were seduced by English ways. They showed themselves incapable of capitalising on the opportunities Sir Patrick procured for them.

Castle Rackrent *and Union*

Maria Edgeworth may not have consciously designed such a criticism of the Irish, but these implications were not far from the surface in the manuscript she

---

65 The title may also suggest that Sir Patrick adopted the word 'Castle' in keeping with the growing interest in Ireland's antiquities during the eighteenth century, what McCormack calls 'the affecta-tions of antiquity practised by gothic revivalists': W.J. McCormack, *Ascendancy and Tradition in Anglo-Irish Literary History from 1789 to 1939* (Oxford, 1985), p. 113. However, it has to be remembered that Sir Patrick had inherited the estate early in the eighteenth century before the gothic revival had permeated to rural Ireland. 66 *Castle Rackrent*, p. 110. 67 Cf. W.J. McCormack, *Ascendancy and Tradition*, p. 106.

had completed in 1798 and sent to her London publisher Joseph Johnson. In the spring of 1799 her father and his new wife Frances took Maria with them on a visit to friends in England during which they were impressed at the support for the proposed Union between England and Ireland. Butler writes,

> Suddenly it must have seemed to the Edgeworths that the onus was on the Irish to prove that the English were getting a bargain; so that the light entertainment Maria was about to produce, which presented the Irish as comic and irresponsible, was anything but timely.[68]

On their return to Edgeworthstown they wrote the glossary and notes which had then to be hastily bound in at the front of the first edition. The stated purpose was to educate English readers in the unfamiliar speech and customs of the Irish and thus to make the novel more accessible to those with little knowledge of Ireland. But there was another purpose which the Edgeworths' visit to England made all the more urgent, and that was to insist that many of the attitudes and practices alluded to were no longer current in Ireland. The world of Castle Rackrent was different from what Ireland now offered England in the Union. Phrases like 'formerly' and 'it was customary' help to set the action back a generation or two. In other words, Maria Edgeworth tries to distance the Ireland of her fiction from Ireland moving towards Union. Because the glossary does not impinge on the plot, it establishes a centre of authority outside the plot, which in turn suggests someone outside looking in. The world of the novel thus becomes a curiosity, which was precisely the Edgeworths' purpose. The same point is evident in the Preface which ends with a clear statement as to how the Edgeworths wanted *Castle Rackrent* to be read:

> When Ireland loses her identity by an Union with Great Britain, she will look back with a smile of good-humoured complacency on the Sir Kits and Sir Condys of her former existence.[69]

The implication is that the novel was being published in a new era. Ireland was facing a new historical direction which Richard Lovell Edgeworth, along with many in England including Adam Smith, believed would bring her prosperity. The follies of the Rackrents were a thing of the past never to recur in the new order.[70]

These attempts by the Edgeworths to rescue themselves and the novel from the embarrassment of seeming to ridicule Ireland at a sensitive moment in history confirm rather than diminish their patronising attitude towards the Irish.

---

68 Butler, *Maria Edgeworth*, p. 355. 69 *Castle Rackrent*, p. 63. 70 Edgeworth's visit to industrialist friends in the English Midlands in 1799 convinced him of the commercial advantages to Ireland of a union (Butler, *Maria Edgeworth*, p. 181). Adam Smith argued that union would bring free trade, and release Ireland from an 'oppressive aristocracy', and 'religious and political prejudices': *An Inquiry into the Nature and Causes of the Wealth of Nations* (1776), 2 vols (Dublin, 1785), ii, 486.

Whether the Rackrents are based on Maria's 'dissipated forebears' or not makes no difference;[71] nor is it the whole truth to say 'the destruction of the Rackrents is self-impelled, altogether wanton and unconcerned'.[72] Thady and the Rackrents are represented as participants in a history plagued by religious and cultural divisions. To image them as carefree, wilful and amusing products of a history they do not comprehend and then add a glossary on the grounds that they merit closer understanding hardly calls for 'a smile of good-humoured complacency'. *Castle Rackrent* is a uniquely ambivalent novel. The Edgeworths claim to be mediating an amusing, even affectionate image of rural Ireland, but in fact confirm English prejudices about the careless, hard-drinking, irrational and crafty Irish. Their patronising, colonial strategy produces a tale about the moral and social chaos at the meeting point between Irish and English culture. In this light *Castle Rackrent* is a novel that runs out of settler control.

This is most clearly evident in Thady who is at once the creation of the settler imagination and the genesis of its subversion. Shocked at his son's transgressions he is the father of transgressions. His voice, a rural, unstudied dialect, is by its own avowal unskilled in argument. His rootedness in local rather than national consciousness means he is less able than the reader to understand the significance of the story he tells – as Burke or O'Conor certainly would – and this adds to rather than detracts from its power because his lack of comprehension is a statement that he is ultimately victim rather than agent of the imperial process which enveloped the O'Shaughlins, the Rackrents and Ireland in the eighteenth century. His transgression is that he pays lip-service to that process while fathering disloyalty. While he fulfils his masters' stereotypical expectations of a faithful, honest and amusing servant, he tells a story about the futility of his and their endeavours. Thady is a living parody of service. The last of the Rackrents fathers no children while his loyal servant fathers the master-to-be.

New directions

The emplotment of *Castle Rackrent* taken together with Edgeworth's own success as an improving landlord could be read as the failure which the settler came to redeem. Taken on its own terms the novel can be read as an indictment of settler history in Ireland. The issues so strenuously debated from Molyneux to Burke are here emplotted in the lives of landlord and servant far removed from the language and concerns of political argument in Dublin and London. *Castle Rackrent* illustrates the reverse side of public rhetoric in Ireland. It locates those conflicting attitudes and issues found in Swift and O'Conor on an estate in the heartland of Ireland. Edgeworth's achievement is that she shifts the focus of

71 Butler, *Maria Edgeworth*, p. 354. 72 Oliver MacDonagh, 'The Nineteenth Century Novel and Irish Social History: Some Aspects', p. 5.

debate from pamphlets, histories, speeches and conventions into imaginative literature. Much that had been said about Ireland from Molyneux to Grattan and
by Catholic writers at home and in exile is reflected in the Rackrent history.
Events on the Rackrent estate, its landlords, their plans, their debts and disap-
pointments, the servant and his son, and the day-to-day tensions between master
and tenants constitute the tissue of Irish life which Irish writers contested.

The absence in *Castle Rackrent* of that radical dimension of Irish politics
which had been gathering momentum since the 1780s and led to the rebellion of
1798 is a reminder of the difference between Maria Edgeworth and the prevailing Irish discourse of the time. Edgeworth deliberately sets the novel prior to
1782: 'these are "tales of other times",' says the Preface. Yet reading about the
hard-drinking Rackrents and the obsequious Thady it is easy to forget that the
novel depicts the years leading into sectarian violence, especially in Ulster
between Protestant Defenders and Catholic Peep o' Day Boys, and revolutionary rhetoric by men determined on major changes in Ireland's relation to
England. Lord Annesley wrote in a panic from County Down in 1792 that
Catholics were buying 'every Gun and all the Powder and Ball that can be got …
a Protestant cant go out of the House but the Bullets are flying about them'.[73] If
the inhabitants of Castle Rackrent have no inkling of the Volunteers or their
conventions, much less of the caustic contempt of say Drennan for the politics of
Edgeworth heroes like Grattan, Burke and Charlemont, they occupy the space
out of which Drennan and Wolfe Tone emerged. Clearly the Edgeworths would
be uncomfortable with Drennan's stark oppositions: 'Every nation under the sun
must be placed in one of two conditions. It must be free, or enslaved.'[74] Drennan's
Ireland had no place for improving landlords like Edgeworth:

> You are all native Irish, under the controul of an English pale, and every
> rotten borough in the kingdom is nothing more or less than a feudal
> castle, and the collection of these petty sovereignties is nothing more or
> less than despotism.[75]

Drennan would include the Rackrents and the Edgeworths in his essentialist dis-
missal of the 'petty sovereignties' and 'despotism' of the settlers, yet they seem
oblivious of such a voice in Ireland. The parochial world of Thady and the
Rackrent estate has no such turbulence to shake it out of its self-concern, though
the pre-1782 period had seen the Whiteboy disturbances of the 1760s and the
execution at Clonmel of a Catholic priest, Fr Sheehy, and four others for sedition.[76]

73 Lord Annesley to Lord Downshire, 1 June 1792 in *Peep o' Day Boys and Defenders: Selected
Documents on the Disturbances in County Armagh, 1784-1796*, p. 112.   74 Drennan, *Letters of an Irish
Helot, signed Orellana: republished by order of the Constitution Society of the City of Dublin* (Dublin, 1785),
p. 8.   75 Ibid., p. 9.   76 See Dickson, *New Foundations*, pp 134-5.

When Maria Edgeworth's father, a member of the Volunteers and a politically involved man, writes in the Preface that the Rackrent era is over and that 'there is a time, when individuals can bear to be rallied for their past follies and absurdities', he makes no mention of the post-Castle Rackrent Ireland of the agitated 1780s and 1790s. He imagines instead that after the Union 'when Ireland loses her identity' readers will look back at the Rackrents with good humour. While he distances the 'follies and absurdities' of the past, he implies that the more recent Ireland has changed from her 'former existence'. The new Ireland was in fact a more disturbed place as Edgeworth had already witnessed during the 1798 rebellion.

Edgeworth wrote the Preface in the aftermath of Drennan and Wolfe Tone's campaigns to contest the identity which the Edgeworths had imagined for Ireland in *Castle Rackrent*. Tone's part in the 1798 rebellion had ended when arriving from France he was captured, put on trial in Dublin and sentenced to a public hanging. In his speech to the court he condemned Ireland's connection with England as 'her bane'. He added, 'I have endeavoured by every means in my power to break that connexion.'[77] Tone as we shall see in the next chapter contested an Ireland quite different from that of the Edgeworths. *Castle Rackrent* can be read as a clear example of what Tone meant when he said England had been the 'bane' of Ireland.

It is to Maria Edgeworth's credit that she turns attention from polemics about Ireland to the pecularities of a specific Irish family and place. She gives Ireland a local habitation. It could be argued that it took a woman's imagination to do this, and in so doing wrest Irish writing away from confrontational rhetoric and a preoccupation with politics and history, away from argument, legal issues, trade, exhortations to liberty and complaints about oppression, and into fiction. The striking difference between the Ireland Maria Edgeworth depicts in the novel and the Ireland she knew while writing it cannot be explained away by the note on the title page that it is set 'before the year 1782'. The swirl of events that prefaced the 1798 rebellion – conventions, treason trials, the Defenders, the United Irishmen and Wolfe Tone – was the masculine face of Ireland.[78] She had come physically close to the rebellion when rebel forces came within a few miles of Edgeworthstown. She regarded that experience as terrifying rather than exhilarating, presumably unlike many women who fought on both sides.[79] The insignia of the day were weapons, public rhetoric, the law courts and executions. Maria Edgeworth posits against those a statement about Ireland that is both feminine, fictional – and therefore beyond legal contention – and only obliquely national. Her feminine pose is as editor of Thady's tale. Her role is to listen, not

77 Cited in Elliott, *Wolfe Tone, Prophet of Irish Independence*, p. 393.   78 For the times of composition see Marilyn Butler, Introduction, *'Castle Rackrent' and 'Ennui'*, pp 4-5.   79 Mitzi Myers gives examples of women in the rebellion, particularly at Wexford; cf. the article cited in note 58 above, p. 391 and also *1798: 200 Years of Resonance*, ed. Mary Cullen, Dublin, 1998.

to speak. She is the only person listening in an Ireland where so many men are busy talking. Yet the Ireland she hears about is the Ireland Drennan and Tone wanted for their own. Paradoxically the tale she hears is about Ireland as an amusing failure. The implication may be that no amount of argument about rights and precedents, or conflict or rebellion would remedy Ireland's careless mismanagement of itself. Ireland had to learn first to listen to itself. And then to resist its worst self. Otherwise it would self-destruct. As Kiberd says of Yeats, 'personal liberation must precede national recovery, being in fact its very condition'.[80] The Edgeworths had no patience with Drennan's exhortation to the people, 'GO, and *be free.*'[81] But Tone did. He is a remarkable example of an Irishman who turned his back on the traditions of Protestant privilege and attempted to rid Ireland of its colonial ties.

80 Kiberd, *Inventing Ireland*, p. 124.   81 Drennan, *Letters of an Irish Helot*, p. 32.

CHAPTER NINE

Wolfe Tone and national independence

Few Irishmen at the end of the eighteenth century make a more striking contrast to Maria Edgeworth than Theobald Wolfe Tone. Although both were Protestant Irish and witnesses to the same political upheavals and debates of the early 1790s and both were engrossed in the character and failings of Ireland, their lives and works seem continents apart. Tone's mission to France was the ultimate cause of the Edgeworths' anxieties in the summer of 1798 when French invaders drew near to Edgeworthstown, and the Edgeworths were the kind of Protestant landed gentry Tone so vilified in his numerous memoranda to the French Directory. Two of Ireland's most celebrated figures at the close of the century had little to say to one another.

Tone brings to a head the century long contest for Ireland by putting the options, continued English control or total independence, in a particularly dramatic way. His testament is most famously the rebellion he inspired rather than his writings, a difference that sets him apart as the Irishman who moved from words to action, from argument to insurrection. And the difference shows in the tenor of his writings. Blunt and clear he argues for Catholic toleration, a sense of nation and, in his last years, a total break from England. Like many Irish Protestants, he had access to the security and privilege that went with the colonising power but chose to identify himself with the Catholics and reform, to situate himself on the margin, not the centre. What reforms had been achieved for Catholics since the 1770s, and they were substantial, did not in Tone's view remove the stigma of second-class citizens. His decision to identify with the marginalised majority together with his belief that England was attempting to mould Ireland into something other than its true national self gives Tone his creative energy.[1] He

---

1 On marginalisation in postcolonial power relations see *The Empire Writes Back*, p. 12.

shifts resistance writing away from the debates about accommodation with the metropole, which had so preoccupied Molyneux and his followers, to a more radical option – armed rebellion.

The last few years of his young life were given so single-mindedly to the liberation of Ireland that the rebellion is often coupled with his name. After leaving Ireland in the summer of 1795 in the wake of government suspicion that he had colluded with the French he settled his family in America. In February 1796 he landed alone in France to pursue the Irish cause. Lonely for the company of his family and close friends like Thomas Russell, often fending off despair, he spent his days and nights in Paris writing memoranda, waiting on French officials, arguing with members of the Directory about Irish affairs, advising them on the size and kind of troops needed for an invasion, pleading for action. In the summer of 1798 when General Kilmaine told him the French Directory had decided to shelve any action on Ireland he wrote in his journal, 'I lost my temper at this, and told him that if the affair was adjourned it was lost. The present crisis must be seized, or it would be too late.'[2] Virtually single-handedly he had persuaded the French to undertake the expedition of 45 ships under General Hoche to Bantry Bay in 1796, which because of accidents and foul weather was a total failure. Despite changes in the French government, the death of Hoche and Tone's loss of influence in Paris, Tone remained ready to contribute to any further plans for invading Ireland, and in the summer of 1798, went with a French force to northern Ireland where he was arrested on landing. He had written in an address to be distributed to the Irish that 'blood shed for the sacred cause of Liberty, shall cement the Independence of Ireland'.[3] He was tried for treason and committed suicide in prison.

Early life and education

Yet Wolfe Tone had not always been a revolutionary. His belief that armed rebellion was the only sure way to rescue Ireland, a remedy far beyond what O'Conor or Burke, much less Molyneux or Swift had envisaged, is all the more extraordinary in the light of his background and education in Dublin and his early years in London. In his relatively brief life he moved through the full gamut of eighteenth-century ideas about how Ireland should relate to England. The early years followed a conventional Protestant pattern. His father was descended from French Protestants and his mother was a Catholic who had conformed to the church of Ireland in 1771.[4] Tone says his parents were 'pretty much like other people'; the children, he adds, with 'a wild spirit of adventure', were not.[5] He was

2 *The Autobiography of Theobald Wolfe Tone 1763-1798*, 2 vols, ed. R. Barry O'Brien (London, 1893), ii, 334 (20 June 1798). 3 Elliott, *Wolfe Tone, Prophet of Irish Independence*, p. 382. I am indebted throughout this chapter to this work. 4 Elliott, *Wolfe Tone*, pp 10-11. 5 *Autobiography of Theobald Wolfe Tone*,

a bright but distracted pupil who found little stimulus in the education that prepared him for Trinity College. He preferred watching the British army parades in Phoenix Park to studying, and had a strong inclination to join the army so that he could go to America and do battle with the colonists. He wanted a much more active life than the College might offer. His father prevailed, however, and Tone entered Trinity College in February 1781.

By the time he graduated in 1786 much had changed: he had won premiums and a scholarship, realised that he could have done much better but for his idleness, had set his heart on marrying Matilda Witherington who was but sixteen, and had decided to become a barrister. So, like Flood and Grattan and Burke he went to London to study at the Middle Temple with a view to returning to practise in Dublin. He was well aware that his time in London would be something of a tedious professional formality: 'I had no great affection for study in general, but that of the law I particularly disliked.'[6] As is well-known, legal training at the Inns of Court was so lax in the eighteenth century that attendance at dinners was the principal, if not only, indicator of a student's progress.[7] In the absence of formal classes students were left to their own devices. Many gave up in despair or boredom. Tone like most of his colleagues spent much of his time in other pursuits than the learning of writs, case law and procedures.

What is striking about Tone's account of his time in London is the pleasure he had from friends like George Knox, later a Westminster M.P. and a supporter of the Irish Catholics, former Trinity acqaintances John Hall and Benjamin Phipps and his brother William recently returned from an expedition to St Helena. Whatever the drudgery of his law studies and his financial difficulties, he liked to be out in the company of lively young men interested in books, politics, walks and new projects. He enjoyed going with Phipps to look at the ships from India or to see the launch of a warship. London was the heart of an empire that his brother William had run away to serve at the age of sixteen. The two were fascinated by British military history. But for the fact that the East India Company were not taking recruits in Setember 1788 Tone would have enlisted with his brother and seen service in India.[8]

A colonial project

Whatever Tone's promise as an intellectual he was an active character who respected thoroughness and had little patience with inefficiency. While studying law his growing interest in politics prompted him to think up a scheme to thwart the power of Spain. What started out as a fanciful project was quickly converted by research and discussion with his brother and Phipps into a detailed proposal

i, 7.   6 Ibid., 16.   7 See e.g. Sir William Holdsworth, *A History of English Law*, 2nd edn, 17 vols (London, 1937), xii, 17.   8 Elliott, *Wolfe Tone*, pp 59–60.

which he addressed to prime minister Pitt and delivered personally to the porter at Downing Street. His plan was to establish a military colony in the South Seas which would be the base for harrying Spanish ships and trade in that area both in times of war and peace. In the light of his later determination to oust the English from Ireland Tone's 'first essay in what I may call politics' makes curiously ironic reading. The fact that Pitt paid no attention so angered him that he vowed to 'make Mr Pitt sorry'.[9]

Although Tone's enthusiasm for the empire had changed dramatically between drafting the plan in 1788 and recalling it in his journal eight years later, he still believed it was a good plan for Britain – if only Pitt could see it that way. His notion of such a colony, as he explains it to Pitt, follows much the same line as Gullliver's and echoes Gulliver's rider that a British colony would not be contaminated by the barbarism associated with other nations' colonial behaviour.

> My idea is to construct a settlement on somewhat of a feudal plan; to reward military exertions by donations of land; to train the rising generation to arms and adventure; to create a small but impenetrable nation of soldiers, an army of sinew and bone, where every man should have a property, and spirit and skill and arms to defend it; to temper the savage ferocity of the natives by the arts of European culture and the mild precepts of the Christian religion; in a word to call from the tomb where for a century it has slept the daring and invincible spirit of our old buccaneers, but uncontaminated by their disgraceful debaucheries in peace or their still more infamous barbarities in war.[10]

The proposal might easily be transferred forward in time to late nineteenth-century British colonies in Africa and backwards to English settlements in Ireland in the sixteenth century. Where he talks about giving 'every man a property' he means the colonisers not the colonised. European culture would go hand in hand with Christianity as the determinant of values. The word 'our', clinching Tone's identification with British interests, is more than a rhetorical gesture. Just as he would put a great deal of effort into the cause of Ireland in the 1790s so now he thought out the scheme with great thoroughness:

> I read every book I could find relating to South America, as Ulloa, Anson, Dampier, Woodes, Rogers, Narborough, and especially the Bucaniers, who were my heroes, and whom I proposed to myself as the archetypes of the future colonists. Many and many a delightful evening did my brother,

9 *Autobiography of Wolfe Tone*, i, 19.   10 Tone to Pitt, 23 August 1788, cited by Frank MacDermot, *Theobald Wolfe Tone and His Times*, p. 20 (a facsimile of the letter is in the National Library of Ireland, MS 3212).

Phipps, and I spend in reading, writing, and talking of my project, in which, if it had been adopted, it was our firm resolution to have embarked.[11]

This air of bravado, the admiration for the buccaneering spirit, the energy that Tone puts into his research would be channelled within a few years into quite the opposite and more serious endeavour of rebellion against England. Between 1788 and 1794, by which time he is deeply involved in Irish politics, Tone goes through a transformation which is very unusual in eighteenth-century Irish politics. It seems remarkable in retrospect that in this early period he gives no inkling of an interest in Ireland as a specific cultural or political entity, much less of a curiosity about its history or its laws. He is a product of Protestant and English culture and institutions and behaves much as energetic young Englishmen out of Oxford or Cambridge might have done. It is difficult to see at this time that 'hatred of England, so deeply rooted in my nature' which he claimed he had always felt.[12]

Political awakening

Tone returned to his wife and family in Dublin for Christmas in 1788 just when debates about Ireland's independence were again in the air. The Regency crisis in the autumn with the king showing signs of mental illness raised the question of whether Ireland had the independent right to appoint a regent for itself if the king was found incapable of ruling. The attorney-general, John Fitzgibbon, later lord chancellor, who came to regard Tone with considerable hostility, argued that in spite of legislative changes in 1782 the statute of Henry VIII still stood which declared that Ireland 'is depending and belonging ... to the imperial crown of England'.[13] Nevertheless Grattan led the parliamentary opposition to invite the Prince of Wales to be regent for Ireland. Although the dispute was resolved in the sense that the king had recovered by early 1789 the arguments were a sign that even though Grattan had achieved legislative independence for Ireland in 1782 there were many including Tone who thought that power still rested with London, and that despite Grattan's renowned parliamentary rhetoric that he had come 'to restore freedom', that 'the nation begins to form; we are moulding into a people', Grattan had missed the point.[14] Tone's friend Drennan had asked some years earlier, 'What ... is this boasted legislative independence? – what but a transference of arbitrary power from despotism abroad to aristocracy at home; from an ostensible power ... to a hidden power which steals away the rights of the nation like a cut-purse.'[15] Tone believed that the problems of decentring

---

11 *Autobiography of Theobald Wolfe Tone*, i, 18-19. 12 Ibid., 55. 13 Cited by Johnston, *Ireland in the Eighteenth Century*, p. 159. 14 19 April, 1780, *The Speeches of the Right Hon. Henry Grattan*, ed. Daniel O. Madden, 2nd edn (Dublin, 1861), p. 48. 15 *Letters of an Irish Helot, signed Orellana*, p. 20.

power from Westminster and of admitting Catholics to the vote and to parliament had yet to be resolved.

As the examples below illustrate Tone was not a strikingly original thinker. His political views evolved largely from the company he moved in and the books he read. He kept up his interest in Trinity College and returned to take part in the affairs of the debating club there, the Historical Society, where the proceedings reflected topical talking points in the streets and coffee houses of Dublin. Tone had a hand in drafting some of the topics for debate such as 'Whether a Union with England would be of advantage to this country?' and 'Whether exiles are justified in bearing arms gainst their country?'[16] He was also a frequent visitor to the strangers' gallery in parliament and was soon impressed by Grattan and the Whig opposition, but he remained on the fringes preferring to debate among friends and subscribe to the *Universal Magazine* with its nationalist leanings than show any deliberate commitment. His first written sally into politics was a pamphlet, *A Review of the Conduct of the Administration during the Seventh Session of Parliament* (1790) in which he praised the Whigs and attacked the government as reneging on the trust of the people.[17] He had been particularly impressed by the speeches of Sir Laurence Parsons who enunciated thoughts Tone would soon assimilate as his own. The present government, said Parsons, was the fulfilment of England's worst curse for Ireland,

> that an arrogant, self-sufficient, incapable and corrupt administration should triumph here, until it blasted every sentiment of affection for the English government, which remained in the bosoms of the Irish.[18]

His meeting with Thomas Russell for the first time in the gallery of parliament in that same year was the start of one of his closest friendships with a man often regarded as more revolutionary than he was and with whom Tone would argue out many of his ideas about Ireland.

Before Tone became involved with the Volunteers or the Catholic Committee or Belfast radicals like Drennan he knew what he opposed in government, he favoured reform, but had no decided political stance for himself.[19] Implicit rather than explicit in his thought at this time is a link with the resistance politics of Protestant patriots going back through Grattan to Molyneux. Much of his thought stemmed from that principle of Molyneux which so changed the empire: 'I have no other Notion of Slavery, but being Bound by a Law to which I did not consent.'[20] He held firmly to Molyneux's contention that

16 Elliott, *Wolfe Tone*, p. 64. 17 *Autobiography of Wolfe Tone*, i, 232-4 and Elliott, *Wolfe Tone*, pp 83-6. 18 Cited by N.D. Atkinson, 'Sir Laurence Parsons, Second Earle of Rosse, 1758-1841', Ph.D. dissertation, Trinity College, Dublin, 1962, p. 113. 19 By the 1790s the Volunteers had become politically active and Tone was made an honorary member by the Belfast Volunteers in 1791. 20 Molyneux, *Case of Ireland*, p. 129.

Ireland and England were separate kingdoms. In 1796 during his stay in Paris, fired with enthusiasm by what he saw in the much changed city, he was struck by the construction of the Pantheon and resolved, 'If we have a Republic in Ireland, we must build a Pantheon, but we must not, like the French, be in too much of a hurry to people it.'[21] Those who come to his mind immediately are Roger O'Moore, active in the rebellion of 1641, Molyneux, Swift and Lucas. In the early stages of his political involvement he thinks within their terms. A change is apparent when he joins a small and short-lived discussion club in late 1790. Debate went well beyond the policies of the opposition Whigs and perhaps prompted him to recognise for the first time how deep-seated was his antagonism to the English presence in Ireland. He remarks of himself in 1791,

> I think it right to mention, that, at this time, the establishment of a Republic was not the immediate object of my speculations. My object was to secure the independence of my country under any form of government, to which I was led by a hatred of England, so deeply rooted in my nature, that it was rather an instinct than a principle. I left to others, better qualified for the inquiry, the investigation and merits of the different forms of government.

That last sentence captures the sense of Tone's self-confessed political innocence. His early writing acknowledges that he was jejeune about the more complex arrangements of politics. Not least among his attractive qualities is this sense of being an amateur among professionals. Having left the finer details to avowedly political minds, he nevertheless continues thinking out his own schemes. There was always something of the political projector in his thinking:

> I contented myself with labouring on my own system, which was luckily in perfect coincidence as to its operation with that of those men who viewed the question on a broader and juster scale than I did at the time I mention.[22]

Despite this claim to 'my own system', his ideas are often the distillation of what he has read and argued about. What he did have was the facility and courage to express and follow his convictions. As Padraic Pearse put it, Tone 'did not inherit or merely accept his principles; he thought himself into them'.[23] Those gifts, so frustrating to his father and presumably to his professors who wanted him to meet conventional academic expectations, were among his greatest strengths. His originality in terms of Ireland's contest with England was that he thought

21 *Autobiography of Theobald Wolfe Tone*, i, 268. 22 Ibid., 55. 23 Padraic H. Pearse, 'The Separatist Idea' (1916), *Political Writings and Speeches* (Dublin, 1966), p. 266.

beyond particular political interests and the terms of previous arguments. He wanted a national solution.

This strength had its flaws. Tone's enthusiasm for his own solution meant not only that he came to abandon the Molyneux tradition: he also gave little thought to the cost in terms of lives, deportations and imprisonments. The point comes out in a passage in the journal where he reflects on friends in the discussion club like Russell, Drennan, Knox, Peter Burrowes, Thomas Emmet and Whitley Stokes. They were men of great wit and ability who disagreed with one another on several issues at a time when, says Tone, 'politics unfortunately enter into everything, even into our private friendships'.[24] What Tone recalls with particular emphasis is that Stokes would not agree to a solution for Ireland that meant the spilling of blood. Tone admired him for that, but disagreed with him:

> We differ on principles which do honour to Stokes' heart. With an acute feeling of the degradation of his country, and a just and generous indignation against her oppressors, the tenderness and humanity of his disposition is such, that he recoils from any measures to be attempted for her emancipation which may terminate in blood.[25]

Tone thought such virtue unrealistic because the chances of a peaceful rebellion or an honourable settlement had long gone: 'I am afraid that in the present state of affairs that is a thing impossible.'[26] The alternative he well knew was blood, yet he seems not to have weighed up the cost of, much less felt responsible for the violence that his rebellion would bring. The shock and distress he feels when a man he admires like Lord Edward Fitzgerald is arrested borders on protest as if some personal outrage had been done, but his response to news in the French newspapers of the dead in the early weeks of the rebellion in 1798 has a different tone. He writes as if galvanised to the cause. He is angered rather than aggrieved by the loss of life on both sides, angry because the loss of life seems a waste when the outcome is in his view assured. He thinks his friend John Keogh's son has been killed:

> if it be so I shall regret him sincerely; but how many other valuable lives must be sacrificed before the fortune of Ireland be decided! Dr. Esmonde and eight other gentlemen of my county have been hanged; at Nenagh the English whip the most respectable inhabitants till their blood flows into the kennel. The atrocious barbarity of their conduct is only to be excelled by the folly of it; never yet was a rebellion, as they call it, quelled by such means ... From the blood of every one of the martyrs of the liberty of Ireland will spring, I hope, thousands to revenge their fall.[27]

24 *Autobiography of Theobald Wolfe Tone*, i, 37.   25 Ibid.   26 Ibid.   27 Ibid., ii, 311 (17/18 June 1798).

The moral energy in this writing takes its strength from the simple opposition between wicked English and martyred Irish, and the dynamics of martyrdom alluded to in the last sentence hold out the prospect of success even in the hour of seeming defeat. Blood is the price of triumph, and the triumph is what matters. This is a nationalist rhetoric unheard of prior to Tone. It belongs more to the romance of those splendid parades he enjoyed watching in Phoenix Park than to the bloodshed seen in Wexford. Johnston argues that Tone epitomises that nationalist idealist in Irish history evident into the last decades of the twentieth century who shows,

> an almost total disengagement from the bloody, often vicious, consequences of inflicting that political idealism on a populace, which may only partially comprehend or even agree with, the theories for which they are compelled to suffer so ruthlessly.[28]

This characteristic, be it romantic or idealist, or both, is that crucial element in Tone's temperament which distinguishes him from Ireland's previous protesters.

Tone and the Catholics

Although much of the protest through the eighteenth century is from Protestants arguing for greater autonomy to let them manage Ireland as they wanted, the second half of the century saw an increasing number of Protestants speaking up for Catholic relief and thereby proposing a new kind of Ireland. In Tone we have the most striking and unorthodox example of this. It is not that his moral indignation fires him to use the privileges open to Protestants to persuade his fellow religionists to reform legislation against the Catholics. Nor is he a turncoat who sides against his own out of sympathy or self-interest for the Catholic majority. Tone, along with O'Conor, is one of Ireland's first nationalists. He thought party and religious differences should be subsumed into and by national concerns. His nationalism is more overtly political than O'Conor's but the two men share a similar vision – an Irish nation with a distinct culture and institutions. Where Tone differs from the patriots like Flood and Grattan is that the Irish nationality he shares with the Catholics supersedes their differences. An extreme feature of his nationalism in terms of the century's debates is that he regards most Protestants with contempt – Grattan was a noted exception – because he sees them as having so entrenched their political power as to deny the very sense of nation he aimed to achieve. He writes of them,

> The Protestants I despaired of from the outset for obvious reasons. Already in possession of an unjust monopoly of the whole power and

28 Johnston, *Ireland in the Eighteenth Century* , p. 170.

patronage of the country, it was not to be supposed they would ever concur in measures the certain tendency of which must be to lessen their influence as a party, how much soever the nation might gain.[29]

His anger turns especially on what he calls 'that execrable and contemptible corps, the country gentlemen of Ireland. I know not whether I most hate or despise them, the tyrants of the people and slaves of the Government.'[30] By thus dismissing his fellow Protestants – his family had been country gentlemen – he was disengaging himself from institutional change. If there was to be change, it would have to come from the Catholics and the Dissenters. The right of self-determination lay with them, not with the Irish gentry or what he calls 'the English party' who are,

> content to sacrifice the liberty and independence of their country to the pleasure of revenge, and their own personal security. They see Ireland only in their rent rolls, their places, their patronage, and their pensions.[31]

He thought the Catholics would support any initiative to improve their condition.

> As no change could make their political situation worse, I reckoned upon their support to a certainty; besides, they had already begun to manifest a strong sense of their wrongs and oppressions; and, finally, I well knew that, however it might be disguised or suppressed, there existed in the breast of every Irish Catholic an inextirpable abhorrence of the English name and power.[32]

This confidence was shaken at times by what he thought a lack of determination, as for example in the negotiations for Catholic relief in 1793 when the Catholic Committee, having set its eye on total emancipation, settled for less. The bill which passed in April 1793 meant they were still barred from sitting in parliament and on the judicial bench, and were not eligible for any of the major offices of state. The result, said Tone, was 'a mortifying state of degradation to men of ardent spirit and generous feelings!'[33] Tone's eagerness for action and success often left him disappointed in the people he pinned his hopes on. He wrote in 1797,

> I do not at all believe that the people are prepared for a serious and general insurrection, and, in short – why should I conceal the fact? – I do not

29 *Autobiography of Theobald Wolfe Tone*, i, 51. 30 Ibid., ii, 55 (25 June 1796). 31 Ibid., 309 (27 April 1798). 32 Ibid., i, 51. 33 Ibid., i, 199.

believe they have the spirit. It is not fear of the army, but fear of the law, and long habits of slavery, that kept them down.[34]

A few months later, as he reflected on the just missed opportunity for rebellion in Dublin, he sensed 'a great want of spirit in the leaders in Dublin ... it seems to me to have been an unpardonable weakness, if not downright cowardice to let such an occasion slip'.[35] But these misgivings never blurred his vision for an Ireland free from English control and that was the source of his unflagging activity on the Catholics' behalf.

Tone first came to the attention of the Catholics as a result of his pamphlet, *Argument on behalf of the Catholics of Ireland*, published in Dublin in August 1791, 'addressed to the People, and more particularly to the Protestants of Ireland'.[36] Within six months the pamphlet had run to five editions and was quickly recognised as one of the major Irish political tracts of the period leading up to the 1798 rebellion.

The Argument *as resistance*

Tone's reasoning in the *Argument* is that Ireland cannot be a nation so long as she is governed by foreigners. 'The people here,' he says, 'are despised or defied; their will does not weigh a feather in the balance, when English influence, or the interest of their rulers, is thrown into the opposite scale.'[37] Ireland must therefore empower her people and that means accepting the Catholics as full citizens. The resolution of Ireland's colonial predicament rests on this point. With Tone those Swiftean phrases in *The Drapier's Letters* like 'My Dear Countrymen' and 'the whole people of Ireland' have to include the Catholics. Echoing Burke rather than Swift he speaks against 'the monstrous injustice which has held for a century three millions of my countrymen in ignorance and bondage'.[38]

The pamphlet is ostensibly an argument for parliamentary reform which had been an issue in the public forum for over a decade and remained so with the parliamentary debates on Catholic emancipation. But Tone's identifying with the Catholics shows he has more urgent business than the 'abstract rights' of people to reform their legislature. He adds, giving a hint of the vigorous voice to come, 'for, after Paine, who will, or who need, be heard on that subject?'[39] He assures readers that he is 'a Protestant of the Church of Ireland as by law established', and adds with typical bluntness that he is also 'a steady detester of tyranny'.[40] His

---

34 Ibid., ii, 225 (4 June 1797). 35 Ibid., 250 (5 Aug. 1797). 36 *An Argument on behalf of the Catholics of Ireland, in which the Present Political State of that Country, and the Necessity of a Parliamentary Reform, are Considered, addressed to the People, and more particularly to the Protestants of Ireland. 1791* in *The Writings of Theobald Wolfe Tone*, 3 vols, eds T.W. Moody, R.B. McDowell and C.J. Woods (Oxford, in press), i, 109-28 (hereafter referred to as *Argument*). 37 Ibid., 115. 38 Ibid., 125. 39 Ibid., 110. 40 Ibid.

attack on corruption in government is nothing new, but when he attributes that to Protestant shibboleths he cuts against the grain of the very Protestantism he claims to belong to.

The reform Tone proposes is more radical than anything the Irish public had yet heard both in its emphasis on the people and its attack on Protestant prejudices. He wants Protestants to apply their loudly proclaimed theories of liberty to the Catholics. There could be no meaningful change unless they did. Tone comes afresh to the problem besetting every postcolonial society – how to transform Ireland from a situation of dominance and oppression to 'an acceptance of difference on equal terms'.[41] Only if Protestants accept the Catholics, jettison centuries of suspicion and think of themselves as citizens of a non-sectarian Ireland, and not just as a privileged class, will Ireland become a nation. This had been the missing factor in Irish politics since Molyneux's *Case*. Its absence had delayed a resolution to Ireland's problems with England. Grattan's parliament of 1782, according to Tone, had achieved little because legislative independence had proven a victory in little more than principle. 'We are free in priciple, we are slaves in fact.'[42] In a hard-hitting criticism of the 1782 reform he blames Grattan's parliament for employing the same compromising tactics as the English had always used: 'They set out with sacrificing the eternal dictates of justice to temporizing and peddling expediency; they failed because they did not deserve to succeed.'[43] At the heart of that failure was neglect of the Catholics. In a phrase that rings back down the previous hundred years of protest Tone puts his finger on the core issue:

> From their failure we are taught this salutary truth, that no reform can ever be obtained which shall not comprehensively embrace Irishmen of all denominations. The exclusion of the Catholics lost the question under circumstances that must have otherwise carried it gainst all opposition.[44]

The problem, however, is not so much with the mechanics of reform but with Protestants themselves. He spends the body of the pamphlet persuading the Protestants to put away their fears. Liberty for Ireland requires justice for the Catholics: 'we must adopt or reject them together'.[45] Without toleration there can be no Irish nation. His overriding vision is of 'an ingenious and a gallant

41 *The Empire Writes Back*, p. 36. Seamus Deane remarks, 'Sectarianism runs deep in this society, as everything, from killings, to corruption of the law, to the corruption of reading, makes perfectly plain. Sectarianism is a kind of limbo into which we have been cast': 'Canon Fodder: Literary Mythologies in Ireland', *Styles of Belonging: The Cultural Identities of Ulster*, eds Jean Lundy and Aodan Mac Poilin (Belfast, 1992), p. 29. 42 *Argument*, 115; he had demonstrated a similar view in his pamphlet *Spanish War! How far Ireland is Bound, of Right, to Embark on the Impending Contest on the Side of Great Britain* (1790) where he remarked, 'We raise the lofty temple of her glory, but we cannot, or dare not, inscribe our name on the entablature' (*Life of Wolfe Tone*, ed. William Theobald Wolfe Tone, i, 336). 43 *Argument*, 116. 44 Ibid. 45 Ibid., 117.

people', diverse in religion but transcending differences so as to stand 'among the nations of the earth'.[46] Instead, he says with some embarrassment, Ireland remains unknown and unrecognised despite its wealth of human and natural resources:

> yet, with all these great advantages, unheard of and unknown, without pride, or power, or name; without ambassadors, army, or navy; not of half the consequence in the empire of which she has the honour to make a part, with the single county of York, or the loyal and well regulated town of Birmingham![47]

To put that right will take a radical change in the hearts of Protestants. As long as they do not admit the Catholics, they will remain subservient to England, so 'that Administration despise and laugh at you, and that while you remain in your present state of apathy and ignorance, they will continue to insult and to contemn you'.[48] Irish parliamentarians fulfil Westminster's construct of Ireland as incompetent and confused. Not much has changed since Swift described them as 'three hundred Brutes/ All involv'd in wild Disputes.'[49] Contempt is the diet of a subject administration.[50] Drennan had a vision of Ireland 'labouring under every corruption in thy domestic government … overlooked by a British Senate, ridiculed by thy own, despised by thy K——, and abandoned in despair by thy children.'[51] Grattan had frequently complained of the slurs: 'Ireland has been represented as the slave of England by the laws of nature.' The task of parliament he said was to 'combat a project to govern this country by corruption', and again, Ireland will not suffer 'such a set of men … to predominate, to insult, to corrupt, and to enslave'.[52] Tone reminded his readers that despite such protests nothing had changed, nor would it until the Irish changed.

Ireland's humiliation can be traced to two causes – first, 'our evil government', second, 'our own intestine division'.[53] The first had been a regular target of the patriots, though it had always been difficult in Dublin's complex political structures to identify who exactly was the 'government'. Tone puts the question,

> What is our Government? It is a phenomenon in politics, contravening all received and established opinions: it is a Government derived from another country, whose interest, so far from being the same with that of the people directly crosses it at right angles.[54]

46 Ibid., 110. 47 Ibid. 48 Ibid., 113. 49 'The Legion Club', *Poems of Jonathan Swift*, iii, 829-39, ll. 113-14. 50 The example of Protestant English despising Protestant let alone Catholic Irish provides a variation on Bhabha, *The Location of Culture*, p. 70: 'The objective of colonial discourse is to continue the colonised as a population of degenerate types on the basis of racial origin, in order to justify conquest and to establish systems of administration and instruction.' 51 *Letters of an Irish Helot*, signed *Orellana*, pp 22-3. 52 6 Sept. 1785, 1 Feb. 1790 and 26 Feb. 1790 in *The Speeches of the Right Hon. Henry Grattan*, pp 106, 138 and 156. 53 *Argument*, 110. 54 Ibid., 111.

Tone vilifies those in high office whose profligacy and corruption are the hall-mark of 'an Administration of boobies and blockheads'.[55] While the rest of Europe is fired by reform Ireland 'is struck with a political paralysis that has withered her strength and crushed her spirit'.[56] The remedy is a united Ireland, a union of Protestants, Dissenters and Catholics. O'Conor had argued that irra-tional religious prejudices of government were at the root of the problem: 'By their Prevalence, Kingdoms are impoverished, the human Mind is distempered, and every Thing valuable carries the Taint of a superstitious Policy.'[57] Government should act not from sectarian motives but for the good of Ireland. Tone would repeatedly come back to the point in the next few years. At this stage he gives no hint that he is thinking of armed insurrection. Nationhood can be achieved by constitutional means:

> My argument is simply this: That Ireland so deriving her Government from another country, requires a strength in the people which may enable them, if necessary, to counteract the influence of that Government, should it ever be, as it indisputably has been, exerted to thwart her prosperity: that this strength may be most constitutionally acquired, and safely and peaceably exerted, through the medium of a Parliamentary reform.[58]

But this constitutional avenue requires Protestant support. Much of the *Argument* is a badgering attempt to shake Protestants out of their old attitudes. The task fires him to a belligerent rhetoric. There is impatience in his mockery and urgency in his imperatives:

> Let us, for God's sake, shake off the old woman, the tales of our nurses, the terrors of our grandams, from our hearts; let us put away childish fears, look our situation in the face like men; let us speak to this ghastly spectre of our distempered imagination, the Genius of Irish Catholicity![59]

That is the opening cry in his appeal to set aside sectarian views. He says point-edly and passionately what Secretary Dundas was soon to tell Lord Lieutenant Westmorland; there would be no solution in Ireland 'unless the Protestants lay aside their prejudices'.[60] What Tone meant by 'our own intestine divisions' was the suspicion and apprehension inculturated into Protestants and Catholics alike which placed their sectarian loyalties ahead of national allegiances. As he wrote

55 Ibid., 112. The point is well illustrated in 1795 over the resignation of Lord Lieutenant Earl Fitzwilliam who favoured Catholic reform but was opposed by Westminster; see for example 'A New Song call'd The Lord Lieutenant's Farewell to the Kingdom of Ireland' in Carpenter, *Verse in English from Eighteenth-Century Ireland*, pp 517-18. 56 *Argument*, 111. 57 O'Conor, *The Case of the Roman-Catholics of Ireland*, p. iv. 58 Ibid., 113. 59 Ibid., 117. 60 Dundas to Westmorland, 26 Dec. 1791, cited by Elliott, *Wolfe Tone*, p. 152.

later in his journal, it was necessary for Catholics and Protestants 'to forget all former feuds, to consolidate the entire strength of the whole nation, and to form for the future but one people'.[61]

Tone takes arguments on behalf of the Catholics by O'Conor and Burke a significant step forward. Burke had insisted that it was not in government's interest, nor indeed moral, to deny the Catholic majority access to land, leases, education and other rights. Burke's feelings of outrage match anything in Tone, as for example when he calls the heads of a new bill for Catholic relief in 1782,

> neither more nor less than a renewd act of universal, unmitigated, indispensible, exceptionless, disqualification. One would imagine, that a Bill inflicting such a multitude of incapacities, had followed on the heels of a conquest made by a very fierce Enemy under the impression of recent animosity and resentment.[62]

Burke's arguments had been addressed to some extent by reform legislation in 1779 and 1782. Nevertheless he demonstrated time and again what Tone also believed that treatment of the Catholics was the product of religious bigotry: 'The great prop of this whole system is not pretended to be its justice or its utility, but the supposed danger to the State which gave rise to it originally, and which they apprehend would return if this system were overturned.'[63] Burke is more discursive and cautious than Tone. In a sense Tone cuts away all Burke's qualifications and presents the basic issue. Burke had asked for toleration of Catholics; Tone wants toleration as a step to national identity. Burke's phrasing has a circuitousness about it which Tone strips away. Burke had said Protestants attempted,

> to shew that a toleration of them is inconsistent with the established Government among us. Now, though this postition be in reality as untenable as the other, it is not altogether such an absurdity on the face of it. All I shall here observe, is, that those who lay it down, little consider what a wound they are giving to that Establishment for which they pretend so much zeal.[64]

Tone has less patience with complexities of argument and none with the fashionable rhetoric of his day. He likes to address what he sees as the bald facts:

> What answer could we make to the Catholics of Ireland, if they were to rise and with one voice demand their rights as citizens and as men? What reply justifiable to God and to our conscience? None. We prate and bab-

---

61 *Autobiography of Theobald Wolfe Tone*, i, 51. 62 'Letter to Lord Kenmare', *Writings and Speeches of Edmund Burke*, ix, 567. 63 'Tracts relating to Popery Laws', ibid., 478. 64 Ibid., 469.

ble, and write books, and publish them, filled with sentiments of freedom and abhorrence of tyranny and lofty praises of *the Rights of Man!* Yet we are content to hold three millions of our fellow creatures and fellow subjects, in degradation and infamy and contempt, or, to sum up all in one word, in *slavery!*[65]

Burke had summed up the principle when he wrote, 'A Law against the majority of the people, is in substance a Law against the people itself … it is not particular injustice, but general oppression.'[66] Tone, like O'Conor, realises he is not dealing with a rational situation. Protestants have to be argued out of their fears. They think Catholics will not keep their oaths, that they will want to take back the land, that ignorant Catholics will be 'incapable of liberty'[67] – a point that has Tone angrily retorting that 'he that is prepared to live is prepared for freedom'[68] – that Catholics pay loyalty to Rome rather than Ireland, that they are Jacobites who if they get the vote will join Ireland to France, form a Catholic parliament, pass laws against Protestant interests and corrupt the system in their own favour. These 'old and hackneyed' arguments Tone dismisses one by one. But worse than any of them, he says, is this,

> There is no one position, moral, physical, or political that I hear with such extreme exacerbation of mind as this which denies to my country the possibility of independent existence.[69]

The barrier to this is sectarianism, and that must be put aside:

> if all barriers between the two religions were beaten down so far as civil matters are concerned, if the odious distinction of Protestant and Presbyterian and Catholic were abolished and the three great sects blended together under the common and sacred title of Irishman, what interest could a Catholic member of Parliament have distinct from his Protestant brother sitting on the same bench, exercising the same function, bound by the same ties?[70]

If the Protestants have any lingering anxieties that the Catholics would be corrupt in government they have only to witness 'the most profligate venality, the most shameless and avowed prostitution of principle' in the present government.[71] Catholic France, he tells them, demonstrates more integrity in government than Protestant Ireland.

This challenge for Protestants to liberate themselves as well as Ireland follows on not only from Burke but from his seemingly irreconcilable opponent Thomas

65 *Argument*, 125. 66 'Tracts relating to Popery Laws', *Writings and Speeches of Edmund Burke*, ix, 454.
67 *Argument*, 119. 68 Ibid., 120. 69 Ibid., 122. 70 Ibid., 124. 71 Ibid., 125.

Paine. It is one of the ironies of the day that whereas Tone found in Burke detailed arguments about the Catholics in Ireland which gave substance to his demand for liberty, he found in Paine and the French Revolution the terms and vision for the Ireland he hoped to bring about. Paine, he says, presents the most recent and compelling argument for liberty, one accepted throughout Europe. But in Ireland the Protestants cry liberty while 'rivetting the fetters of the wretched Roman Catholics.' They keep the Catholics in ignorance and then blame their bigotry on their ignorance. Paine had written, 'Reason obeys itself; and ignorance submits to whatever is dictated to it.'[72] Tone taunts the Protestants in the guise of a Catholic spokesman, much as Paine had taunted Burke on the origin of the rights of man. He echoes Paine's dictum that the principle of equal rights 'has its origin from the Maker of man.'[73] He then builds a devastating plea on behalf of the Catholics:

> Are we not men, as ye are, stamped with the image of our Maker, walk-
> ing erect, beholding the same light, breathing the same air as Protestants.
> Hath not a Catholic hands; hath not a Catholic eyes, dimensions, organs,
> passions?[74]

Admit the Catholics as men and the whole of Paine's argument on liberty has to apply. With measured sarcasm Tone ends his plea saying that if Catholics are to remain in slavery for some time it may be because God 'thinks fit to continue us a little longer under the rod of our oppressors, the ministers of his wrath'.[75] But these 'ministers' must put away their generations of prejudice. They have to resist their past. Only that way will Ireland become a nation.

His faith in constitutional reform was short-lived. A year later Tone thought Ireland was fast approaching a moment of choice: 'the Government of Ireland must either alter their whole system, or be subverted by force'.[76] He would be a major influence in that attempted subversion.

Aftermath to the Argument

The *Argument* appeared at the start of a tense political winter in Ireland. On the national level the English administration in Dublin and Westminster were wrangling over the right policy for Ireland. The British parliament was increasingly aware of the pressures within Ireland for reform and had already adopted relief measures for Catholics in England. In the light of anti-clerical events in Revolutionary France English attitudes towards Catholic clergy turned more tolerant. Burke had assured his readers in his *Reflections on the Revolution in France*

---

72 Thomas Paine, *The Rights of Man* (1791-2; London, 1969), p. 130. 73 Ibid., p. 42. 74 *Argument*, 126.
75 Ibid. 76 *Autobiography of Theobald Wolfe Tone*, i, 147 (24 Oct. 1792).

(1790) that the Catholic priests he had met in France were 'liberal and open; with the hearts of gentlemen, and men of honour; neither insolent nor servile in their manners and conduct'.[77] Attitudes towards the Catholics, be they French, English or Irish, were softening. The opposite was the case in Dublin. The lord lieutenant, Westmorland, looked with alarm at the arguments coming from England that the franchise should be extended to Irish Catholics so as to ensure their continued loyalty. That, said Westmorland, ran counter to English policy in Ireland. It ran in the face of the Williamite revolution of the 1690s which had given the constitution, as Hill notes, 'a firm and permanent protestant character'.[78] Westmorland asked Pitt with some desperation, 'Do you believe England can govern Ireland by the popularity of government? … Is it not the very essence of your imperial policy to prevent the interests of Ireland clashing and interfering with the interests of England?'[79] A reform bill introduced to the Irish parliament by Sir Hercules Langrishe was passed in February 1792 but it did not include the franchise. That had been the subject of a petition to the House framed by Richard Burke, agent to the Catholic Committee, and it was rejected along with one from the Belfast Presbyterians.[80] The turbulent parliamentary session of early 1792 was a triumph for the Ascendancy and the administration, who appeared to have routed the supporters of Catholic reform from any significant power base in parliament. But by March Tone's *Argument*, sponsored by the United Irishmen, had gone into its fifth edition. The contest had moved out of parliament into the popular domain.

The *Argument* had been published just when Tone was also involved in the foundation of the United Irishmen in Belfast in October 1791. Started as a club this organisation brought together radical elements among Catholics and Protestants who believed in religious liberty, and in the more liberal and anti-authoritarian climate of northern Ireland, influenced by events in France, they soon sought a major overhaul of the Irish political system. They wanted 'Irishmen of every religious persuasion in parliament.'[81] Several members of the Catholic Committee were also members of the United Irishmen. Drennan had already thought of setting up a society in Dublin to promote 'the Rights of men, and the Greatest Happiness of the Greatest Number its end – its general end Real Independence to Ireland, and Republicanism its particular purpose'.[82] On

---

77 *Reflections on the Revolution in France* in *Writings and Speeches of Edmund Burke*, viii, ed. L.G. Mitchell (1989), 194.   78 Jacqueline Hill, '1641 and the Quest for Catholic Emancipation, 1691-1829', *Ulster 1641: Aspects of the Rising*, ed. Brian Mac Cuarta (Belfast, 1993), p. 168. Hill argues that this change in the British government did more for Catholic relief than Tone or the United Irishmen in 1791.   79 Westmorland to Pitt, 18 Jan. 1792, cited by R.B. McDowell, 'The Age of the United Irishmen: Reform and Reaction, 1789-94', *New History of Ireland*, iv, 309.   80 See ibid., 310-11.   81 Declaration and Resolutions of the Society of United Irishmen of Belfast, cited by Elliott, *Wolfe Tone*, p. 140.   82 Drennan to Samuel McTier [21 May 1791], *The Drennan Letters*, ed. D.A. Chart (Belfast, 1931), p. 54. Neither Russell, who was based in Belfast, nor Tone took much part in the Dublin society.

the understanding that religious toleration was the necessary foundation for political reform the movement drafted a policy which included male suffrage, more equitable electoral districts and annual parliaments.

In this climate of fresh initiatives invigorated by the philosophy of the rights of man coming from France Tone's *Argument* was welcomed by the Catholics. They helped distribute it, and Tone, an avowed supporter of the Catholic franchise, found himself introduced to their leaders and attending their dinners. In April 1792 they approached him to serve as assistant secretary to the Catholic Committee to replace Richard Burke, whom leading Catholics had found ineffectual as their London agent and a tactless embarrassment when he visited Dublin.[83] They invited Tone not least because he was known for the pamphlet and for his links with the newly formed United Irishmen and their campaign for Catholic relief.[84] Tone was willing not least because his none too successful career at the bar found him restless for more steady employment and he also wanted to distance himself from the internal wrangles which had developed within the Dublin Society of the United Irishmen. The appointment gave him the chance to participate directly in the day-to-day politics of Catholic reform and thus provided a context in which to assess the radical nationalist vision which he had begun to formulate.

He took the post already convinced by Molyneux, Swift and more recently Parsons that 'England was the radical vice of our Government.' His 'great discovery' was that Ireland would never be 'free, prosperous, or happy, until she was independent'.[85] The feasibility and logistics of this were not at all clear even while he worked in his secretarial and often humdrum capacity for the Catholic Committee. But the principle gnawed at him as he drew up memoranda and petitions for the Committee, wrote to the papers, visited Belfast with John Keogh to strengthen ties with the Ulster Dissenters, helped resuscitate the Volunteers, organised the convention of its members in December 1792, and witnessed the internal disputes between conservative and more radical members of the Committee.[86] There were times during this work, and even more so after he had to leave Ireland with his family for America in 1795, when nationhood and independence seemed little more than a dream.

From words to rebellion

Tone breaks away from previous protest in eighteenth-century Ireland in that he comes to advocate rebellion. But that idea took time to mature. It was nurtured

---

83 For the Committee's letter to Richard Burke, drafted by Tone, see Burke, *Correspondence*, vii, 164–6 (30 July 1792). 84 McDowell, 'The Age of the United Irishmen', *New History of Ireland*, iv, 325. 85 *Autobiography of Theobald Wolfe Tone*, i, 26. 86 Tone had a major part in organising the Catholic Convention of Dec. 1792 of which the aim was to make representation on the Catholic Committee as democratic as possible with representatives delegated by their parishes.

during the period he was working on the *Argument* and for the Catholic Committee, stimulated both by changes going on in post-revolutionary France and by conversations with Russell. An early indicator of this maturation is in a postscript to the resolutions he drafted for the Volunteer meeting in Belfast to celebrate Bastille Day on 14 July 1791. These resolutions have a business-like tone of reform, an air of challenge: they state it is 'indispensably necessary' to extend the franchise to Catholics; English influence in politics and commerce must be balanced by Irish interests; divisions between Irishmen shoud be abolished as they have been 'the source of weakness and misery and disgrace to the country'.[87] Tone then tells Russell that he would personally want Ireland to separate from England, but 'truth itself must sometimes condescend to temporise.' What follows, he says, is not for publication. Starting with an argument well-worn through the century, he moves quickly to the admission that his thinking is ahead of the times. He writes,

> My unalterable opinion is that the bane of Irish prosperity is in the influence of England. I believe that influence will ever be extended while the connexion between the countries continues. Nevertheless, I know that opinion is for the present too hardy, though a very little time may establish it universally. I have not made it a part of the resolutions. I have only proposed to set up a reformed Parliament as a barrier against that mischief which every honest man that will open his eyes must see in every instance overbears the interest of Ireland. I have not said one word that looks like a wish for separation, though I give it to you and your friends as my most decided opinion that such an event would be a regeneration for this country.[88]

The postscript is typical of postcolonial resistance writing, both in its plan to put a stop to English 'mischief' and its desire for Ireland's 'regeneration'. Yet in 1793 he still talked in public about accepting a settlement with England, albeit with reservations. He wrote to the editor of *Faulkner's Journal* that he did not wish Ireland to break the connection with England 'provided it can be, as I am sure it can, preserved consistently with the honor, the interests, and the happiness of Ireland'. If that were not possible, he 'would hold it a sacred duty to endeavour, by all possible means, to break it'.[89]

As secretary to the Catholic Committee he kept a low profile. He discussed his republican sympathies with but a few friends like Russell, Drennan and Sam

---

87 MacDermot, *Theobald Wolfe Tone and His Times*, pp 60-1. The meeting eventually adopted another set of resolutions drafted by Drennan (McDowell, 'The Age of the United Irishmen', *New History of Ireland*, iv, 293). 88 Cited by MacDermot, *Theobald Wolfe Tone and His Times*, pp 61-2. 89 *Life of Wolfe Tone*, ed. William Theobald Wolfe Tone, i, 500. When accused of sedition by Lord Chancellor Fitzgibbon in 1793 Tone said Ireland's problems could not be resolved without total separation from England (Elliott, *Wolfe Tone*, p. 228).

Neilson of the *Northern Star*, but while with such friends he was excited by the notion of total independence. He records with enthusiasm his American friend Thomas Digges' vison of an independent Ireland,

> If Ireland were free, and well governed, being that she is unencumbered with debt, she would in arts, commerce, and manufactures spring up like an air balloon, and leave England behind her at an immense distance. There is no computing the rapidity with which she would rise.[90]

Tone took such visions of independence more seriously after Catholic expectations of relief were disappointed by the Relief bill of 1793 which failed to allow Catholics to sit in parliament. Many lost hope in political reform. Tone and other radicals realised however they could do nothing until Dissenters and Catholics were reconciled. If England was then sufficiently pressurised by a war with France, that would make substantial reform if not rebellion feasible. But the administration's increasing vigilance, the introduction of the Militia bill of 1793 and the lack of forward thinking among the United Irishmen left Tone pessimistic.[91]

His private thoughts about rebellion were brought to light during the visit to Dublin by an agent from France in April 1794. Dublin-born William Jackson arrived on a fact-finding mission for the French Directory.[92] He had met up with an old friend John Cockayne in London who accompanied him to Dublin but, unbeknown to Jackson, was an informer for the British government. When Jackson asked about reactions in Ireland to a possible French invasion, Tone said he thought it 'a grievous remedy', but 'the people had no way left to expose their sentiments but by open resistance'.[93] Fellow United Irishman Archibald Hamilton Rowan asked Tone to draw up a position paper for Jackson on the current state of Ireland. Tone immediately did this and a copy was handed to Jackson. There was talk of sending Tone to France, but he declined. Government were quickly apprised of Jackson's agenda and of Tone's memorandum. After some hesitation the authorities arrested Jackson. Rowan later fled the country and there was a crack-down on the United Irishmen.[94] Although Tone had been implicated, he was regarded as 'a nuisance rather than a threat', and thanks to influential connections in government, he was not charged.[95] In return for a full

---

90 *Autobiography of Theobald Wolfe Tone*, i, 79 (16 October 1792). Digges was later suspected of betraying Tone by handing over a confidential letter to the Irish administration.   91 The bill allowed for the compulsory enlistment of 16,000 men for local defence thus releasing trained troops for the war against France.   92 Jackson (c.1759-94), a one-time Protestant clergyman, radical journalist and supporter of the American colonists, committed suicide during his trial for treason.   93 *Autobiography of Theobald Wolfe Tone*, ii, 204.   94 Rowan escaped from prison following a two year sentence. He had been charged *inter alia* with planning 'to overturn the established constitution of this kingdom, and to overawe and intimidate the legislature of this kingdom by an armed force': 29 Jan. 1794, *The Speeches of the Right Honourable John Philpot Curran*, ed. Thomas Davis, 5th edn (Dublin, n.d.), p. 160.   95 Elliott, *Wolfe Tone*, p. 243; the Attorney-General Arthur Wolfe was a family friend and the Lord-

statement of his involvement in the affair he was granted immunity from prosecution. Jackson was tried in April 1795 and committed suicide.

The memorandum for Jackson

The memorandum, although a short, informal and confidential document, distills a new thrust in Irish resistance thinking. It proved to be the basis of Tone's thought for the remaining few years of his life. It assesses divisions, points to where the real grievances and injustices lie and talks of how to redress them by forcibly changing the power structures. The tenor of the document makes previous resistance writing sound long-winded, oblique if not hesitant, even timid. The memorandum gives resistance a fresh aggressive direction. The French Directory wanted to know not what the Irish thought of their plight but whether they would react positively to a French invasion. Tone, more interested in action than talk, responded with a sketch of present problems in Ireland and indicated to the French what should be done in the event of an invasion.[96]

The decidedly clandestine air about Tone writing a memorandum for Rowan, who revises it and hands it over to Jackson, who will convey it secretly to the French Directory, gives the memorandum that postcolonial characteristic of being illicit. It justifies and facilitates a dramatic subversion of Ireland as he knows it. It is a conspiratorial step towards the creation of an Ireland that does not yet exist, an Ireland quite different from that of the administration, an Ireland that would confront the administration in rebellion.[97]

These are Tone's more personal thoughts about Ireland's independence. He elaborates on them a year later in a memorandum to the French minister in Philadelphia and in his several memoranda to the French Directory while he was in Paris. They constitute his credo through until the rebellion. When he sat down to write the memorandum for Jackson Tone had not previously written for an audience sympathetic to a rising and his excitement is reflected in the terse pointed style of the opening which starts almost in point form with curt, informative sentences for the benefit of his French readers:

> The situations of England and Ireland are fundamentally different in this: The Government of England is national; that of Ireland provincial. The

Chancellor John Fitzgibbon was a cousin of Tone's wife Matilda. A witness at Jackson's trial stated that 'there was a compromise with Mr. Tone by government that he was not to be prosecuted': *A Complete Collection of State Trials*, eds T.B. and T.J. Howell, 33 vols (London, 1809), xxv, 880. The Irish Chief Secretary, Sylvester Douglas, was among those who thought Tone should have been hanged. 96 'I went home and that evening made a sketch of the state of Ireland' (Tone's Confession, MacDermot, *Theobald Wolfe Tone and His Times*, p. 139). Elliott argues that much of the memorandum echoes what Tone had been saying since 1791 (*Wolfe Tone*, p. 239). 97 Cf. Ernest Gellner, 'Nationalism is not the awakening of nations to self-consciousness; it *invents* nations where they do not exist' (cited by Childs and Williams, *An Introduction to Post-Colonial Theory* , p. 207).

interest of the first is the same with that of the people. Of the last, directly opposite.[98]

He had made the point in the *Argument*, but seldom had it been given with such economy and clarity. Tone was at pains to make the same point again and again to various members of the French Directory and to French generals during his stay in France from 1796 to 1798. We are back to the colonial predicament of Molyneux, only worse. The imposition of English over Irish interests remains foremost in the Protestant mind. The memorandum looks to displace those with a non-sectarian national consciousness. In his assessment of the main religious groups Tone indicates where the French can or need not expect support. The Protestants, he says,

> infinitely the smallest portion, [they] have engrossed, besides the whole Church patronage, all the profits and honours of the country and a very great share of the landed property. They are, of course, all aristocrats, adverse to any change, and decidedly enemies to the French Revolution.

The adverbs 'infinitely' and 'decidedly' and adjectives like 'whole' and 'very great' indicate his anger at them, and a noted souring from his hectoring attitude in the *Argument*. The Protestants are a static entity, unwilling to change from within. Force is the only way to get them out. By 1796 he was telling General Clarke in Paris that his feelings were so shared by the populace of Ireland that, though he hoped it would not happen, he feared 'a general massacre of the gentry, and a distribution of the entire of their property'. He was sure 'the just resentment of the people' would demonstrate itself.[99] The Dissenters, with whom he had worked in Ulster, were much more to be relied on: they were both 'the most enlightened body of the nation', dedicated to liberty and 'enthusiastically attached to the French Revolution.' His view of the Catholics, 'the great body of the nation', is typically ambiguous: he sees 'they are ready for any change, because no change can make them worse', yet his positive remarks about them have the air of wishing rather than knowing their commitment to rebellion. They live in the wake of the 'political paralysis' he mentioned in the *Argument*.[100] He here identifies them with the Defenders, those Catholic agitators originating in Ulster who had spread their activities by 1794 into several southern counties, but by no means throughout Ireland.[101] As Johnston notes,

98 MacDermot provides Tone's initial text in *Theobald Wolfe Tone and His Times*, pp 121-3, which is also found in *Life of Wolfe Tone*, i, 271-9; Rowan's revised version is given in *A Complete Collection of State Trials*, xxv, 841-3. 99 *Autobiography of Theobald Wolfe Tone*, ii, 85 (18 July 1796). 100 *Argument*, 111. 101 The Defenders, a grass-root organisation of Catholics, originated in Ulster in local sectarian feuds with Protestants in the 1780s, and in the 1790s came to identify more closely with the aspirations of the United Irishmen contributing significantly to the 1798 rebellion. Tone was involved on

Tone's patriotism is sometimes tinged with romance and his idealism vulnerable to self-deception.[102]

But Tone's hopes, open to whatever practical misgivings, envisage a resistance aimed at overthrowing the English. In his eyes disturbances by the Defenders are but a sign of a new spirit in the people, and no entrenched English system nor landed interest will be able to withstand it. It is difficult to say whether what follows in the memorandum for Jackson is rhetorically geared to persuade the French to land – his targets of vilification are similar to those in France during the French Revolution – or whether the anti-English sentiment does not carry Tone into a visionary prospect of retribution and justice which he has not fully thought out.

> In Ireland, a conquered and oppressed and insulted country, the name of England and her power is universally odious, save with those who have an interest in maintaining it, such as the Government and its connexions, the Church and its dependencies, the great landed property, etc; but the power of these people, being founded on property, the first convulsion would level it with the dust. On the contrary the great bulk of the people would probably throw off the yoke, if they saw any force in the country sufficiently strong to resort to for defence.

Such were the sentiments that boosted Tone's image as a revolutionary. But that image was foisted on him. At Jackson's trial, which he did not attend, his name was linked with the treasonable charges. As Curran noted, Jackson was accused of trying to persuade 'Theobald Wolfe Tone to go beyond the seas to incite France to invade this kingdom'.[103] The case against Jackson was indirectly a case against Tone. He quickly resigned from the Catholic Committee, rented out his property and left for America in the belief that the cause of independence was dead. Only in hindsight does it become clear that by escaping Ireland Tone gave the cause new hope.

The memorandum echoes through much of his later journal writings and he held to that argument until his own landing in 1798. His attacks on the aristocracy and the propertied gentry simply get more vicious with the years. In France in 1796 he recounts the case of the gentry of Meath raising the wages of their labourers for fear of the Defenders, and then raising rents and grazing fees.

> Such is the honesty of the Squirearchy of Ireland. No! no! it is we who will better the condition of the labouring poor, if ever we get into that country; it is we that will humble the pride of that execrable and contemptible corps, the country gentlemen of Ireland. I know not whether I

behalf of Defenders in a trial in Drogheda at the time of Jackson's visit. 102 Johnston, *Ireland in the Eighteenth Century*, p. 169. 103 *Speeches of John Philpot Curran*, p. 215.

most hate or despise them, the tyrants of the people and slaves of the Government.[104]

In 1794 his language suggests that change will only come by force. He had warned of violence in the *Argument*. Previous protest had regarded that as either unnecessary or futile. Protestants kept appealing to the moral foundations of British justice, Catholics with Jacobite sympathies had long despaired of military resistance. Tone does the reverse: he despairs of English justice and resuscitates hopes of rebellion. He considers that Ireland has been greatly changed by the French Revolution which it watched 'very diligently' and France now has the opportunity which Louis XIV had a hundred years earlier – and didn't take – of making Ireland independent. If France had attacked then, 'the navy of England would never have grown to what it is at this day'.[105] Here therefore is the opportunity for both France and Ireland to right the wrongs of the last hundred years.

Why then he asks in the memorandum are the Irish people so depressed and why have they done nothing? Again the answer is hope rather than fact. In the *Argument* he had said that after a century in 'slavery' it was no wonder 'they may have lost the wish for freedom'.[106] He now argues that the people have no outlet for civil protest, but the recent 'numberless local insurrections' are the best indicator of their discontent. That evidence together with a hatred of the English generated by 'the tyranny of nearly seven hundred years' leaves 'little doubt' that an invasion 'in sufficient force' would be supported. The hesitancy indicates his anxiety, a tussle within himself between the rebellion he hopes for and his doubts about the people's will to rise up.

In the rush of producing the memorandum Tone is aware that the situation is more complex than he says. The anomaly is that he wants the people of Ireland to rebel but he cannot force them to it. On one side he sees independence, on the other the spectre of further colonial domination. He stands in the uncertain space between, and in his few remaining years this anxiety continues to haunt him. By 1797 he is convinced there is well-organised support for a rebellion: he believes 'the organisation is ... much more complete than when I left Ireland' and that 'there are over 100,000 United Irishmen in the North of Ireland'; even so,

> I do not at all believe that the people are prepared for a serious and general insurrection, and in short – why should I conceal the fact? – I do not believe that they have the spirit. It is not fear of the army, but fear of the law, and long habits of slavery, that keep them down; it is not fear of the General, but fear of the Judge.[107]

104 *Autobiography of Theobald Wolfe Tone*, ii, 55 (25 June 1796). 105 Ibid., i, 289–90 (21 March 1796). 106 *Argument*, 125. 107 *Autobiography of Theobald Wolfe Tone*, ii, 225.

That system of subjugation which thirty years earlier Burke had warned might incite the people to violence has in Tone's view dulled the people into submission. His worst fears proved right when in 1798 many leading Catholics condemned the rising. For example, Dr Francis Moylan, Catholic bishop of Cork, warned his flock on 26 April, 'that secret associations for the subversion of the order and peace of society are unlawful and criminal'. He goes on,

> I know, Beloved Brethren, that efforts have been made by evil minded men, to weaken your attachment to the Constitution of your country, and your allegiance to the best of Kings, by circulating impious and seditious writings, and encouraging you to outrage and riot.

The faithful were to 'renounce all those wicked associations'.[108]

On the other hand, nationalist ballads and verses of the 1790s suggest that some looked to the possibility of a rising, supported by the French, with exhilirating confidence, as in these well-known lines,

> Oh! may the wind of Freedom soon send young Boney o'er,
> And we'll plant the tree of Liberty upon our Shamrock shore;
> Oh! we'll plant it with our weapons while the English tyrants gape,
> To see their bloody flag torn down, to Green on the cape!
> Oh! the wearing of the Green. Oh! the wearing of the Green!
> God grant us soon to see that day, and freely wear the Green![109]

Of all Ireland's protestors in the eighteenth century Tone brings out most clearly Ireland's ambivalence to armed resistance. Burke and O'Conor had foreseen the possibility and warned of the threat, but Tone was the person who gave the people the option to turn words into action. The irony is he wondered at times whether they would take it.

If he feared their apathy in 1794, he kept resolutely to his dictum: 'I am sworn not to despair.'[110] In the final two paragraphs of the memorandum he instructs the French what to do on landing. They are to have ready a statement to distribute to the people. Perhaps those earlier misgivings are what prompt him to be very specific about what this document should say. The people must realise that the landing force has not come to conquer but to liberate them, 'to enable the people to redress their grievances, to assert their rights, to subvert the ancient tyranny of their oppressors, and to establish on a permanent basis the independence of their country.'

108 Rt Rev. Dr Francis Moylan, *Pastoral Instruction to the Roman Catholics of the Diocese of Cork* (Cork, 1798), pp 5, 10, 13   109 Anon., 'Green upon the Cape', *Verse in English from Eighteenth-Century Ireland*, pp 573-4.   110 *Autobiography of Theobald Wolfe Tone*, ii, 329.

In addition there should be no room to doubt that this was war – those who support the government would suffer for it. 'Such persons as might be troublesome' would be seized. Here in the first formulation of his plan he is confident that with a force of no less than ten thousand the landing would be successful. That figure was to drop to five thousand as over the next few years the French delayed, and then to two thousand. General Humbert set sail in August 1798 with 1,019 men, followed too late by Hardy's expedition of 2,291 with Tone aboard the *Hoche*.[111]

These details in the final paragraphs of the memorandum were plainly treasonous and Rowan removed them from the version given to Jackson. Discussion of discontent and opinions on rebellion were one thing, but detailed advice on how to effect the rebellion was another. He was encouraging the French to give 'a conquered and oppressed and insulted country' the chance to overthrow 'a Government of force.' No wonder some officials thought Tone should have hanged. Certainly in hindsight, if not at the time, Tone understood these implications and he made no apology for them. At his trial in Dublin he was unequivocal about his conduct:

> Whatever I have said, written, or thought on the subject of Ireland I now reiterate: looking upon the connexion with England to have been her bane I have endeavoured by every means in my power to break that connexion; I have laboured in consequence to create a people in Ireland by raising three Millions of my Countrymen to the rank of Citizens.[112]

He forgets that during his youth he had wanted to fight for Britain in America and the South Seas, but by this stage he thinks of the break from England as a lifetime's work. The fact that so much had gone wrong gives him not a moment of remorse. His confidence of purpose remains clear to the end.

The most obvious and dramatic sign that he had made his own severance from the Ireland that England governed was that he came ashore at Buncrana in the uniform of a French officer. He presumed that if captured he would be treated as an officer in the French army. Instead, he was imprisoned in chains, dubbed a traitor and taken, 'to receive the punishment due to the crimes he had been guilty of committing against his King and his country'.[113] Tone's attempt to distance himself, to claim that different Irelands were in contention here was abortive. Having failed to bring into existence the Ireland he dreamed of, he found himself a prisoner of the Ireland he abhorred.

111 Ibid., 347-9; Elliott, *Wolfe Tone*, pp 382-3. 112 I follow the version of the speech given by Elliott, *Wolfe Tone*, p. 393; for an alternative version of this passage see *Autobiography of Theobald Wolfe Tone*, ii, 357. 113 Cornwallis' secretary Captain Herbert Taylor to General Jean Hardy, cited by Elliott, *Wolfe Tone*, p. 389.

As he waited in prison to hear the outcome of his application to be shot rather than hanged, he wrote to the Directory in Paris proud to affirm that he had given his life for Ireland, 'the Republic':

> I have served the Republic faithfully, and my death, as well as that of my brother, a victim like myself, and condemned in the same manner about a month ago, will sufficiently prove it.[114]

He then pleads for assistance to his family and reminds the Directory, 'I was expelled from my own country in consequence of my attempts to serve the Republic ... I have sacrificed for the Republic all that man holds dearest – my wife, my liberty, my life ...'[115] Sacrifice leaves an onus on the living. What he had said of Keogh's son now applies to himself, 'From the blood of every one of the martyrs of the liberty of Ireland will spring, I hope, thousands to revenge their fall.'[116]

The language is a forerunner of the nationalist rhetoric Ireland produced over the next hundred and twenty years. Elliott identifies in it 'the belief in the sanctity of the blood sacrifice, of victory in defeat'.[117] That rhetoric reaches down to the last decades of British rule, to writers and activists caught up in the 1916 rising like Padraic Pearse and Maud Gonne – sometimes defiant, sometimes aggressive, often romantic, but unflinching in the principle that Ireland must be totally independent. The temper of Tone's writings from 1794 onwards is clearly discernible in Pearse's remarks about what freedom means to Ireland:

> It has meant not a limited freedom, a freedom conditioned by the interests of another nation, a freedom compatible with the suzerain authority of a foreign parliament, but absolute freedom, the sovereign control of Irish destinies.[118]

In Pearse's view Tone brought to a head all that Keating, Swift, O'Conor and many others had begun to utter. He was 'the first to formulate in worthy terms' the gospel of Irish nationalism.[119] By giving his life in 1798 Tone gave nationalists the example they so revered more than a hundred years later, when as Pearse reminded his audience in 1913, 'his work is still unaccomplished'.[120] Nevertheless Tone's death and the failure of the rebellion meant more immediately the collapse of a century-long contest for Ireland, be it the Ireland of Molyneux, or O'Conor, or Tone.

---

114 Tone's brother Matthew had sailed from France with Humbert's force and was hanged after their defeat in September. 115 Letter to the Directory, in MacDermot, *Theobald Wolfe Tone and His Times*, pp 270-1. 116 *Autobiography of Theobald Wolfe Tone*, ii, 311. 117 Elliott, *Wolfe Tone*, p. 379. 118 Pearse, *Political Writings and Speeches* (Dublin, 1962), pp 228-9. 119 Pearse, 'Address at Wolfe Tone's grave, 1913', *Political Writings and Speeches*, p. 55. 120 Ibid., p. 62.

Index